CARL
ROGERS:
DIALOGUES

CARL
ROGERS:
DIALOGUES

*Conversations with Martin Buber,
Paul Tillich, B. F. Skinner, Gregory Bateson,
Michael Polanyi, Rollo May, and Others*

Edited by
HOWARD KIRSCHENBAUM *and*
VALERIE LAND HENDERSON

Constable · London

First published in Great Britain 1990
by Constable and Company Limited
3 The Lanchesters, 162 Fulham Palace Road
London W6 9ER
Copyright © 1989 Howard Kirschenbaum
and the estate of Carl Rogers
Reprinted 1994, 1997
ISBN 0 09 469830 9
Printed in Great Britain by
St Edmundsbury Press Limited
Bury St Edmunds, Suffolk

A CIP catalogue record for this book
is available from the British Library

Acknowledgments

We sincerely thank the following individuals for their gracious assistance: B. F. Skinner, Rollo May, Mary Catherine Bateson, and William Coulson, for their permission to publish four of the dialogues or written exchanges; Professor Gerald Gladstein, for his help on the Rogers-Skinner dialogue; Neil Kramer, Rita Bottoms, and Gregory Williams, for their help in locating the Rogers-Bateson dialogue and correspondence; Mary Catherine Bateson, for reviewing the Rogers-Bateson dialogue; Virginia Conard for transcribing the Skinner and Bateson dialogues; Natalie Rogers and David Rogers, for their support of this entire project; Ruth Hapgood and Chris Jerome, for their editorial assistance; and our agent, Donald Cutler.

HOWARD KIRSCHENBAUM
VALERIE LAND HENDERSON

Contents

I / CARL ROGERS
AND HIS WORK

I
Introduction

Carl Rogers's entire professional life was devoted to enhancing human communication. He strove to understand and promote "the characteristics of helping relationships" throughout a sixty-year career, from the mid-1920s until his death in 1987 at age eighty-five. In our introduction to *The Carl Rogers Reader*,[1] we summarize his most significant achievements:

He pioneered a major new approach to psychotherapy, known successively as the "nondirective," "client-centered," and "person-centered" approach.

He was the first person in history to record and publish complete cases of psychotherapy.

He carried out and encouraged more scientific research on counseling and psychotherapy than had ever been undertaken anywhere.

More than any individual, he was responsible for the spread of professional counseling and psychotherapy beyond psychiatry and psychoanalysis to all the helping professions — psychology, social work, education, ministry, lay therapy, and others.

He was a leader in the development and dissemination of the intensive therapeutic group experience, sometimes called the "encounter group."

He was a leader in the humanistic psychology movement of the 1960s to 1980s, which continues to exert a profound influence on society and the professions.

He was a pioneer in applying the principles of effective interpersonal communication to resolving intergroup and international conflict.

He was one of the helping professions' most prolific writers, authoring sixteen books and more than two hundred professional articles and research studies. Millions of copies of his books have been printed, including more than sixty foreign-language editions of his works.

Ironically, the man who was to become the most influential psychotherapist in the United States began his life as a shy child. Growing up in suburban and rural Illinois, he was a sensitive boy in a family in which teasing was the norm. He had no close friends outside the family until he went away to college at the University of Wisconsin, where he majored in agriculture. Coming from a religious family, he was inspired by the evangelical movement on campus and decided to enter the ministry. After marrying a childhood friend, Helen Elliott (a union that lasted more than fifty years), Rogers and his wife moved to New York City, where he enrolled in Union Theological Seminary.

Discouraged by some of the more doctrinaire aspects of ministerial training, Rogers soon became attracted to the field of psychology and transferred to Teachers College, Columbia University, from which he received his doctorate in 1931. He later acknowledged that his shifting from agriculture to ministry to counseling psychology could be explained in no small part by his personal need for closer human contact within a structured situation.

From 1928 to 1940 he worked in Rochester, New York, as staff member and then director of the Rochester Society for the Prevention of Cruelty to Children and the Rochester Child Study Center. In this practical laboratory, treating hundreds of children and their families, he began to clarify his thinking about the counseling relationship. Here he came to recognize the resources individuals have within them for solving their own problems, and that the counselor can serve as helpful companion rather than director in that process.

At Ohio State University (1940–1944), the USO where he worked with returned servicemen (1944–1945), the University of Chicago (1945–1957), and the University of Wisconsin (1957–1963), he steadily pursued his pioneering research, clarified his theory of psychotherapy and personality change, and developed his methods of counseling and psychotherapy. Throughout this period, his counseling experience and research encompassed the continuum of mildly disturbed students through hospitalized schizophrenics. Some of his major publications from this period were *Counseling and Psychotherapy*, 1942; *Client-Centered Therapy*, 1951; *Psychotherapy and Personality Change*, 1954; *On Becoming a Person*, 1961; and *The Therapeutic Relationship and Its Impact: A Study of Psychotherapy with Schizophrenics*, 1967.[2,3,4,5,6] The following chapter, written by Rogers in 1959 and updated in 1966,[7] is an excellent summary of his work from this period. It describes the basic theory and approach that was the foundation for all his subsequent work.

After leaving Wisconsin, Rogers moved to La Jolla, California, where he joined the staff of the new Western Behavioral Sciences Institute, a nonprofit think tank and training organization. A few years later, he and a number of his colleagues left WBSI and formed the Center for Studies of the Person, Rogers's primary professional affiliation until his death. In La Jolla he expanded his focus beyond counseling and psychotherapy to fields he had begun exploring earlier, and also to entirely new arenas of human communication and concern. Titles of his major books from this period illustrate some of the areas his work grew to encompass: *Freedom to Learn: A View of What Education Might Become*, 1969 and 1983; *On Encounter Groups*, 1970; *Becoming Partners: Marriage and Its Alternatives*, 1972; *On Personal Power*, 1977; and *A Way of Being*, 1980.[8,9,10,11,12,13]

Rogers won numerous honors and awards throughout his long career and served as president or officer of some of the leading national organizations in his field. The honor he prized the most was the American Psychological Association's first Distinguished Scientific Contribution Award. A few years later he also received its Distinguished Professional Contribution Award, the first person ever to win both honors from the psychology profession's leading organization. In polls in two leading professional journals, he was voted the most influential American psychologist.[14,15]

Whether exploring therapy, education, marriage, or international relations, Rogers's contribution always centered on the person-to-person relationship. Almost everyone who knew him, personally or professionally, from Ohio State onward, regarded him as the best listener they had ever met. Rogers not only popularized the term *empathy*, but more than anyone else demonstrated its potency in therapy, education, and all human relationships. Also of paramount importance, though less well understood, was his concept of congruence — open, authentic, and genuine communication. Rogers emphasized that congruence by the counselor, teacher, parent, or other helper was an essential condition for helping relationships, and was just as important for couples, work groups, or international negotiations, however risky it might seem. These concepts are explored more fully in Rogers's essay and the dialogues that follow.

As Rogers developed a reputation as the generation's leading proponent of good listening and clear communication, it was not surprising that participating in or witnessing a conversation with Carl Rogers became a memorable and sought-after experience. He was often invited to participate in panel discussions and dialogues with leading members of the helping professions, and eventually he was asked to participate in dialogues with some of the leading intellectual figures of the twentieth century.

Fortunately, a number of these dialogues were taped. A few were transcribed, printed in small journals, and then mostly forgotten. The lengthy dialogue with B. F. Skinner — not to be confused with their often-reprinted 1956 symposium on "Some Issues Concerning the Control of Human Behavior"[16] — has never before been published, although a six-cassette recording of the conversation is available.[17]

While researching material for *The Carl Rogers Reader*,[18] our collection of readings representing Rogers's lifework, we rediscovered these dialogues and were impressed with their cumulative impact. Martin Buber, Paul Tillich, B. F. Skinner, Gregory Bateson, Michael Polanyi — their brief biographies indicate their stature among this century's intellectual elite. Additional written exchanges in the form of a symposium on the work of theologian Reinhold Niebuhr and published correspondence with psychotherapist Rollo May, while not dialogues in the true sense, add significantly to the collection.

To a degree, the dialogues and correspondence can be categorized by Rogers's interaction with the theologians (Buber, Tillich,

Niebuhr), the psychologists (Skinner, Bateson, May), and the scientist (Polanyi). However, as the dialogues richly reveal, such a division would be misleading. All three theologians were vitally concerned with helping relationships, with succoring the psychologically and spiritually troubled, with the "I-Thou" encounter, with forgiveness and the state of grace as it may be experienced between the person and God or person to person. The three psychologists were concerned with the "nature of man," with helping their clients find meaning in life, with understanding the "good life," and with the question of free choice and free will versus determinism — all profound and perennial theological questions. And all seven of Rogers's counterparts cared deeply about science — how we know, the relation between knowledge and faith, and the role of values and beliefs in the pursuit of science.

Ironically, Carl Rogers — the student minister turned agnostic, the psychologist, the scientist — became the fulcrum for a series of fascinating exchanges that sometimes touched lightly upon and at other times delved deeply into many of the most profound questions of religion, psychology, and philosophy. In each instance, the entire dialogue or written exchange is included in this volume. Although some minor editing of the Skinner and Bateson dialogues was done to improve the readability of the spoken word, we have tried to retain their conversational tone.

Another editing dilemma presented itself with the Bateson and Skinner dialogues, in which there was considerable joking by the protagonists and laughter from the audience. In an early draft, we noted each instance of laughter — "Audience laughs," "Rogers laughs," "Both laugh," and so on — to try to capture the real flavor of the occasion. This turned out to read so awkwardly that in the end we eliminated the audience laugh track, as it were, letting the reader determine for him- or herself what is amusing. We *do* indicate when the protagonists themselves laughed aloud, as this seems an important part of their communication. For the record, though, Rogers, Bateson, and Skinner all had excellent rapport with their audiences.

REFERENCES

1. Kirschenbaum, H., and Henderson, V. L. (eds.), *The Carl Rogers Reader*. Boston: Houghton Mifflin, 1989.

2. Rogers, C. R., *Counseling and Psychotherapy: New Concepts in Practice.* Boston: Houghton Mifflin, 1942.
3. Rogers, C. R., *Client-Centered Therapy: Its Current Practice, Implications and Theory.* Boston: Houghton Mifflin, 1951.
4. Rogers, C. R., and Dymond, R. (eds.), *Psychotherapy and Personality Change.* Chicago: University of Chicago Press, 1954.
5. Rogers, C. R., *On Becoming a Person.* Boston: Houghton Mifflin, 1961.
6. Rogers, C. R., Gendlin, E. T., Kiesler, D. J., and Truax, C. B. (eds.), *The Therapeutic Relationship and Its Impact: A Study of Psychotherapy with Schizophrenics.* Madison: University of Wisconsin Press, 1967.
7. Rogers, C. R., Client-centered therapy. In Arieti, S. (ed.), *American Handbook of Psychiatry, Vol. 3.* New York: Basic Books, 1959 and 1966.
8. Rogers, C. R., *Freedom to Learn: A View of What Education Might Become.* Columbus, OH: Charles Merrill, 1969.
9. Rogers, C. R., *Freedom to Learn in the 80s.* Columbus, OH: Charles Merrill, 1983.
10. Rogers, C. R., *Carl Rogers on Encounter Groups.* New York: Harper and Row, 1970.
11. Rogers, C. R., *Becoming Partners: Marriage and Its Alternatives.* New York: Delacorte Press, 1972.
12. Rogers, C. R., *Carl Rogers on Personal Power: Inner Strength and Its Revolutionary Impact.* New York: Delacorte Press, 1977.
13. Rogers, C. R., *A Way of Being.* Boston: Houghton Mifflin, 1980.
14. Heesacker, M., Heppner, P., and Rogers, M. E., Classics and Emerging Classics in Counseling Psychology. *Counseling Psychology,* Vol. 29, No. 4, July 1982.
15. Smith, D., Trends in Counseling and Psychology. *American Psychologist,* Vol. 37, No. 7, July 1982.
16. Rogers, C. R., and Skinner, B. F., Some issues concerning the control of human behavior. *Science,* Vol. 124, No. 3231, November 1956, 1057–1066.
17. Rogers, C. R., and Skinner, B. F., A dialogue on education and the control of human behavior. A six-cassette album edited by Gerald Gladstein. Available from Jeffrey Norton Publishers, 145 E. 49th St., New York, NY 10017.
18. Kirschenbaum, H., and Henderson, V. L. (eds.), *The Carl Rogers Reader.* Boston: Houghton Mifflin, 1989.

2

Client-Centered Therapy

BY CARL ROGERS*

A CHANGING APPROACH TO PSYCHOTHERAPY

From its inception, the orientation that has come to be called
client-centered psychotherapy has been noted for its growing,
changing, developing quality. It has not been a fixed or rigid
school of thought. The changes have emerged as a result of the
increasing experience of a group of therapists and out of the
findings of a continuing and multifaceted program of research.
The following description focuses on the developments in this
orientation, as well as on the relatively unchanged aspects that
have stood the test of time and of research.

It has never been my intention to inaugurate a "school" of
psychotherapy. It has been my purpose, and that of a growing
number of therapists holding congenial ideas, to endeavor to
identify the essential elements of any effective psychotherapy
or personal counseling. But because the resultant ideas have
departed somewhat radically from conventional approaches to
therapy, client-centered therapy has come to be regarded by out-
siders as a separate school of therapy, and in this chapter they are

*Dr. William R. Coulson has assisted me in every phase of the development and
writing of this article, and I am much indebted to him for his help. Dr. Charles
Truax assisted in drafting the section on the therapeutic climate.

Reprinted from Arieti, S. (Ed.), *American Handbook of Psychiatry, Vol. 3.* New York:
Basic Books, 1959 and 1966, 183–200.

presented as a distinct and definable approach to the process of facilitating constructive change in the troubled person.

The client-centered point of view has a number of distinguishing characteristics. These include the developing hypothesis that certain attitudes in the therapist constitute the necessary and sufficient conditions of therapeutic effectiveness; the developing concept of the therapist's function as being immediately present to his client, relying on his moment-to-moment felt experience in the relationship; the continuing focus on the phenomenal world of the client; a developing theory that the therapeutic process is marked by a change in the client's manner of experiencing and an ability to live more fully in the immediate moment; a continuing stress on the self-actualizing quality of the human organism as the motivating force in therapy; a concern with the process of personality change, rather than with the structure of personality; a stress on the necessity of research to discover the essential truths of psychotherapy; the hypothesis that the same principles of psychotherapy apply to the competently functioning business executive, the maladjusted and neurotic person who comes to a clinic, and the hospitalized psychotic on the back ward; a view of psychotherapy as one specialized example of all constructive interpersonal relationships, with the consequent generalized applicability of all our knowledge from the field of therapy; and, finally, a concern with the philosophical and value issues that grow out of the practice of therapy. Each of these distinguishing elements is dealt with in this chapter.

THE THERAPEUTIC CLIMATE

Contrary to the opinion of a great many psychotherapists, I have long held that it is not the technical skill or training of the therapist that determines his success — not, for example, his skillful dream interpretations, his sensitive reflections of feeling, his handling of the transference, his subtle use of positive reinforcement. Instead, I believe it is the presence of certain *attitudes* in the therapist, which are communicated to, and perceived by, his client, that effect success in psychotherapy.

A number of years ago,[26] I tended to refer to these attitudes in relatively loose, general terms as the therapist's belief in the worth and dignity of the individual and the therapist's capacity to provide a relationship of safety and freedom in accord with his basic respect for his client. During the last decade, those of us in the client-centered group have advanced more specific thoughts about these conditions.[6, 10, 34, 36] We have hypothesized that, if the therapist can provide three definable conditions in his relationship with the client and if the client can perceive to some degree the presence of these conditions, then therapeutic movement will ensue. These three conditions are the therapist's congruence or genuineness; unconditional positive regard, a complete acceptance; and a sensitively accurate empathetic understanding.

Therapist's Congruence

The order in which these therapeutic conditions are described has some significance because they are logically intertwined. In the first place, the therapist must achieve a strong, accurate empathy. But such deep sensitivity to the moment-to-moment "being" of another person requires that the therapist first accept, and to some degree prize, the other person. That is to say, a sufficiently strong empathy can scarcely exist without a considerable degree of unconditional positive regard. However, since neither of these conditions can possibly be meaningful in the relationship unless they are real, the therapist must be, both in these respects and in others, integrated and genuine within the therapeutic encounter. Therefore, it seems to me that genuineness or congruence is the most basic of the three conditions. I shall try to describe its meaning.

We readily sense this quality of congruence in everyday life. We all know persons who always seem to operate from behind a front, who play a role, who tend to say things they do not feel. They are exhibiting incongruence. We tend not to reveal ourselves too deeply to such people. On the other hand, we all know individuals whom we trust because we sense that they actually are as they present themselves to be, openly and transparently — that we are dealing with the person himself, not a polite or professional façade. This is genuineness.

Genuineness in therapy means that the therapist is his actual self during his encounter with his client. Without façade, he openly has the feelings and attitudes that are flowing in him at the moment. This involves self-awareness; that is, the therapist's feelings are available to him — to his awareness — and he is able to live them, to experience them in the relationship, and to communicate them if they persist. The therapist encounters his client directly, meeting him person to person. He is *being* himself, not denying himself.

Since this concept is liable to misunderstanding, let me state that it does not mean that the therapist burdens his client with overt expression of all his feelings. Nor does it mean that the therapist discloses his total self to his client. It does mean, however, that the therapist denies to himself none of the feelings he is experiencing and that he is willing to experience transparently any *persistent* feelings that exist in the relationship and to let these be known to his client. It means avoiding the temptation to present a façade or hide behind a mask of professionalism, or to assume a confessional–professional attitude.

It is not simple to achieve such reality. Being real involves the difficult task of being acquainted with the flow of experiencing going on within oneself, a flow marked especially by complexity and continuous change. So, if I sense that I am feeling bored by a client and if this feeling persists, I think I owe it to him and our relationship to share my feeling with him. The same will hold if my feeling were fear, or if my attention were so focused on my own problems that I could scarcely listen to him. But, as I attempt to share such feelings with him, I want also to be constantly in touch with what is going on in me. If I am, I will recognize that I am expressing my own feeling of being bored and not some supposed fact about him as a boring person. When voiced as my own reaction, such an expression can lead to a deep relationship. But my feeling exists in the context of a complex and changing flow, which also needs to be communicated. I would like to share with him my distress at feeling bored and my discomfort in expressing it. As I do, I find that my boredom arises from my sense of remoteness from him and that I would like to be in closer touch with him; and even as I try to express these feelings they change. I am certainly not bored as I wait with eagerness, and perhaps a bit of apprehension, for his response. I also feel a new sensitivity to him now that I have shared this feeling which has been a barrier between us. I am far more able to hear the surprise, or perhaps the hurt, in his voice as he now finds himself speaking more genuinely because I have dared to be real with him. I have let myself be a person — real, imperfect — in my relationship with him.

It should be clear from this lengthy description that the concept of congruence implies that it is helpful to be genuine even when negative feelings toward the client are involved. It would probably be most helpful if these feelings did not exist in the therapist. However, our theory implies that it would be more harmful if these negative feelings were hidden. Even with such negative attitudes, which seem so potentially damaging but which all therapists have from time to time, I am suggesting that it is preferable for the therapist to be real than to put on a false posture of interest, concern, and liking that the client is likely to sense as false.

It is not easy for a client, or for any human being, to entrust his most deeply shrouded feelings to another person. It is even more difficult for a disturbed person to share his deepest and most troubling feelings with a therapist. The genuineness of the therapist is one of the elements in the relationship that make the risk of sharing easier and less fraught with dangers.

Unconditional Positive Regard

The second condition that seems to me essential for therapeutic movement and change is an unconditional positive regard for the client. This means that the therapist communicates to his client a deep and genuine caring for him as a person with human potentialities, a caring uncontaminated by evaluations of the patient's thoughts, feelings, or behavior. The therapist experiences a warm acceptance of the client's experience as a part of that person and places no conditions on his acceptance and warmth. He prizes the client in a total, rather than a conditional, way. He does not accept certain feelings in the client and disapprove of others. He feels an unconditional positive regard for this person. This is an outgoing, positive feeling without reservations and without evaluations. It means making no judgments. It involves as much feeling of acceptance for the client's expression of painful, hostile, defensive, or abnormal feelings as for his expression of good, positive, mature feelings. For us as therapists, incidentally, it may be easier to accept painful and negative feelings than the positive and self-confident feelings that sometimes come through. These latter we almost automatically regard as defensive. But unconditional positive regard involves a willingness to share equally the patient's confidence and joy, or his depression and failure. It is an un-possessive caring for the client as a separate person, which allows the client freely to have his own feelings and his own experiencing. One client describes the therapist as "fostering my possession of my own experience and that I am actually having it; thinking what I think, feeling what I feel, wanting what I want, fearing what I fear; no 'ifs,' 'buts,' or 'not reallys.' " This type of acceptance, I hold, can lead to a relationship that both facilitates the engagement of the client in the process of therapy and leads to constructive personality change.

Unconditional positive regard, when communicated by the therapist, serves to provide the nonthreatening context in which the client can explore and experience the most deeply shrouded elements of his inner self. The therapist is neither paternalistic, nor sentimental, nor superficially social and agreeable. But his deep caring is a necessary ingredient of the "safe" context in which the client can come to explore himself and share deeply with another human being.

Our recent experience in psychotherapy with chronic and un-motivated schizophrenics raises the question whether we must modify our conception of this condition. Very tentatively it appears to me at the present time that, in dealing with the extremely immature or regressed individual, a conditional re-gard may be more effective in getting a relationship under way, hence therapy under way, than an unconditional posi-tive regard. It seems clear that some immature or regressed clients may perceive a conditional caring as constituting more acceptance than an unconditional caring. The therapist who expresses the theme, "I don't like it when you act in such and such a way: I care for you more when you act in a more grown-up fashion," may be perceived as a "better parent" than one whose caring is unconditional. This may be especially true of the person from a lower socioeducational group. Yet, for the achievement of full maturity, I still believe that an unconditional positive regard on the part of the therapist is the most effective element. In any event, this particular speculation is an example of the way in which our theoretical formulations have at times changed on the basis of more complete experience.

Accurate Empathic Understanding

The ability of the therapist to perceive experiences and feelings accurately and sensitively, and to understand their meaning to the client during the moment-to-moment encounter of psychotherapy, constitutes what can perhaps be described as the "work" of the therapist after he has first provided the contextual base for the relationship by his self-congruence or genuineness and his unconditional positive regard.

Accurate empathic understanding means that the therapist is completely at home in the universe of the client. It is a moment-to-moment sensitivity in the here and now, in the immediate present. It is a sensing of the client's inner world of private personal meanings as if it were your own, while never forgetting that it is not yours. Accurate sensitivity to the client's being is of primary value during the moment-to-moment encounter of therapy; it is of limited use to the individual if the therapist only arrives at this insightful and empathic understanding of the client's experience after the interview. Such a delayed insight may be of value if the therapist has a further chance to respond to the same theme, but its value would be in formulating the moment-to-moment response to the client's immediate living of this later relationship.

The ability and sensitivity required to communicate these inner meanings again to the client in a way that allows them to be "his" experiences are the other major part of accurate empathic understanding. To sense the client's fear, his confusion, his anger, or his rage as if it were a feeling you might have (but which you are not currently having) is the essence of the perceptive aspect of accurate empathy. To communicate this perception in a language attuned to the client, which allows him more clearly to sense and formulate his fear, confusion, rage, or anger, is the essence of the communicative aspect of accurate empathy.

An accurate empathic grasp of the client's conflicts and problems perhaps contrasts most sharply with the more usual diagnostic formulation of the client's experiences. This diagnostic understanding, which is so different but so common, involves the implication, "I understand what is wrong with you," or "I understand the dynamics that make you act this way." Such evaluative understandings are external and sometimes even impersonal. Although they may at times be very useful in developing an understanding of the self as an *object*, they are in sharp contrast to an accurate and sensitive grasp of the personal meanings and perceptions that form the client's private world. External and evaluative understanding tends to focus the client's being on himself as object or upon intellectualizations that remove him from an ongoing contact with the experiencing going on within him. Empathic understanding, when it is accurately and sensitively communicated, seems crucially important in enabling the client more freely to experience his inward feelings, perceptions, and personal meanings. When he is thus in contact with his inward experiencing, he can recognize the points at which his experience is at variance with his concept of himself and, consequently, where he is endeavoring to live by a false conception. Such recognition of incongruence is the first step toward its resolution and the revision of the concept of self to include the hitherto denied experiences. This is one of the major ways in which change becomes possible and a more complete integration of self and behavior is inaugurated.

The Significance of These Attitudes

Considerable space has been given to these three attitudinal conditions because I believe they come close to representing the heart of the client-centered approach. Because they have proved effective, because they have actually worked in the therapist's confrontation with troubled or disturbed individuals, they have led to a theory of the process of personality change, a personality theory, a concern for philosophic issues, and a recognition of their implications for other areas. The core elements of therapeutic success, I believe, can be couched in terms of these three attitudinal conditions, and consequently they deserve considerable attention in any description of client-centered therapy. They are also worthy of continued scientific scrutiny toward their further modification, refinement, or exposition.

Several studies, completed or in process, tend to confirm the hypothesis that congruence, unconditional positive regard, and sensitive empathic understanding are important antecedents of therapeutic movement and progress. A pilot project in the training of mental health counselors conducted by Rioch[23] at the National Institute of Mental Health tends to confirm the hypothesis that it is not the technical professional training of the therapist, but his attitudes, that make him effective or ineffective. A study by Halkides[18] indicated that the existence of these three attitudes in the therapist, as judged by raters listening to the therapeutic interviews, was significantly correlated with therapeutic success. A series of investigations of this hypothesis completed by Barrett-Lennard[2, 3] has added further confirmation. A paper-and-pencil instrument, the Relationship Inventory, was used in these studies to measure the attitudes perceived in the relationship. Those clients who eventually showed more therapeutic change perceived more of these attitudinal conditions in their relationship with their therapist, even at the time of the fifth interview, than did those who eventually showed less change. The correlation between the client's perception of these conditions, as measured by the Relationship Inventory, and the degree of change eventually achieved, as measured by other tests, was positive and significant. The data in a current research program of psychotherapy with schizophrenics,[47, 56] so far as they have been analyzed as of this writing, also lend support to our theorizing about therapeutic conditions. Ratings of therapists' attitudes were made on four-minute segments of the therapeutic interviews by raters who knew nothing about the cases. It is interesting that, in this study, a higher level of these attitudes in the relationship is positively associated with constructive personality change, whereas a lower level of such attitudes is associated with regression. The evidence indicates

that patients who received a high level of therapeutic conditions did significantly better on process and outcome measures
than did the matched control group. Moreover, the group of
patients for whom the ratings of conditions were lower actually showed a deterioration in personality integration during the
period of therapy and afterward. Clinically this is a very sober-
ing finding, for it means that sincere attempts by experienced
therapists to carry on therapy with schizophrenics may actually
result in harm or decreased personality integration. Scientifically
it is an exciting finding, because it seems we have put our finger
on some of the genuinely crucial elements in successful psychotherapy.

THE THERAPIST'S WAY OF FUNCTIONING

Seeman[60] has pointed to the recent considerable freeing in
the response mode of client-centered therapists. In an earlier
study,[61] he found that 85 percent of all therapists' responses
among a sample of the client-centered group were in the
category of "reflection of feeling." However, along with the
recent stress on the importance of the therapist's genuineness
has come a corresponding divergence in method among client-
centered therapists. As client-centered thinking has advanced
from detailed concern over the difference between "reflection
of feeling" and "restatement of content,"[21, 28] and from a central
preoccupation with the technical problem of getting inside the
client's frame of reference[26] to the broader concern that the
therapist use his whole person in the relationship, we have
moved toward a greater variety of techniques among individual
therapists. The recent work with unmotivated, deeply disturbed,
and often highly uncommunicative persons has pushed this
development further.[9, 13, 14, 46] Gendlin's important "theory
of experiencing"[10, 11, 12] has also contributed to this elaboration
of the therapist's function.

In our work with hospitalized persons diagnosed as schizophrenic — individuals who were often at the same time of
low socioeconomic status and relatively meager education —
we found that therapists had to call on resources other than
the patients' verbalizations if they were to establish meaningful

relationships. The reason for this was that these withdrawn, in-articulate patients often found themselves unable or unwilling to take any initiative whatsoever in establishing communication. Thus, if there was to be a relationship at all, the therapist found it necessary to call upon his own feelings. When the patient offered no verbalization, the therapist could at least share, tentatively and without imposing, his own ongoing flow of feelings — his own concern for the patient, his hope for the establishment of a rela-tionship, his imaginings about what was going on in the patient at that moment.

This new way of being with the client or patient requires of the therapist a heightened awareness of the shifting flow of felt ex-periencing within himself. When the patient expresses feelings of his own, a sensitive therapist finds his experiential awareness filled with empathy for the patient's meanings. But when the patient is silent, the therapist can make direct reference to his own experiencing and communicate the meanings found there; again, if he is at all sensitive, these meanings inevitably involve the patient and the relationship. Thus, the expression of the im-plicit meanings found in his own felt experiencing allows the client-centered therapist to build a bridge to a meaningful re-lationship. The therapist uses his experiencing as a source to which he can turn for meanings to express. This is illustrated in the following excerpt from an interview between a therapist and an inarticulate, somewhat depressed, hospitalized male schizo-phrenic, Mr. Vac:

THERAPIST: And I guess your silence is saying to me that either you don't wish to or can't come out right now and that's okay. So I won't pester you but I just want you to know, I'm here.

A very long silence of seventeen minutes.

T: I see I'm going to have to stop in a few minutes.

Brief silence.

T: It's hard for me to know how you've been feeling, but it looks as though part of the time maybe you'd rather I didn't know how you were feeling. Anyway it looks as though part of the time it just feels very good to let down and . . . relax the tension. But as I say I don't really know . . . how you feel. It's just the way it looks to me. Have things been pretty bad lately?

Brief silence.

T: Maybe this morning you just wish I'd shut up . . . and maybe I should but I just keep feeling I'd like to, I don't know, be in touch with you in some way.

Silence of two minutes. Mr. Vac yawns.

T: Sounds discouraged or tired.

Silence of forty seconds.

CLIENT: No, just lousy.

T: Everything's lousy, huh? You feel lousy?

Silence of forty seconds.

T: Want to come in Friday at twelve at the usual time?

C: *Yawns and mutters something unintelligible.*

Silence of forty-eight seconds.

T: Just kind of feel sunk way down deep in these lousy, lousy feelings, huh? Is that something like it?

C: No.

T: No?

Silence of twenty seconds.

C: No. I just ain't no good to nobody, never was, and never will be.

T: Feeling that now, huh? That you're just no good to yourself, no good to anybody. Never will be any good to anybody. Just that you're completely worthless, huh? . . . Those really are lousy feelings. Just feel that you're no good at *all*, huh?

C: Yeah. That's what this guy I went to town with just the other day told me.

T: This guy that you went to town with really told you that you were no good? Is that what you're saying? Did I hear that right?

C: Uh-hum.

T: I guess the meaning of that, if I get it right, is that here's somebody that meant something to you and what does he think of you? Why, he's told you that he thinks you're no good at all. And that just really knocks the props out from you. (*Vac weeps quietly.*) It just brings the tears.

Silence of twenty seconds.

C: I don't care though.

T: You tell yourself that you don't care at all, but somehow I guess some part of you cares because some part of you weeps over it.

The responses are clearly client-centered in their respect for the person of the client, but the categories are no longer those of the earlier period of concern with standardized technique.

THE FOCUS ON THE CLIENT'S PHENOMENAL WORLD

It has already been pointed out that, in spite of the changes reflected in client-centered therapy by the development of the theory of the three therapeutic conditions, the communication of accurate empathic understanding remains the actual work of the client-centered therapist. This indicates the continued belief among client-centered therapists that understanding the client's world as the client sees it is central in effecting therapeutic change. It is this belief that, as Seeman has pointed out,[60] is signified by the term "client-centered."

All therapeutic approaches are of course centrally interested in the client, and in this sense might be thought of as client-centered. But the term "client-centered" has, for our group, a technical meaning not often explicated. Many therapeutic systems consider the achievement of an empathic grasp of the client's private world only a preliminary to the real work of the therapist. For these therapists, coming to understand the client's phenomenal universe is rather like taking a history; it is a first step. Instead, the client-centered therapist aims to remain within this phenomenal universe throughout the entire course of therapy and holds that stepping outside it — to offer external interpretations, to give advice, to suggest, to judge — only retards therapeutic gain.

This is not to say, however, that the client-centered therapist responds only to the obvious in the phenomenal world of his client. If that were so, it is doubtful that any movement would ensue in therapy. Indeed, there would be no therapy. Instead, the client-centered therapist aims to dip from the pool of implicit meanings just at the edge of the client's awareness. And in this sense — but in this sense only — the work of the client-centered therapist is like that of Fenichel's skillful Freudian interpreter:

> Since interpretation means something unconscious become con-
> scious by naming it at the moment it is striving to break through,
> effective interpretations can be given only at one specific point,
> namely, where the patient's immediate interest is momentarily
> centered.[8]

The analyst, in other words, works at the edge of his patient's focused awareness. He facilitates the breakthrough into
consciousness of those feelings that are about to become conscious in any event, as a result of the therapeutic process. The
client-centered therapist works somewhat similarly. He does not
merely repeat his client's words, concepts, or feelings. Rather, he
seeks for the meaning implicit in the present inner experiencing
toward which the client's words or concepts point. As Gendlin has
put it:

> The client-centered response at its best formulates something
> which is not yet fully formulated or conceptualized. . . . It formu-
> lates the meaning which the client has not yet symbolized explicitly
> but which he does now feel and which is implied in what he says.
> Sometimes it formulates the felt whole which the client has been
> trying to get at by various verbalizations.[12]

Thus, the client-centered therapist aims to concentrate on the
immediate phenomenal world of the client. For he believes that it is
in confusions or contradictions within this world that the client's
difficulties lie. This exclusive focus in therapy on the present
phenomenal experience of the client is the meaning of the term
"client-centered."

THE THEORY OF THE THERAPEUTIC PROCESS

Since client-centered therapy originated in the experience of
psychologists who were oriented toward theory and research
as well as toward clinical practice, it is not surprising that we
have from the first been interested in discerning the order that
underlies the process of personality change. This interest has

led us to a slowly changing series of formulations as to what constitutes the process of therapy. These formulations have been enriched by experience with an ever wider range of clients and by attempts to study the process of change empirically.

In the earliest description of client-centered therapy, I pictured the process as composed primarily of three steps. As it seemed to my colleagues and me at that time, a client-centered approach resulted, first, in the release of expression, the release of personal feelings in the interview. Following this emotional catharsis, insight tended to develop into the origin and nature of the difficulties being experienced by the client. Such insight was followed by the making of positive choices and decisions in regard to the problem elements of the client's life — an emotional re-education involved in the practice of applying the newly gained insights in reality. This practice led to an increased capacity for personal problem-solving in various areas. Research investigations in the 1940s by Snyder[67] and Seeman[61] tended to confirm this theory. Statements categorized as discussion of problem situations declined from more than half of the total client conversation during the first fifth of counseling to approximately one-fourth of the statements during the final fifth of the counseling interviews. Statements of insight, and changed perceptions experienced as a result of counseling, increased from 4 to 19 percent from the first to last quintile of the counseling interviews. The discussion of plans and the making of decisions, almost nonexistent during the early aspects of therapy, came to occupy a significant portion of the client's conversation. During the same time, the balance shifted from largely negative attitudes to largely positive ones. This latter tendency was even more marked when the study was limited to statements in the present tense, indicating the client's current feelings, and omitting his descriptions of past feelings.

Although this description of the process seemed adequate as far as it went, further attention to the data of therapy made it seem imperative that more attention be paid to the place of the self in the client's experience of personality disorganization and subsequent change and reintegration. As I have stated elsewhere:

... those doing therapeutic work from a client-centered orientation certainly had no initial leaning toward the self as an explanatory construct. Yet so much of the verbal interchange of therapy
had to do with the self that attention was forcibly turned in this direction. The client felt that he was not being his real self, often felt
he did not know what his real self was, and felt satisfaction when
he had become more truly himself.[26]

Raimy[22] was the first to attempt a theoretical formulation of
the kind of changes that occurred within the self. He also made
an empirical study of the changing attitudes toward the self during therapy, finding that self-attitudes became more positive.
Gradually other studies were undertaken, particularly with the
Q-sort developed by Stephenson,[69] which enabled us to make
a far more refined measurement of the self-concept and its
changes.[55] Gradually a coherent theory and a body of supporting
evidence developed in this area. We came to see the troubled or
neurotic individual as one whose self-concept had become structured in ways incongruent with his organismic experience. (As
one very brief example, a mother may be experiencing feelings
of dislike and rejection toward her child, but her self-concept
may contain only perceptions of herself as a good and loving
mother.) Thus there may be a sharp discrepancy between the
client's organismic experiencing and his self-concept. Such a discrepancy between experience and the conceptualized self is the
source of anxiety.

In therapy, with its climate of acceptance and safety and its
freedom to explore one's feelings whatever they may be, it becomes possible for the client to experience the feelings that have
not been admitted into his concept of self. Once experienced in
an accepting climate, they can gradually be incorporated into his
self-picture, and he thereby achieves more unity and integration
between the person he organismically is and the self he perceives
himself as being.[26] This theory of therapeutic change has been
far more rigorously described in a formal statement of client-
centered theory,[49] in which it is pointed out that the origin of
the inaccuracies in the self-concept lies primarily with the individual's attempt to retain love. In order to hold the love of a parent, the child introjects values and perceptions that he does not

actually experience. He then denies to his awareness the organismic experiencings that contradict these introjections. Thus his self-concept contains false elements that are not based on what he is, in his experiencing.

More recently[40,41,70] we have moved toward a new theory of process that builds on two previous descriptions. Based on the study of a large number of recorded interviews, a fresh picture of the process of change has been developed that sees change occurring along a number of continua. This newer picture of the process has borrowed significantly from Gendlin's theory of experiencing.[10,11,12] It may be briefly delineated by presenting some of the closely related continua on which change occurs. No matter where the client may be on each of these continua at the outset of his therapy, he moves in a directional fashion toward the latter end of the continuum. For example, in regard to his feelings and personal meanings, he moves away from a state in which feelings are unrecognized, unowned, unexpressed. He moves toward becoming a flowing process in which ever-changing feelings are experienced in the moment, knowingly and acceptingly, and may be accurately expressed.

The process of therapy also involves a change in the manner of his experiencing. At the initial point on the continuum, he is remote from his experiencing. An example would be the intellectualizing client who talks only in abstractions, leaving one quite ignorant of what is actually going on within him. From such remoteness, he moves toward an immediacy of experiencing in which he lives openly in his feelings and knows that he can turn to his experiencing to discover its current meaning.

The process also involves a loosening of the cognitive maps of experience. From construing experience in rigid ways that are perceived as external facts, the client moves toward developing loosely held construings of meanings in experience, constructs modifiable by each new experience.

In general, the evidence from a number of research studies shows that the process moves away from fixity, remoteness from feelings and experience, rigidity of self-concept, remoteness from people, impersonality of functioning. It moves toward fluidity, changingness, immediacy of feelings and experience, acceptance of feelings and experience, tentativeness of constructs,

discovery of a changing self in one's changing experience, realness and closeness of relationships, a unity and integration of
functioning.

A number of studies are currently attempting to delineate even
more sharply the various facets of this therapeutic process.

THE MOTIVATION FOR CHANGE:
THE "GROWTH HYPOTHESIS"

Many years ago, Kurt Goldstein recorded the following observation, based on his work with brain-injured war veterans:

> Normal behavior corresponds to a continual change of tension of
> such a kind that over and over again that state of tension is reached
> that enables and impels the organism to actualize itself in further
> activities, according to its nature. Thus, experience with patients
> teaches us that we have to assume only one drive, the drive of self-
> actualization.[15]

My own experience with disturbed individuals and that of my
colleagues in psychotherapy amply corroborate Goldstein's observation, and early in our development we formulated, and
have since found no reason to abandon, what has been called
the "growth hypothesis":

> . . . in most if not all individuals there exist growth forces, ten-
> dencies toward self-actualization, which may act as the sole mo-
> tivation for therapy. . . . The individual has the capacity and the
> strength to devise, quite unaided, the steps which will lead him
> to a more mature and more comfortable relationship to his real-
> ity.[42]

One phrase in this quotation has led to a regrettable misunderstanding, the phrase "quite unaided." I meant, and would still
maintain, that no direct aid in the way of suggestions, advice,
and the like is necessary. The phrase was not intended, however, to rule out the fact that the growth-promoting therapeutic
climate is the very thing that makes these steps toward maturity
possible.

The emphasis on the self-directive capacity of the individual and the release of this potential through a suitable growth-promoting climate have for some reason stirred much criticism. Some have thought of the client-centered therapist as an optimist. Others have felt that this line of thought follows Rousseau. Neither criticism seems to me to be true. The hypothesis in regard to the capacity of the individual is, rather, distilled out of an accumulated experience with many mildly and deeply disturbed individuals, who often display destructive or self-destructive tendencies. Contrary to those therapists who see depravity at men's core, who see men's deepest instincts as destructive, I have found that when man is truly free to become what he most deeply is, free to actualize his nature as an organism capable of awareness, then he clearly appears to move toward wholeness and integration. As I have put this elsewhere:

> When [man] is most fully man, when he is his complete organism, when awareness of experience, that peculiarly human attribute, is most fully operating, then he is to be trusted, then his behavior is constructive. It is not always conventional. It will not always be conforming. It will be individualized. But it will also be socialized.[36]

I have attempted to deal with two different aspects of this tendency toward growth, first, by describing far more fully the actualizing tendency and its place in psychological dynamics.[24] I have also held that, if we paid attention to the directions in which the individual moves when he is safe enough to function freely, we would then have a picture of the trends that would operate in the optimal person, whom I have termed the "fully functioning person." I have tried to describe not only what such an individual would be like[29, 36] but also the organismic valuing process by which he would guide his life.[51]

The concept of the fully functioning person — the personal tendency toward growth when it is most fully lived out — can best be presented in two recent quotations on this topic. It will be clear that this concept leads to quite a different picture of the optimal person than would be true, for example, in psychoanalytic thinking.

I have little sympathy with the rather prevalent concept that man is basically irrational, and that his impulses, if not controlled, will lead to destruction of others and self. Man's behavior is exquisitely rational, moving with subtle and ordered complexity toward the goals his organism is endeavoring to achieve. The tragedy for most of us is that our defenses keep us from being aware of this rationality, so that consciously we are moving in one direction, while organismically we are moving in another. But in our person who is living the process of the good life, there would be a decreasing number of such barriers, and he would be increasingly a participant in the rationality of his organism. The only control of impulses which would exist, or which would prove necessary, is the natural and internal balancing of one need against another, and the discovery of behaviors which follow the vector most closely approximating the satisfaction of all needs. The experience of extreme satisfaction of one need (for aggression, or sex, etc.) in such a way as to do violence to the satisfaction of other needs (for companionship, tender relationship, etc.) — an experience very common in the defensively organized person — would be greatly decreased. He would participate in the vastly complex self-regulatory activities of his organism — the psychological as well as physiological thermostatic controls — in such a fashion as to live in increasing harmony with himself and with others. . . . This process of living in the good life involves a wider range, a greater richness, than the constricted living in which most of us find ourselves. To be a part of this process means that one is involved in the frequently frightening and frequently satisfying experience of a more sensitive living, with greater range, greater variety, greater richness. It seems to me that clients who have moved significantly in therapy live more intimately with their feelings of pain but also more vividly with their feelings of ecstasy; that anger is more clearly felt but so also is love; that fear is an experience they know more deeply but so is courage. And the reason that they can thus live fully in a wider range is that they have this underlying confidence in themselves as trustworthy instruments for encountering life. . . . [Such a process] involves the stretching and growing of becoming more and more of one's potentialities. It involves the courage to be. It means launching oneself fully into the stream of life. Yet the deeply exciting thing about human beings is that when the individual is inwardly free he chooses as the good life this process of becoming.[36]

FOCUS ON THEORY OF CHANGE

Although a theory of personality has developed from our experience in client-centered therapy,[26,49] it is quite clear to anyone closely associated with this orientation that this is not our central focus. Rather, the manner in which change comes about in the human personality has been the central core of our interest. In this respect, client-centered therapy represents a "field-theory approach" rather than a genetic or trait approach to issues regarding personality, which means that we are centrally concerned with all of the elements in an immediately present situation that appear to be involved in the process of change. We are far less interested in the manner in which these elements and characteristics have developed over the years. It seems to us that far more intelligent and answerable questions can be raised in regard to the *process* of personality change than in regard to the *causes* of the person's present personality characteristics.

In any event, this central focus explains why the type of research instruments developed has to do with the measurement of immediate attitudes, of relationship qualities existing in the present, of current indexes of a process of change. Such indexes have been incorporated in a number of process scales by which we are currently endeavoring to find, in the manner of expression of the client at the moment, an indirect measure of the quality of change occurring within him.

THE EXPANSION OF RESEARCH

One distinctive aspect of client-centered therapy is that, from the beginning, it has placed a strong emphasis on research. We have been committed to the belief that the phenomena of therapy can and should be subjected to rigorous research investigation. To this end, thousands of therapeutic interviews have been recorded, providing the raw data for many studies.

Sound-motion pictures of interviews have been made to subject the process to even more microscopic investigation.[57,58] An annotated bibliography published in 1957[7] shows more than one hundred published investigations on all phases of therapy — the relationship, the process, the outcomes, the theoretical formulations and predictions.

Since the publication of that bibliography, there has been an increased development of research in all its phases. New instruments have been devised for the measurement of therapeutic conditions. Various scales have been prepared for assessing the therapeutic process. A program of research in psychotherapy with hospitalized schizophrenics has been carried through. A volume has been published investigating the therapeutic relationship.[68] Time-limited therapy has been exhaustively studied.[65,66] Many individual investigations of different aspects of therapy or of hypotheses growing out of client-centered theory have been completed.

This large body of research cannot be presented in this brief article, although references to a number of studies have already been made, showing something of the way in which both a research orientation and the findings from research investigations interpenetrate all our work. A more comprehensive knowledge of the studies growing out of the client-centered approach can be obtained through Cartwright's annotated bibliography,[7] already mentioned. A good analysis of the earlier research is contained in a chapter on research perspectives in client-centered therapy, by Seeman and Raskin.[62] A cluster of studies, carried out at the Counseling Center of the University of Chicago, is contained in a 1954 volume.[55] It presents objective measures of the changes in the self-perceptions, personality structure, and social behavior of clients that result from therapy. It is hoped that a volume reporting our study of the therapeutic relationship and its effects with hospitalized schizophrenics will be available in 1966.[56]

Seeman summarizes the progress already made:

> If we take a long view of the research that has been reported we can see that much has been done in two decades. The studies have gone from simple descriptive studies to theory-oriented studies of

the therapeutic process. Outcome studies have grown in sophistication, and linkages between process and outcome have been made. The problem of controls, always a stubborn problem, is now being met on a satisfactory basis. These are solid and durable gains.[60]

THE BROADENED RANGE OF CLIENTS

Initially, there was some justification for the belief that client-centered therapy developed only from experience with college students and hence was applicable only to such a group. During the ensuing years, a client-centered approach has been utilized with children in play therapy,[1] with clients in speech clinics, with troubled parishioners who have come to their clergyman,[19] with deeply disturbed neurotics, with individuals in marital difficulty, with industrial executives, with borderline psychotics, and with hospitalized schizophrenics. This attempt to work with many types of individuals has led to a stretching and broadening of our thinking, and has brought about many of the developments reported here. Though our work has changed in a number of significant ways it is a matter of some interest that we have seen no reason to alter in any basic way either our concept of the therapeutic relationship or our concept of the directional tendency of the human organism when given a suitable climate for growth and development.

THE GENERALITY OF APPLICATION

Client-centered therapy has always seen the therapeutic relationship as a special instance of interpersonal relationships in general. It has also seen change and growth in therapy as a special instance of growth and development in any human being. Perhaps it is because of these two aspects of our point of view that client-centered theories and methods have been utilized in a wide variety of settings having nothing to do with the formal therapy situation. The client-centered approach has had a wide and receptive audience not simply among therapists but among school and vocational counselors, leaders in group dynamics, industrial counselors, speech therapists,

teachers, business executives, clergymen of many faiths, social
caseworkers, and other groups. It is somewhat surprising, for
example, to find school counselors in Japan and social caseworkers in Belgium and Italy receiving training along client-
centered lines. Of equal interest are the classes set up in some
experimental schools in which client-centered principles are
being consciously applied to the group process. Workers in
the field of community development have drawn upon client-
centered theory and practice to facilitate the independent growth
of community responsibility and problem-solving skill. Wide
application, of course, is of itself no adequate index of the truth
of any given point of view. Some individuals are doubtless endeavoring to use a client-centered approach when it is irrelevant.
I think, however, that it is not unimportant that this point of view
has been perceived as having significance for so many people in
such a diversity of settings.

In my own professional work I have experienced something of
the range of applicability of the theories and practices we have
developed. Initially considering them applicable only in individual therapy with clinic clients, I began to recognize their
relevance to the facilitation of learning in the classroom and
developed a very different approach with students.[26, 43] It also
followed that, if this point of view resulted in the growth and
development of individuals, then it had relevance for administration of a staff in which the development of the individual was
one of the goals.[45] It has been very rewarding to see this same
point of view adopted by executives in some industrial organizations.[16] It appeared to me that a client-centered approach, having these implications and applications, should also apply to the
chronic hospitalized psychotic, and I have spent several recent
years testing this hypothesis. As that work comes to its conclusion, I find myself wanting to test our hypotheses in still another
field, namely, that of the intensive group experience. "Sensitivity
training groups," "T-groups," "basic encounter groups," are different labels for a relatively new type of intensive group experience. Much of this development in group work has come about
entirely independently of my own thinking, but the principles arrived at are in many respects very similar. I am eagerly looking
forward to testing our hypotheses more fully in such intensive

group encounters and also assisting in the development of a theory for this field. Some of the impact of client-centered thinking on this development is already evident in recent books dealing with this area.[5]

THE CONCERN WITH PHILOSOPHICAL ISSUES

In recent years many of my own writings, and those of others in our group, have focused on broad philosophical questions, the human problems on which the data of psychotherapy seem to bear.[10, 11, 31, 36, 39, 50, 52, 64]

Some of the issues to which we have directed ourselves can only be listed here. In a world that teeters on the brink of annihilation and in which new problems are developing at an incredible rate, it has seemed only natural to endeavor to throw whatever light we can on some of the broad social questions faced by modern man. Thus we have presented a point of view as to the basic nature of man, an issue that goes to the heart of much social philosophy.[35] There has been the attempt to delineate the characteristics of the optimal human being as we see him.[29] Society, as well as our clients, has the right to know how we have come to define the healthy person, and to decide whether this concept outlines a desirable goal. There has also been an attempt to define the way in which the mature person develops a sensitive, organismic valuing process rather than a rigid set of values.[51] To me it seems that some change in our valuing approach is essential if mankind is to exist in a rapidly changing world. There have been several articles about the control of human behavior, a goal toward which behavioral scientists seem to be moving.[31, 39, 59] A public dialogue with B. F. Skinner in 1956 and some later encounters with him have helped to clarify for the public both sides of this important issue. Partly growing out of this concern has come an interest in the philosophy of science that operates in the behavioral sciences. A recent article has held that the advances in both other sciences and the field of psychotherapy indicate that the behavioral sciences are operating on an outmoded philosophy that has come to have a highly constrictive effect.[52] Out of our interest in the learning process have come papers presenting a view of education that seems congenial with the client-centered point of view.[26,37,43,54] Another broadly philosophical topic that has engaged attention has been the close relationship between client-centered therapy, with its emphasis on the significance of the present moment, and various strands of existential philosophy in both this country and Europe.[53] A related development is the alignment of many in the client-centered group with the so-called "third force" in American psychology — the more humanistically, existentially oriented psychology taking its place beside behaviorism and Freudian psychoanalysis. These are some of the directions in which our broader interests are carrying us.

REFERENCES

1. Axline, Virginia. *Play Therapy*. Boston: Houghton Mifflin, 1947.
2. Barrett-Lennard, Godfrey. "Dimensions of Perceived Therapist Response Related to Therapeutic Change." Unpublished dissertation, University of Chicago, 1959.
3. ———. "Dimensions of Therapist Response as Causal Factors in Therapeutic Change," *Psychological Monographs*, 76 (1962), Whole No. 562.
4. Bergman, Daniel. "Counseling Method and Client Responses," *Journal of Consulting Psychology*, 15 (1951), 216–224.
5. Bradford, Leland P., Jack R. Gibb, and Kenneth D. Benne. *T-Group Theory and Laboratory Method: Innovation in Re-education*. New York: Wiley, 1964.
6. Butler, John. "Client-Centered Counseling and Psychotherapy," in Daniel Brower and Leonard Abt, eds., *Progress in Clinical Psychology*, Vol. 3. New York: Grune & Stratton, 1958.
7. Cartwright, Desmond. "Annotated Bibliography of Research and Theory Construction in Client-Centered Therapy," *Journal of Counseling Psychology*, 4 (1957), 82–100.
8. Fenichel, Otto. *The Psychoanalytic Theory of the Neuroses*. New York: W. W. Norton, 1945.
9. Gendlin, Eugene T. "Client-Centered Developments in Psychotherapy with Schizophrenics," *Journal of Counseling Psychology*, 9 (1962), 205–211.
10. ———. *Experiencing and the Creation of Meaning*. New York: The Free Press of Glencoe, 1962.
11. ———. "Experiencing and the Nature of Concepts," *The Christian Scholar*, 46 (1963), 245–255.
12. ———. "Experiencing: A Variable in the Process of Therapeutic

Change," *American Journal of Psychotherapy*, 15 (1961), 233–245.
13. ———. "Initiating Psychotherapy with 'Unmotivated' Patients," *Psychiatric Quarterly*, 35 (1961), 134–139.
14. ———. "Sub-verbal Communication and Therapist Expressivity: Trends in Client-Centered Psychotherapy with Schizophrenics," *The Wisconsin Psychiatric Institute Bulletin*, 1 (1961).
15. Goldstein, Kurt. *The Organism.* New York: American Book, 1939.
16. Gordon, Thomas. *Group-Centered Leadership.* Boston: Houghton Mifflin, 1955.
17. Grummon, Donald. "Client-Centered Theory," in Buford Steffire, ed., *Theories in Counseling.* New York: McGraw-Hill, 1965.
18. Halkides, Galatia. "An Experimental Study of Four Conditions Necessary for Therapeutic Personality Change." Unpublished doctoral dissertation, University of Chicago, 1958.
19. Hiltner, Seward, and Lowell Colston. *The Context of Pastoral Counseling.* New York: Abingdon Press, 1961.
20. Kirtner, William, and Desmond Cartwright. "Success and Failure in Client-Centered Therapy as a Function of Client Personality Variables," *Journal of Consulting Psychology*, 22 (1958), 259–264.
21. Porter, Elias. *An Introduction to Therapeutic Counseling.* Boston: Houghton Mifflin, 1950.
22. Raimy, Victor. "Self Reference in Counseling Interviews," *Journal of Consulting Psychology*, 12 (1948), 153–163.
23. Rioch, Margaret, et al. "NIMH Pilot Project in Training Mental Health Counselors: Summary of First Year's Work 1960–61," mimeographed report. Bethesda, Md.: National Institute of Mental Health Adult Psychiatry Branch, undated.
24. Rogers, Carl R. "The Actualizing Tendency in Relation to 'Motives' and to Consciousness," in Marshall Jones, ed., *Nebraska Symposium on Motivation.* Lincoln, Neb.: University of Nebraska Press, 1963.
25. ———. "The Characteristics of a Helping Relationship," *Personnel and Guidance Journal*, 37 (1958), 6–16.
26. ———. *Client-Centered Therapy.* Boston: Houghton Mifflin, 1951.
27. ———. "Client-Centered Therapy: A Current View," in Frieda Fromm-Reichmann and J. L. Moreno, eds., *Progress in Psychotherapy.* New York: Grune & Stratton, 1956.
28. ———. *Counseling and Psychotherapy.* Boston: Houghton Mifflin, 1942.
29. ———. "The Concept of the Fully Functioning Person," *Psychotherapy: Theory, Research and Practice*, 1 (1963), 17–26.
30. ———. "The Essence of Psychotherapy: A Client-Centered View," *Annals of Psychotherapy*, 1 (1959), 51–57.

31. ———. "Implications of Recent Advances in the Prediction and Control of Behavior," *Teachers College Record*, 57 (1956), 316–322.

32. ———. "The Interpersonal Relationship: The Core of Guidance," *Harvard Educational Review*, 32 (1962), 416–429.

33. ———. "Learning to Be Free," in Seymour M. Farber and Robert H. Wilson, eds., *Conflict and Creativity: Control of the Mind*, Part 2. New York: McGraw-Hill, 1963.

34. ———. "The Necessary and Sufficient Conditions of Therapeutic Personality Change," *Journal of Consulting Psychology*, 21 (1957), 95–103.

35. ———. "A Note on the Nature of Man," *Journal of Counseling Psychology*, 4 (1957), 199–203.

36. ———. *On Becoming a Person*. Boston: Houghton Mifflin, 1961.

37. ———. "Personal Thoughts on Teaching and Learning," *Merrill-Palmer Quarterly*, 3 (1957), 241–243.

38. ———. "Persons or Science? A Philosophical Question," *American Psychologist*, 10 (1955), 267–278.

39. ———. "The Place of the Person in the New World of the Behavioral Sciences," *Personnel and Guidance Journal*, 39 (1961), 442–451.

40. ———. "A Process Conception of Psychotherapy," *American Psychologist*, 13 (1958), 142–149.

41. ———. "The Process Equation of Psychotherapy," *American Journal of Psychotherapy*, 14 (1961), 27–45.

42. ———. "Significant Aspects of Client-Centered Therapy," *American Psychologist*, 1 (1946), 415–422.

43. ———. "Significant Learning: In Therapy and in Education," *Educational Leadership*, 16 (1959), 232–242.

44. ———. "Significant Trends in the Client-Centered Orientation," in Daniel Brower and Leonard Abt, eds., *Progress in Clinical Psychology*, Vol. 4. New York: Grune & Stratton, 1960.

45. ———. "Some Implications of Client-Centered Counseling for College Personnel Work," *Educational and Psychological Measurement*, 8 (1948), 540–549.

46. ———. "Some Learnings from a Study of Psychotherapy with Schizophrenics," *Pennsylvania Psychiatric Quarterly* (1962), 3–15.

47. ———. "A Study of Psychotherapeutic Change in Schizophrenics and Normals: The Design and Instrumentation," *Psychiatric Research Reports*, 15 (1962), 51–60.

48. ———. "A Tentative Scale for the Measurement of Process in Psychotherapy," in E. Rubinstein, ed., *Research in Psychotherapy*. Washington, D.C.: American Psychological Association, 1959.

49. ———. "A Theory of Therapy, Personality, and Interpersonal Re-

lationships as Developed in the Client-Centered Framework," in Sigmund Koch, ed., *Psychology: A Study of a Science, Vol. 3: Formulations of the Person and the Social Context.* New York: McGraw-Hill, 1959.

50. ———. "A Therapist's View of the Good Life," *The Humanist*, 17 (1957), 291–300.

51. ———. "Toward a Modern Approach to Values: The Valuing Process in the Mature Person," *Journal of Abnormal and Social Psychology*, 68 (1964), 160–167.

52. ———. "Toward a Science of the Person," in T. W. Wann, ed., *Behaviorism and Phenomenology: Contrasting Bases for Modern Psychology.* Chicago: University of Chicago Press, 1964.

53. ———. "Two Divergent Trends," in Rollo May, ed., *Existential Psychology.* New York: Random House, 1961.

54. ———. "What Psychology Has to Offer to Teacher Education." Paper prepared for Conference on Educational Foundations, Cornell University, 1964.

55. ———, and Rosalind Dymond, eds. *Psychotherapy and Personality Change.* Chicago: University of Chicago Press, 1954.

56. ———, Eugene T. Gendlin, Donald J. Kiesler, and Charles B. Truax. *The Therapeutic Relationship and Its Impact: A Study of Psychotherapy with Schizophrenics.* Madison, Wisc.: University of Wisconsin Press. In press.

57. ———, and R. H. Segel. "Psychotherapy Begins: The Case of Mr. Lin." 16-mm. sound motion picture, State College, Pennsylvania Psychological Cinema Register, 1955.

58. ———, and R. H. Segel. "Psychotherapy in Process: The Case of Miss Mun." 16-mm. sound motion picture, State College, Pennsylvania Psychological Cinema Register, 1955.

59. ———, and B. F. Skinner. "Some Issues Concerning the Control of Human Behavior," *Science*, 124 (1956), 1057–1066.

60. Seeman, Julius. "Perspectives in Client-Centered Therapy," in *Handbook of Clinical Psychology.* In press.

61. ———. "A Study of the Process of Nondirective Therapy," *Journal of Consulting Psychology*, 13 (1949), 157–168.

62. ———, and Nathaniel Raskin. "Research Perspectives in Client-Centered Therapy," in O. H. Mowrer, ed., *Psychotherapy: Theory and Research.* New York: Ronald, 1953.

63. Shlien, John. "A Client-Centered Approach to Schizophrenia," in Arthur Burton, ed., *Psychotherapy of the Psychoses.* New York: Basic Books, 1960.

64. ———. "The Phenomenological Perspective," in J. M. Wepman and

R. W. Heine, eds., *Perspectives in Personality*. Chicago: Aldine Press, 1963.

65. ———. "Time-Limited Psychotherapy: An Experimental Investigation of Practical Values and Theoretical Implications," *Journal of Counseling Psychology*, 4 (1957), 318–322.

66. ———, Harold Mosak, and Rudolph Driekurs. "Effect of Time-Limits: A Comparison of Client-Centered and Adlerian Psychotherapy," *University of Chicago Counseling Center Discussion Paper*, 6 (1960).

67. Snyder, William U. "An Investigation of the Nature of Non-Directive Psychotherapy," *Journal of Genetic Psychology*, 33 (1945), 193–223.

68. ———. *The Psychotherapy Relationship*. New York: Macmillan, 1961.

69. Stephenson, William. *The Study of Behavior: Q-Technique and Its Methodology*. Chicago: University of Chicago Press, 1953.

70. Walker, Alan, Rickard A. Rablen, and Carl R. Rogers. "Development of a Scale to Measure Process Changes in Psychotherapy," *Journal of Clinical Psychology*, 16 (1960), 79–85.

II / THE DIALOGUES

3
Martin Buber

Martin Buber was born in Vienna in 1878. From age three, when his parents divorced, he lived with his grandfather, a wealthy businessman, respected scholar, and leader in the Jewish community. Buber was schooled in the Western European intellectual tradition of reason, logical criticism, and historical research. In contrast, during summers in Eastern Europe, he was deeply impressed by the Hasidic Jewish tradition, which emphasizes man's direct, mystical, spontaneous, and joyful relationship with God.

After studying philosophy and the history of art at the Universities of Vienna (Ph.D., 1904), Berlin, Leipzig, and Zurich, he taught philosophy and religion at several institutes and universities. From 1923 to 1933 he was professor of Jewish theology (the only such chair in a German university), history of religion, and ethics at the University of Frankfurt. When Jewish students were excluded from German universities in 1933, he became director of the Central Office for Jewish Adult Education. He married Paula Winkler, who later became a respected novelist.

Early in the century, Buber became the leading interpreter of Hasidism and Jewish mysticism (e.g., *Tales of Rabbi Nachman*, 1906, translated 1956; *The Legend of the Baal-Shem*, 1908, translated 1955), explaining the vitality of the Jewish mystical tradition and writing his own versions of some one hundred Hasidic tales and parables. Gradually moving beyond mysticism, but certainly influenced by Hasidism, Buber developed a philosophy centered around the "encounter" between the person, the "I," and God, the "Thou." God as "Thou" has no boundaries, and

includes everything. A true encounter between persons or between a person and art could also be an I-Thou relationship,
as the other person or the art is experienced without labels or
bounds and is therefore connected to everything, to God. "I-It"
relationships, on the other hand, were more typical of everyday
living, with the other person or medium perceived as object, as
separate.

Buber's major thesis was that "life is meeting." He described a
tragic incident in which a troubled young man came to seek his
advice. Buber was preoccupied and talked with him, but did not
really "meet" him. The young man went away and committed
suicide. Salvation, for Buber, could not be found by glorifying
the individual or the collective, but in relationship. In "open dialogue," not an "unmasking" of the "adversary," he saw the only
hope for the future.

His staggering literary output included more than sixty volumes on theology, Jewish history, philosophy, comparative religion, art, and education, including *Daniel* (1913), *Ich und Du*
(1923; *I and Thou*, 1937), *The Kingship of God* (1932), *For the Sake
of Heaven* (a novel, 1945), and *The Prophetic Faith* (1950). In 1925,
with Franz Rosenzweig, he began a major new translation of the
Bible into German, which he eventually completed in 1962.

From 1899 on, Buber was also a leading Zionist, serving as
cultural editor for the Zionist paper *Die Welt* and as founder
and editor for ten years of *Der Jude*, the leading periodical for
German-speaking Jewry, in which he sought to clarify the spiritual destiny of the Jewish people in Europe and Palestine. In
1926 *Der Jude* was broadened to *Die Kreatur*, which he co-edited
with a German Catholic and Protestant.

Forced to flee Germany in 1938, he emigrated to Israel, where
he became professor of social philosophy at Hebrew University
in Jerusalem. In addition to his writing and teaching on religion
and social philosophy, Buber directed the Institute for Adult
Education (from 1949 to 1953), which dealt with the cultural as-
similation of the vast wave of Jewish immigrants in the four years
following Israel's independence. As it had for half a century, his
Zionism included the consistent advocacy of Palestinian civil and
religious rights.

After retirement in 1951, Buber traveled widely, including

Martin Buber

Martin Buber

several trips to the United States, where he lectured at many leading theological schools and universities. Although Israel was slow to appreciate him, in the fifties his work achieved international acclaim. In Germany he received many prestigious prizes and honors. Reinhold Niebuhr called him "the greatest living Jewish philosopher." Other reviewers wrote that he "profoundly influenced contemporary thought, including Christian theology" and that "His relevance to the work of almost every major writer of the century . . . is indisputable." *Commonweal* wrote that Buber had "an immense influence on diverse thinkers of all faiths, including . . . Paul Tillich." Hermann Hesse said Buber was "one of the leading and most valuable personalities in contemporary world literature." *Yale Review* said his thinking "entered as a vital ingredient into the newer Christian theology as well as into a good deal of the most significant social philosophy of our day."

Described as "a tiny man with a huge head and a flowing white beard, who resembles a prophet of old," Buber was eventually recognized as a seer and sage by his countrymen. Israelis mourned his passing on June 13, 1965, at age eighty-seven. In honor of the man who had fought so consistently for their rights, Arab students at the Hebrew University laid a wreath at his bier as he lay in state.

Martin Buber's dialogue with Carl Rogers took place in Ann Arbor, Michigan, on April 18, 1957, at a conference on Buber's work organized by the University of Michigan. The dialogue is moderated by Maurice Friedman, a prominent American philosopher.

REV. DEWITT BALDWIN: This will be an unusual opportunity — a session where we can enjoy an hour of time when you can think with two men who want to come to closer grips with their own ideas. I just want to introduce one person and let him speak of the others. Your moderator is Professor Maurice S. Friedman, professor of philosophy at Sarah Lawrence College, Bronxville, New York. Professor Friedman is one of the best American interpreters of Martin Buber. He had his undergraduate work at Harvard, his graduate work at Ohio State and the University of Chicago, where he took his doctor's degree. He is best known in

44   *The Dialogues*

relation to Martin Buber for his book *Martin Buber, the Life of Dialogue*. And so, Maurice, I'll turn it over to you and I know you will have a good time.*

MAURICE FRIEDMAN: Thank you, DeWitt Baldwin. It gives me a great deal of pleasure to moderate this because I could say that perhaps I initiated the dialogue between Professor Buber and Professor Rogers some years ago when someone pointed out to me some resemblances in their thought. I wrote to Dr. Rogers and he kindly supplied me with some papers and we corresponded a while. Then I sent this material to Professor Buber, including some of Dr. Rogers' articles, and so I was very happy indeed when the idea of the two of them speaking here in dialogue came up. I think it is a most significant meeting, not just in terms of psychotherapy, but of the fact that both these men have won our admiration as persons with an approach to personal relations and personal becoming. There are so many remarkable similarities between their thoughts that it is awfully intriguing to have the privilege of hearing them talk with one another and seeing what issues may also come out. My role as moderator is only, if the occasion should arise, to sharpen these issues or interpret one way or another. I don't think you need any introduction to Professor Buber since the conference is centered around him. And I'm sure you don't need an introduction to Dr. Rogers either. He, of course, has been famous for a great many years as the founder of the once so-called nondirective therapy, now, I believe, rechristened client-centered therapy, and is the director of the University of Chicago Counseling Center, where he has had very fruitful relations with the theological faculty and the personality and religion courses there. The form of this dialogue is that Dr. Rogers will raise questions with Dr. Buber and Dr. Buber will respond, perhaps with a question, perhaps with a statement. We'll let them carry it from there. Dr. Rogers.

CARL ROGERS: One thing I would say to the audience before starting to talk with Dr. Buber is that this is most certainly an unrehearsed dialogue. The weather made it necessary for me to spend all day arriving here and so it was only an hour or two ago

Psychologia, 1960, 3, 208–221.

that I met Dr. Buber, even though I had met him a long time ago in his writing.

I think that the first question I would like to ask you, Dr. Buber, may sound a trifle impertinent, but I would like to explain it and then perhaps it won't seem impertinent. I have wondered, How have you lived so deeply in interpersonal relationships and gained such an understanding of the human individual without being a psychotherapist? (*Buber laughs.*) The reason I ask is that it seems to me that a number of us have come to sense and experience some of the same kinds of learnings that you have expressed in your writing, but very frequently we have come to those learnings through our experience in psychotherapy. I think that there is something about the therapeutic relationship that gives us permission, almost formal permission, to enter into a deep and close relationship with a person, and so we tend to learn very deeply in that way. I think of one psychiatrist friend of mine who says that he never feels as whole, or as much of a person, as he does in his therapeutic interviews. And I share that feeling. And so, if it is not too personal, I would be interested in hearing what were the channels of knowing that enabled you to learn so deeply of people and of relationships?

MARTIN BUBER: Hmmm. That is rather a biographical question. I think I must give instead of one answer, two. One is that I'm not entirely a stranger in, let me say, psychiatry, because when I was a student long ago I studied three terms psychiatry and what they call in Germany *Psychiatrische-Klinique*. I was most interested in the latter. You see, I have not studied psychiatry in order to become a psychotherapist. I studied it three terms first with —— in Leipzig, where there were students of Wundt. Afterwards in Berlin with Mandel, and a third term with Bleuler, which was the most interesting of the three. I was just then a very young, inexperienced, and not very understanding young man. But I had the feeling that I wanted to know about man, and man in the so-called pathological state. I doubted even then if it is the right term. I wanted to see, if possible to meet, such people and, as far as I can remember, to establish relations, a real relation between what we call a sane man and what we call a pathological man. And this I learned in some measure — as far as a boy of twenty or so can learn such things. (*Chuckles.*)

About what mainly constituted what you ask, it was something other. It was just a certain inclination to meet people. And as far as possible to, just to change if possible something in the *other*, but also to let *me* be changed by *him*. At any event, I had no resistance . . . put no resistance to it. I began as a young man. I felt I had not the right to want to change another if I am not open to be changed by him as far as it is legitimate. Something is to be changed and his touch, his concept is able to change it more or less. I *cannot* be, so to say, above him and say, "No! I'm out of the play. *You* are mad." And so from my — let me see. There were two phases of it. The first phase went until the year 1819 [1918], meaning until I was about forty. And then I, in 1819, felt something rather strange. I felt that I had been strongly influenced by something that came to an end just then, meaning the First World War.

ROGERS: In 1918?

BUBER: M-hmmm. It ended then, and in the course of the war, I did not feel very much about this influence. But at the end I felt, "Oh, I have been terribly influenced," because I could not resist what went on, and I was compelled to, may I say, to live it. You see? Things that went on just at this moment. You may call this *imagining* the *real*. Imagining what was going on. This imagining, for four years, influenced me terribly. Just when it was finished, it finished by a certain episode in May 1919 when a friend of mine, a great friend, a great man, was killed by the antirevolutionary soldiers in a very barbaric way, and I now again once more — and this was the last time — I was compelled to imagine just this killing, but not in an optical way alone, but, may I say so, just with my *body*. And this was the decisive moment, after which, after some days and nights in this state, I felt, "Oh, something has been done to me." And from then on, these meetings with people, particularly with young people, were, became, in a somewhat different form. I had a decisive experience, experience of four years, many concrete experiences, and from now on, I had to give something more than just my inclination to exchange thoughts and feelings, and so on. I had to give the fruit of an experience.

ROGERS: M-hmmm. Sounds as though you're saying that the knowledge, perhaps, or some of it, came in your twenties, but

then some of the wisdom you have about interpersonal relationships came from wanting to meet people openly without
wanting to dominate. And then — I see this as kind of a three-
fold answer — and then third, from really living the world war,
but living it in your own feelings and imagination.

BUBER: Just so. Because this latter was really, I cannot say it in
another language, it was really a *living* with those people. People
wounded, killed in the war.

ROGERS: You felt their wounds.

BUBER: Yes. But feeling is not sufficiently strong — the word
feeling.

ROGERS: I'm going to make one suggestion, even though it in-
terrupts us a little. I can't face the mike and face you at the same
time. Would you mind if I turned the table just a little? (*Moves table.*)

BUBER: Is this all right?

ROGERS: That seems better to me.

MAURICE FRIEDMAN: While he's changing, I want to admit that
Professor Rogers' question reminded me of a theological stu-
dent from a Baptist seminary who talked to me about Professor
Buber's thought, and when he left he said, "I must ask you a ques-
tion. Professor Buber is so good. How is it he's not a Christian?"
(*Laughter.*)

BUBER: Now may I tell you a story, not about me, one that is
a true story, too, not just an anecdote. A Christian officer had
to explain to some people in the war, in the Second War, to explain to them — soldiers — about the Jews. He began, of course,
with the explanation of what Hitler means and so on, and he explained to them that the Jews are not just a barbarous race, they
had a great culture, and so on, and then he addressed a Jewish
soldier who was there and knew something and told them, "Now
you go on and tell them something." And this young Jew told
them something about Israel and even about Jesus. And to that
one of the soldiers answered, "Do you mean to tell us that before
your Jesus we have not been Christian people?" (*Laughter.*)

ROGERS: Well, I'd like to shift to a question that I have often
wondered about. I have wondered whether your concept of what
you have termed the I-Thou relationship is similar to what I see
as the effective moments in a therapeutic relationship? If you

would permit me, I might take a moment or two to say what I see as essential in that and then perhaps you could comment on it from your point of view. I feel that when I'm being effective as a therapist, I enter the relationship as a subjective person, not as a scrutinizer, not as a scientist. I feel, too, that when I am most effective, then somehow I am relatively whole in that relationship, or the word that has meaning to me is transparent. To be sure there may be many aspects of my life that aren't brought into the relationship, but what is brought into the relationship is transparent. There is nothing hidden. Then I think, too, that in such a relationship I feel a real willingness for this other person to *be what he is*. I call that acceptance. I don't know that that's a very good word for it, but my meaning there is that I'm willing for him to possess the feelings he possesses, to hold the attitudes he holds, to be the person he is. And then another aspect of it which is important to me is that I think in those moments I am able to sense with a good deal of clarity the way his experience seems to him, really viewing it from within him, and yet without losing my own personhood or separateness in that. Then, if in addition to those things on *my* part, my client or the person with whom I'm working is able to sense something of those attitudes in me, then it seems to me that there is a real, experiential meeting of persons, in which each of us is changed. I think sometimes the client is changed more than I am, but I think both of us are changed in that kind of an experience. Now, I see that as having some resemblance to the sort of thing you have talked about in the I-Thou relationship. Yet I suspect there are differences. I would be interested very much in your comments on how that description seems to you in relation to what you have thought of in terms of two persons meeting in an I-Thou kind of relationship.

BUBER: Now I may try to ask questions, too, about what you mean. First of all, I would say, this is the action of a therapist. This is a very good example for a certain moment of dialogic existence. I mean, two persons have a certain situation in common. This situation is, from your point of view — point is not a good word, but let's see it from your point of view — it is a sick man coming to you and asking a particular kind of help. Now —

ROGERS: May I interrupt there?

BUBER: Please do.

ROGERS: I feel that if from my point of view, this is a *sick* person, then probably I'm not going to be of as much help as I might be. I feel this is a *person*. Yes, somebody else may call him sick, or if I look at him from an objective point of view, then I might agree, too, "Yes, he's sick." But in entering a relationship, it seems to me if I am looking upon it as "I am a relatively well person and this is a sick person" . . .

BUBER: Which I don't mean.

ROGERS: . . . it's no good.

BUBER: I don't mean . . . Let me leave out this word sick. A man coming to you for help. The essential difference between your role in this situation and his is obvious. He comes for help to you. You don't come for help to him. And not only this, but you are *able*, more or less, to help him. He can do different things to you, but not help you. And not this alone. You *see* him, *really*. I don't mean that you cannot be mistaken, but you *see* him, just as you said, as he *is*. He cannot, by far, cannot *see you*. Not only in the degree, but even in the kind of seeing. You are, of course, a very important person for him. But not a person whom he wants to see and to know and is able to. You're important for him. You're . . . he is floundering around, he comes to you. He is, may I say, entangled in your life, in your thoughts, in your being, your communication, and so on. But he is not interested in you as you. It cannot be. You are interested, you say so and you are right, in him as this person. This kind of detached presence he cannot have and give. Now this is the first point as far as I see it. And the second is — now please, you may interrupt me any moment.

ROGERS: I really want to understand that. The fact that I am able to see him with less distortion than he does me, and that I do have the role of helping him and that he's not trying to know me in that same sense — that's what you mean by this detached presence? I just wanted to make sure.

BUBER: Yes, only this.

ROGERS: OK.

BUBER: Now, the second fact, as far as I see, is in this *situation* that you have in common with him, but from two sides. You're on one side of the situation on the, may I say so, more or less active, and he in a more or less patient, not entirely active, not entirely passive, of course — but relatively. And this situation, let us now look on this common situation from your point of view and from his point of view. The same situation. You can see it, feel it, experience it, from the two sides. From your side, seeing him, observing him, knowing him, helping him . . . from your side and from his side. You can experience, I would venture to say, bodily, his side of the situation. When you do, so to speak, something to him, you feel yourself touched first by what you do to him. He cannot do it at all. You are at your side and at his side at the same time. Here and there, or let's rather say, there and here. Where he is and where you are. He cannot be but where he is. And this, you will, you not only will, you want, your inner necessities may be as you are. I accept that. I have no objection at all. But the *situation* has an objection. You have necessarily another attitude to the situation than he has. You are able to do something that he is not able. You are not equals and cannot be. You have the great task, self-imposed — a great self-imposed task to supplement this need of his and to do rather more than in the normal situation. But, of course, there are limits, and I may be allowed to tell you certainly in your experience as a therapist, as a healing person or helping to healing, you must experience it again and again — the limits to simple humanity. To simple humanity meaning being I and my partner, so to speak, *alike* to one another, on the same plane. I see you *mean* being on the same plane, but you cannot. There is not only you, your mode of thinking, your mode of doing, there is also a certain situation — we are so and so — which may sometime be tragic, even more terrible than what we call tragic. You *cannot* change this. Humanity, human will, human understanding, are not everything. There is some reality confronting us. We cannot forget it for a moment. . . .

ROGERS: Well, what you've said certainly stirs up lots of reactions in me. One of them, I think, is this. Let me begin first on a point that I think we would agree on. . . . I suspect that you would agree, that if this client comes to the point where he can experience what he is expressing, but also can experience my understanding of it and reaction to it, and so on, then really therapy is just about over.

BUBER: Yes. This is not what I mean.

ROGERS: OK. But one other thing that I feel is this. I've some-times wondered whether this is simply a personal idiosyncrasy of mine, but it seems to me that when another person is really ex-pressing himself and his experience and so on, I don't feel, in the way that you've described, different from him. That is, I don't know quite how to put this, but I feel as though in that moment his way of looking at his experience, distorted though it might be, is something I can look upon as having equal authority, equal va-lidity with the way I see life and experience. It seems to me *that* really is the basis of helping, in a sense.

BUBER: Yes.

ROGERS: And I do feel there's a real sense of equality between us.

BUBER: No doubt of it. But I am not speaking now about your feeling but about a real situation. I mean you, too, look, as you just said, on *his* experience. Neither you nor he look on *your* ex-perience. The subject is exclusively he and his experience. He cannot in the course of, let's say, a talk with you, he cannot change his position and ask you, "Oh, Doctor, where have you been yesterday? Oh, you have been in the movies? What was it and how were you impressed?" He *cannot* do it. So, I see and feel very well your feeling, your attitude, your taking part. But you cannot change the given situation. There is something objective-ly real that confronts you. Not only he confronts you, the person, but also the situation. You cannot change it.

ROGERS: Well now, now I'm wondering, Who is Martin Buber, you or me, because what I feel . . . (*Laughter.*)

BUBER: I'm not, so to say, "Martin Buber" as, how do you say, with quotes.

ROGERS: In that sense, I'm not "Carl Rogers," either. (*Laughter.*)

BUBER: You see, I'm not a quoted man who thinks so and so and so.

ROGERS: I know. I realize that. Aside from that facetious re-mark, what I wanted to say is this. That I think you're quite right, that there is an objective situation there, one that could be mea-sured, one that is real, one that various people could agree upon if they examine the situation closely. But it has been my experi-ence that that is reality when it is viewed from the outside, and that that really has *nothing* to do with the relationship that produces therapy. That is something immediate, equal, a meeting of two persons on an equal basis — even though, in the world of I-It, it could be seen as a very unequal relationship.

BUBER: Now, Dr. Rogers, this is the first point where we must say to one another, "We disagree."

ROGERS: OK.

BUBER: You see, I cannot only look on you, on your part of things, on your experience. Let's take the case where I could talk to *him*, to the patient, too. I would, of course, hear from him a very different tale about this same moment. Now, you see, I am not a therapist. I'm interested in you *and* in him. I must see the situation. I must see you and him in this dialogue bounded by tragedy. Sometimes, in many cases, a tragedy that can be overcome. Just in your method. I have no objection at all to your method, you see? There is no need to speak about it. But sometime, method is not enough. You cannot do what is necessary to do. Now, let me ask you a question that seemingly has nothing to do with this, but it's the same point. You have certainly much to do with schizophrenics. Is it so?

ROGERS: Some.

BUBER: You have . . . have you also to do, let me say, with paranoiacs?

ROGERS: Some.

BUBER: Now, would you say that the situation is the same in the one case and in the other? Meaning, the situation as far as it has to do with the relationship betwen you and the other man. Is this relationship that you describe the same kind of relationship in the one case and in the other? This is a case, a question, which interests me very much, because I was interested very much by paranoia in my youth. I know much more about schizophrenia, but I often am very much interested, and I would like to know, have you — this would mean very much — can you meet the paranoiac just in the same kind?

ROGERS: Let me first qualify my answer to some degree. I haven't worked in a psychiatric hospital [yet]. My dealings have been with people for the most part who are able to at least make some kind of an adjustment in the community, so that I don't see the really chronically ill people. On the other hand, we do deal with individuals who are both schizophrenic and others who are certainly paranoid. One of the things that I say very tentatively, because I realize this is opposed by a great weight of psychiatric and psychological opinion, I would say that there is no difference in the relationship that I form with a normal person, a schizophrenic, a paranoid — I don't really feel any difference. That doesn't mean, of course, that when . . . Well, again, it's this question of looking at it from the outside. Looking at it from the outside, one can easily discern plenty of differences. But it seems to me that if therapy is effective, there is this same kind of meeting of persons no matter what the psychiatric label. One minor point in relation to something you said that struck me. It seems to me that the moment where persons are most likely to change, or I even think of it as the moments in which people *do* change, are the moments in which perhaps the relationship is experienced the same on both sides. When you said that if you talked to my patient you would get a very different picture, I agree, that would be true in regard to a great many of the things that went on in the interview. But I should expect that in those moments when real change occurred, that it would be because there had been a real meeting of persons in which it was experienced the same from both sides.

BUBER: Yes. This is really important.

MAURICE FRIEDMAN: Can I interpose a question here?

BUBER: No. Will you wait a moment? I only want to explain to Dr. Rogers why this question is particularly important to me and your answer, too. A very important point in my thinking is the problem of limits. Meaning, I do something, I try something, I will something, and I give all my thoughts in existence into this doing. And then I come at a certain moment to a wall, to a boundary, to a limit that I cannot, I *cannot* ignore. This is true, also, for what interests me more than anything, human effective dialogue. Meaning by dialogue not just a talking. Dialogue can be silence. We would perhaps, without the audience. I would recommend to do it without an audience. We could sit together, or rather walk together in silence and that could be a dialogue. But so, even in dialogue, full dialogue, there is a limit set. This is why I'm interested in paranoia. Here is a limit set for dialogue. It is sometimes very difficult to talk to a schizophrenic. In certain moments, as far as my experience with this, which is, of course, how may I say, dilettante? — I can talk to a schizophrenic as far as he is willing to let me into his particular world that is his own, and that in general he does not want to have you come in, or other people. But he lets some people in. And so he may let me in, too. But in the moment when he shuts himself, I cannot go on. And the same, only in a terrible, terribly strong manner, is the case with a paranoiac. He does not open himself and does not shut himself. He *is* shut. There is something else being done to him that shuts him. And this terribility of this fate I'm feeling very strongly because in the world of normal men, there are just analogous cases, when a sane man behaves, not to everyone, but behaves to some people *just so*, being *shut*, and the problem is if he can be opened, if he can open himself, and so on. And this is a problem for the human in general.

ROGERS: Yes, I think I see that as . . .

BUBER: Now Dr. Friedman wants to get into . . .

MAURICE FRIEDMAN: This is my role as moderator. I'm not quite satisfied as to whether, in this interchange just before the paranoiac and schizophrenic, to what extent it's an issue, to what extent that it may be a different use of terms, so let me ask Dr. Rogers one step further. As I understood, what Buber said was that the relationship is an I-Thou one, but not a fully reciprocal one, in the sense that while you have the meeting, nonetheless you see from his standpoint and he cannot see from yours. And in your response to that, you pointed again and again to the meeting that takes place and even to the change that may take place on both sides. But I didn't hear you even point to the suggestion that he does not see from your standpoint, or that it is fully reciprocal in the sense that he also is helping you. And I wondered if this might not be perhaps just a difference, if not of words, of viewpoint, where you were thinking of how you feel toward him, that he is an equal person and you respect him.

BUBER: There remains a *decisive* difference. It's not a question of objecting to helping the other. It's one thing to help the other. He is a man wanting to help the other. And his whole attitude is this active, helping attitude. There is, I wish to say, a difference by the whole heaven, but I would rather prefer to say by the whole *hell*, a difference from your attitude. This is a man in health. A man *helped* cannot think, cannot imagine helping another. How could he?

ROGERS: But that's where some of the difference arises. Because it seems to me again that in the most real moments of therapy I don't believe that this intention to help is any more than a substratum on my part either. Surely I wouldn't be doing this work if that wasn't part of my intention. And when I first see the client that's what I hope I will be able to do, is to be able to help him. And yet in the interchange of the moment, I don't think my mind is filled with the thought of "now I want to help you." It is much more "I want to understand you. What person are you behind that paranoid screen, or behind all these schizophrenic confusions, or behind all these masks that you wear in your real life? Who are you?" It seems to me that is a desire to meet a *person*, not "now I want to help." It seems to me that I've learned through my experience that when we *can* meet, then help does occur, but that's a by-product.

MAURICE FRIEDMAN: Dr. Rogers, would you not agree, though, that this is not fully reciprocal in the sense that that man does not have that attitude toward you, "I want to understand *you*. What sort of a person are *you*?"

ROGERS: The only modification I made of that was that perhaps in the moment where real change takes place, then I wonder if it isn't reciprocal in the sense that I am able to see this individual as he is in that moment and he really senses my understanding and acceptance of him. And that I think is what is reciprocal and is perhaps what produces change.

BUBER: Hmmm. You see, I, of course, am entirely with you as far as your experience goes. I cannot be with you as far as I have to look on the whole situation, your experience and his. You see, you give him something in order to make him equal to you. You supplement his need in his relation to you. May I say so personally, out of a certain fullness you give him what he wants in order to be *able* to be, just for this moment, so to speak, on the same plane with you. But even that is very — it is a tangent. It is a tangent which may not last but one moment. It is not the situation as far as I see, not the situation of an hour; it is a situation of minutes. And these minutes are made possible by you. Not at all by him.

ROGERS: That last I would thoroughly agree with — but I do

sense some real disagreement there, because it seems to me that what I give him is permission to *be*. Which is a little different somehow from bestowing something on him.

BUBER: I think no human being can give more than this. Making life possible for the other, if only for a moment. I'm with you.

ROGERS: Well, if we don't look out, we'll agree. (*Laughter.*)

BUBER: Now let's go on.

ROGERS: I really would like to shift this to another topic because as I understand what you've written, it seems to me that I discern one other type of meeting which has a lot of significance to me in my work, that as far as I know, you haven't talked about. Now I may be mistaken on that, I don't know. And what I mean is that it seems to me that one of the most important types of meeting or relationship is the person's relationship to himself. In therapy again, which I have to draw on because that's my background of experience, there are some very vivid moments in which the individual is meeting some aspect of himself, a feeling which he has never recognized before, something of a meaning in himself that he has never known before. It could be any kind of thing. It may be his intense feeling of aloneness, or the terrible hurt he has felt, or something quite positive like his courage, and so on. But at any rate, in those moments, it seems to me that there is something that partakes of the same quality that I understand in a real meeting relationship. He is in his feeling and the feeling is in him. It is something that suffuses him. He has never experienced it before. In a very real sense, I think it could be described as a real meeting with an aspect of himself that he has never met before. Now I don't know whether that seems to you like stretching the concept you've used. I suppose I would just like to get your reaction to it. Whether to you that seems like a possible type of real relationship or a meeting? I'll push this one step further. I guess I have the feeling that it is when the person has met himself in that sense, probably in a good many different aspects, that then and perhaps only then, is he really capable of meeting another in an I-Thou relationship.

BUBER: Now here we approach a problem of language. You call something dialogue that I cannot call so. But I can explain why I cannot call it so, why I would want another term between dialogue and monologue for this. Now for what I call dialogue, there is essentially necessary the moment of surprise. I mean . . .

ROGERS: You say "surprise"?

BUBER: Yes, being surprised. A dialogue . . . let's take a rather trivial image. The dialogue is like a game of chess. The whole charm of chess is that I do not know and cannot know what my partner will do. I am surprised by what he does and on this surprise the whole play is based. Now you hint at this, that a man can surprise himself. But in a very different manner from how a person can surprise another person.

(While the tape was being changed, Dr. Buber went on with his description of the characteristics of a true dialogue. A second feature is that in true meeting, or dialogue, that which is different in the other person, his otherness, is prized.)

ROGERS: The first two aspects of that . . . I hope that perhaps sometime I can play recordings of interviews for you to indicate how the surprise element can be there. That is, a person can be expressing something and then suddenly be hit by the meaning of that which has come from someplace in himself which he doesn't recognize. He really is *surprised* by himself. That can definitely happen. But the element that I see as being most foreign to your concept of dialogue is that it is quite true that this otherness in himself is not something to be prized. I think that in the kind of dialogue I'm talking about, within the person, that it is that otherness which probably would be broken down. And I do realize that in part the whole discussion of this may be based on a different use of words, too.

BUBER: And you see, may I add a technical matter? I have learned in the course of my life to appreciate terms. And I think that in modern psychology, this does not exist in a sufficient measure. When I find something that is essentially different from another thing, I want a new term. I want a new concept. You see, for instance, modern psychology in general says about the unconscious that it is a certain mode of the psyche. It has no sense at all for me. If something is so different from . . . if two things are so different from one another as this strain of the soul, changing in every moment, where I cannot grasp anything when I try to grasp its way from one side — this *being* in pure time; and over against this what we call the unconscious, that is not a phenomenon at all, we have no access to it at all, we have only to deal with its effects and so on. We cannot say the first is psychic and the second is psychic; that the unconscious is something in which psychic and physiologic are, how may I say, mixed, it's not enough. They penetrate one another in such a manner that we see in relation to this the terms body and soul are to speak late terms, late concepts, and concepts are never reality. Now, how can we comprehend this one concept?

ROGERS: I agree with you very much on that. I think when an experience is definitely of a different sort, then it does deserve a different term. I think we agree on that. Perhaps, since I see time is going by . . . I'd like to raise one other question that has a great deal of meaning to me and I don't know quite how to put it. Let me express it something like this. As I see people coming together in relationships in therapy, I think that one of the things I have come to believe and feel and experience is that what I think of as human nature or basic human nature — that's a poor term and you may have a better way of putting it — is something that is really to be *trusted*. And it seems to me in some of your writings I catch something of that same feeling. At any rate, it's been very much my experience in therapy that one does not need to supply motivation toward the positive or toward the constructive. That exists in the individual. In other words, if we can release what is most basic in the individual, that it will be constructive. Now I don't know . . . again, I just hope that perhaps that would stir some comments from you.

BUBER: I don't yet see the exact question.

ROGERS: The only question that I'm raising is, Do you agree? Or if I'm not clear, please ask me other questions. I'll try to put it in another way. It seems to me that orthodox psychoanalysis at least has held that when the individual is revealed, when you really get down to what is within the person, he consists mostly of instincts and attitudes and so on which must be *controlled*. That runs diametrically contrary to my own experience, which is that when you get to what is deepest in the individual, that is the very aspect that can most be trusted to be constructive or to tend toward socialization or toward the development of better interpersonal relationships. Does that have meaning for you?

BUBER: I see. I would put it in a somewhat different manner.

As far as I see, when I have to do with, now let me say, a problematic person, or just a sick person, a problematic person, a person that people call, or want to call, a bad person. You see, in general, the man who has really to do with what we call the spirit is called not to the good people, but just to the bad people, to the problematic, to the unacceptable, and so on. The good people, they can be friends with them, but they don't need them. So I'm interested just in the so-called bad, problematic, and so on. And my experience is if I succeed to, and this is near to what you say, but somewhat different, if I come near to the reality of this person, I experience it as a *polar* reality. You see, in general we say this is either A or Non-A. It cannot be A and Non-A at the same time. It can't. It can't. I mean what you say may be trusted, I would say this stands in polar relation to what can be least trusted in this man. You cannot say, and perhaps I differ from you in this point, you cannot say, "Oh, I detect in him just what can be trusted." I would say now when I see him when I grasp him more broadly and more deeply than before, I see his whole polarity and then I see how the worst in him and the best in him are dependent on one another, attached to one another. And I can help, I may be able to help him just by helping him to change the relation between the poles. Not just by choice, but by a certain strength that he gives to the one pole in relation to the other. The poles being qualitatively very alike to one another. I would say there is not as we generally think in the soul of a man good and evil opposed. There is again and again in different manners a polarity, and the poles are not good and evil, but rather yes and no, rather acceptance and refusal. And we can strengthen, or we can help him strengthen, the one positive pole. And perhaps we can even strengthen the force of direction in him because this polarity is very often directionless. It is a chaotic state. We could bring a cosmic note into it. We can help put order, put a shape into this. Because I think the good, what we may call the good, is always only direction. Not a substance.

ROGERS: And if I get the last portion of that particularly, you're saying that perhaps we can help the individual to strengthen the yes, that is to affirm life rather than refuse it. Is that . . . ?

BUBER: M-hmmm. You see, I differ only in this word, I would not say life. I would not put an object to it.

ROGERS: (*to Dr. Friedman*) You're looking as though you want to say something. I guess we could go on forever on this.

MAURICE FRIEDMAN: My function as moderator is to sharpen issues and I feel that there are two interrelated things that have been touched on here, but maybe not brought out, and I feel that it's so important, I'd like to see. When Dr. Rogers first asked Professor Buber about his attitude toward psychotherapy, he mentioned as one of the factors which entered into his approach to therapy, acceptance. Now, Professor Buber, as we saw last night, often used the term *confirmation,* and it is my own feeling both from what they said tonight and my knowledge of their writings, that it might be of real importance to clarify whether they mean somewhat the same. Dr. Rogers writes about acceptance, in addition to saying that it is a warm regard for the other and a respect for his individuality, for him as a person of unconditional worth, that it means "an acceptance of and regard for his attitudes of the moment, no matter how much they may contradict other attitudes he has held in the past. And this acceptance of each fluctuating aspect of this other person makes it for him a relationship of warmth and safety." Now, I wonder whether Professor Buber would look on confirmation as similar to that, or would he see confirmation as including, perhaps, *not* being accepted, including some demand on the other that might mean in a sense a nonacceptance of his feelings at the moment in order to confirm him later.

BUBER: I would say every true existential relationship between two persons begins with acceptance. By acceptance, I mean — perhaps the two concepts are not just alike — that by acceptance I mean being able to tell, or rather not to tell, but only to make it felt to the other person, that I accept him just as he is. I take you just as you are. Well, so, but it is not yet what I mean by confirming the other. Because accepting, this is just accepting how he ever is in this moment, in this actuality of his. Confirming means, first of all, accepting the whole potentiality of the other and making even a decisive difference in his potentiality, and of course we can be mistaken again and again in this, but it's just a chance between human beings. I can recognize in him, know in him, more or less, the person he has been — I can say it only in this word — *created* to become. In the simple factual language,

we find not the term for it because we don't find in it the term,
the concept *being man to become*. This is what we must, as far as we
can, grasp, if not in the first moment, then after this. And now I
not only accept the other as he is, but I confirm him, in myself,
and then in him, in relation to this potentiality that is meant by
him, and it can now be developed, it can evolve, it can answer the
reality of life. He can do more or less to this scope but I can, too,
do something. And this is with goals even deeper than acceptance. Let's take, for example, man and a woman, man and wife.
He says, not expressly, but just by his whole relation to her, that
"I accept you as you are." But this does *not* mean "I don't want
you to change." But it says, "I discover in you just by my accepting love, I discover in you what you are meant to become." This
is, of course, not anything to be expressed in massive terms. But
it may be that it grows and grows with the years of common life.
This is what you mean?

ROGERS: Yes. And I think that sounds very much like this quality that is in the experience that I think of as acceptance, though
I have tended to put it differently. I think that we do accept the
individual *and* his potentiality. I think it's a real question whether we could accept the individual as he is, because often he is in
pretty sad shape, if it were not for the fact that we also in some
sense realize and recognize his potentiality. I guess I feel, too,
that acceptance of the most complete sort, acceptance of this
person as he is, is the strongest factor making for change that I
know. In other words, I think that does release change or release
potentiality to find that as I am, exactly as I am, I am fully accepted — then I can't help but change. Because then I feel there is no
longer any need for defensive barriers, so then what takes over
are the forward-moving processes of life itself, I think.

BUBER: I'm afraid I'm not so sure of that as you are, perhaps because I'm not a therapist. And I have necessarily to do with that
problematic type. I cannot do in my relationship to him without
this polarity. I cannot put this aside. As I said, I have to do with
both men. I have to do with the problematic in him. And I have
. . . there are cases when I must help him against himself. He
wants my help against himself. He wants . . . you see, the first
thing of all is that he trusts me. Yes, life has become baseless for
him. He cannot tread on firm soil, on firm earth. He is, so to say,

suspended in the air. And what does he want? What he wants is a being not only whom he can trust as a man trusts another, but a being that gives him now the certitude that "there *is* a soil, there *is* an existence. The world is not condemned to deprivation, degeneration, destruction. The world *can* be redeemed. *I* can be redeemed because there is this trust." And if this is reached, now I can help this man even in his struggle against himself. And this I can only do if I distinguish between accepting and confirming.

ROGERS: I feel that one difficulty with a dialogue is that there could easily be no end, but I think that both in mercy to Dr. Buber and to the audience, this is . . .

BUBER: What did you say?

ROGERS: I say that out of consideration to you . . .

BUBER: Not to me.

ROGERS: All right . . . (*Laughter*) . . . out of consideration to the audience.

MAURICE FRIEDMAN: May I be so unmerciful as to just ask one last question. That is, my impression is that on the one hand there has been more insistence by Dr. Rogers on the fuller reciprocity of the I-Thou relation in therapy and less by Dr. Buber, but on the other, I get the impression that Dr. Rogers is more client-centered . . .

BUBER: What?

MAURICE FRIEDMAN: More client-centered . . . (*Laughter*) . . . more concerned with the becoming of the person. And he speaks in a recent article of being able to trust one's organism that it will find satisfaction, that it will express me. And he speaks of the locus of value as being inside one, whereas I get the impression from my encounter with Dr. Buber that he sees value as more in the between. I wonder, is this a real issue between the two of you?

ROGERS: I might give an expression of my view on that. It puts it in quite different terms than those you've used, but I think it is related to the same thing. As I've tried to think about it in recent months, it seems to me that you could speak of the goal toward which therapy moves, and I guess the goal toward which maturity moves in an individual, as being *becoming,* or being knowingly and acceptingly that which one most deeply is. That, too, expresses a real trust in the process which we are, that may not entirely be shared between us tonight.

BUBER: Perhaps it would be of a certain aid if I ask a problem that I found when reading just this article of yours, or a problem that approached me. You speak about persons, and the concept "persons" is seemingly very near to the concept "individual." I would think that it is advisable to distinguish between them. An individual is just a certain uniqueness of a human being. And it can develop just by developing with uniqueness. This is what Jung calls individuation. He may become more and more an individual without making him more and more human. I have a lot of examples of man having become very very individual, very distinct of others, very developed in their such-and-such-ness without being at all what I would like to call a man. Individual is just this uniqueness, being able to be developed so and so. But a person, I would say, is an individual living really with the world. And with the world, I don't mean *in* the world. But just in *real contact*, in real reciprocity with the world in all the points in which the world can meet man. I don't say only with man, because sometimes we meet the world in other shapes than in that of man. But this is what I would call a person and if I may say expressly yes and no to certain phenomena, I'm *against* individuals and *for* persons. (*Applause.*)

MAURICE FRIEDMAN: We are deeply indebted to Dr. Rogers and Dr. Buber for a unique dialogue. It is certainly unique in my experience; first because it is a *real* dialogue, taking place in front of an audience, and I think that it is in part because of what they were willing to give us and did give us, and part was because you took part in a sort of a triologue, or adding me, a quatralogue in which you silently participated. (*Applause.*)

4
Paul Tillich

Paul Johannes Tillich was born in Prussia in 1886. At an early age, he was forced to reconcile the traditional Protestantism of his Lutheran minister father with the training in classical humanism he received at the *gymnasia* he attended. Intrigued by these issues, he studied theology and philosophy at the Universities of Berlin, Tübingen, Breslau, and Halle from 1904 to 1912. He received his Ph.D. in 1911 and was ordained a Lutheran minister in 1912.

After serving as field chaplain in the German army from 1914 to 1918 and receiving the Iron Cross for bravery, he was active in the movement to create a German republic. The movement collapsed, however, when Hitler came to power. An active religious socialist, he tried to reconcile Christianity with a dialectic sense of history and social and political concerns. He was a faculty member from 1919 and professor of theology from 1924 at several German universities. When Tillich's activities and writings alienated the Nazi regime, he was dismissed in 1933 from his Chair of Philosophy at the University of Frankfurt. He later said, "I had the honor of being the first non-Jewish professor dismissed from a German university."

His friend Reinhold Niebuhr was in Germany at the time and invited Tillich to join him at Union Theological Seminary, an invitation he readily accepted, becoming a naturalized citizen in 1940. He remained at Union until retirement age in 1955, then joined the faculty at Harvard University until 1963, and then the University of Chicago Divinity School, where he remained until his death. Tillich eventually wrote approximately thirty volumes on theology, in German and English, including a number of collections of his sermons. His most notable works include *The Religious Situation* (1926, English 1932); *The Interpretation of History* (1936); *The Protestant Era* (1948); his magnum opus, the three-volume *Systematic Theology* (1952, 1959, 1963), and *The Courage to Be* (1952), which one critic said "may be his most representative, enduring masterpiece."

Whether considering society or the individual, Tillich came to believe that the struggle between religious authoritarianism and secular autonomy is ultimately transcended in a genuine freedom grounded in religious depth. He once said, "People who listen to me are those who declare they don't understand the Christian symbols that were given by the church and need them translated into modern language." His theology attempted to reconcile the abstract questions of religion with direct religious experience, that is, philosophy with revelation. He also related theological questions to disciplines as wide-ranging as philosophy, contemporary art, political theory, business, and literature. An early interest stemming from his career in Germany, which was maintained throughout his life, was the interrelationship of psychoanalysis, existentialism, and religion. One writer said, "Erich Fromm, Rollo May and Abraham Maslow were indebted to him for key analytic concepts such as 'existential anxiety' and the 'demonic'."

"A short, gentle, white-haired philosopher," Paul Tillich has been described as "the most significant contemporary theologian," "a seminal figure in the Protestant thought of this century," "perhaps the principal molder of modern Christian thought." It has been said that "what Whitehead was to American philosophy, Tillich has been to American theology." Others have pointed out that "Tillich's philosophies concerned all religious groups, for he was not just interpreting Protestantism, but human existence and the interrelations of love, power and justice."

The dialogue between Paul Tillich and Carl Rogers occurred on March 7, 1965, in the radio/television studio of San Diego State College in California. It was Tillich's last public appearance. He died on October 22, 1965.

CARL ROGERS: The importance of self-affirmation: I think that would be one area where we agree. Then I have been much impressed with your thinking about the courage to *be*, because I see that in psychotherapy; the courage of being something, the risk that is involved in knowing. . . . I've also liked your phrase about the antimoral act being one that contradicts the self-realization of the individual, and it seems to me both of us are trying to push beyond some of the trends that are very prominent in the modern world; the logical positivistic, the ultrascientific approach, the stress of the mechanistic and highly deterministic point of view which, as I see it, makes man just an object trying to find some alternative stance in relation to life. I wonder if you feel that we're in some agreement on issues of that sort?*

PAUL TILLICH: Yes, of course. In all these points I heartily agree, and I am very glad you enumerate them for me.

ROGERS: Well, perhaps we could push into some areas where I am not quite so sure. I wonder what some of your views are about the nature of man. When I've been asked about that — I think some of the existentialists take the point of view that man really has no nature, but it seems to me that he has — I have taken the point of view that man belongs to a particular species. He has species characteristics. One of those, I think, being the fact that he is incurably social; I think he has a deep need for relationships. Then I think that simply because man is an organism he tends to be directional. He's moving in the direction of actualizing himself. So, for myself, I really feel man does have a describable nature. I have been interested, for example, in the fact that you discuss the demonic aspects of man. I don't know whether you see that as a part of his nature — at any rate I would be interested in your views in regard to the nature of man.

TILLICH: Your question is very far-reaching and demands of me a little bit longer answer. The first point I want to make is that man, definitively, has a nature, and I think the best way to prove this is negatively, by showing how impossible the argument is if somebody *denies* that man has a nature. I think of the famous

---

Paul Tillich and Carl Rogers: A Dialogue. Pamphlet. San Diego, California: San Diego State College, 1966. The pamphlet appears to have been edited slightly, as the beginnings and endings are rather abrupt.

French existentialist, Sartre, who has denied that man has a nature and has emphasized that man is everything he makes of himself and this is his freedom. But, if he says that this is man's freedom to make himself, then this, of course, means that he has the nature of freedom, which other species do not have. To make such statements is somehow self-contradictory. Even if you attribute to man what medieval theology attributed to God, namely to be by himself, and not conditioned by anything else, even then you cannot escape the statement that man has a nature. Now that's my answer to the first element in your question, but there are two more and I want to get at them.

The second is that I distinguish, so to speak, two natures of man, or one which one rightly calls his nature and the other which is a mixture of accepting and distorting his true nature. The first one I would call, with a very vague term, his true nature, but to make it less vague I usually call it his *essential* nature. If I speak theologically, then I call it man's created nature, and you remember that this is one of the main points about which the early church was tremendously fighting — namely, that man's essential or created nature is good. According to the biblical word, "God looked at everything he had created and behold! it was very good." There is an even more philosophical, reformulated affirmation of this by Augustine, namely, *Esse qua esse bonum est,* which means in English, "being as being is good." Now that is what I would call man's essential nature and then, from this, we must distinguish man's existential nature, of which I would say it has a characteristic of being estranged from his true nature. Man, as he is in time and space, in biography and history, *this* man is not simply the opposite of man's essential nature, for then it wouldn't be man any longer. But his temporal, historical nature is a distortion of his essential nature, and in attempting to reach it, he may be contradicting his true nature. It is a tremendous mixture, and in order to understand the real human predicament, we must distinguish these two elements. I believe that in Freud, himself, and much Freudianism and psychotherapy generally, there is no clear distinction of these two points. This was your second element. Now shall I answer your third element also . . . ?

ROGERS: First . . . let me make one comment on this. I find in my work as a therapist that if I can create a climate of the ut-most of freedom for the other individual, I can really trust the directions that he will move. That is, people sometimes say to me, "What if you create a climate of freedom? A man might use that freedom to become completely evil or antisocial." I don't find that to be true, and this is one of the things that makes me feel that — I don't know whether this is essentially or existentially — in a relationship of real freedom the individual tends to move not only toward deeper self-understanding, but toward more social behavior.

TILLICH: Yes, now I would put a question mark to this, and I would say that first of all, who is free enough to create this situa-tion of freedom for the others? And since I call this mixture of man's essential nature and his estranged nature ambiguous — the realm of the ambiguity of life — I would say under the con-dition of this ambiguity, nobody is able to create this sphere of freedom. But now let's suppose that it exists in some *other* way. I can come to this later when we speak of the demonic. Then I still would say the individual who lives in such a social group in which freedom is given to him remains an ambiguous mix-ture between essential and existential being. He is, as the English language expresses it beautifully, "in a predicament," and this predicament is a universal, tragic estrangement from one's true being. Therefore, I don't believe in the power of the individual to use his freedom in the way in which he should — namely, fulfill-ing one's own essential potentialities, or essentialities; these two words are here the same. So I am more skeptical, both about the creation of such a situation and about the individuals who are in such a situation.

ROGERS: I would agree on the difficulty of creating complete freedom. I am sure none of us is ever able to really create that for another person in its completeness. . . . Yet what impresses me is that even imperfect attempts to create a climate of freedom and acceptance and understanding seem to liberate the person to move toward really social goals. I wonder if it is your thinking about the demonic aspect that makes you put a question mark af-ter that.

TILLICH: Now, let me first answer you about what you just said, and here I would very much agree. I would say there are fragmentary actualizations in history and I agree especially with the deep insight we have gained, largely by psychotherapy, about the tremendous importance of love in earliest ages of the development of children. So the question would come here: "Where are the forces which create a situation in which the child receives that love which gives him, later on, the freedom to face life and not to escape from life into neuroses and psychoses?" I leave that question open.

But now you are interested about the demonic, and you are not the only one. I myself was, and everybody is in some way, so let me say how I came to this concept. I wrote in the year 1926, when I was still professor at the University of Dresden in Germany, a little article, a little pamphlet, *The Demonic*, and the reason not to speak of the "fallen" or the "sinful men" or any of these phrases was that I saw from two points of view structures which are stronger than the good will of the individual, and one of these structures was the neurotic-psychotic structure. I came into contact after the First World War, since 1920 about, with the psychoanalytic movement, coming from Freud at that time, and changing the climate of the whole century — already in Europe at that time. The second was the analysis of the conflicts of society by the Socialist movement and especially by the early writings of Karl Marx, and in both cases, I found a phenomenon for which these traditional terms, like "fallen men" and "sinful men," are not sufficient. The only sufficient term I found was in the New Testament use of the term "demonic," which is in the stories about Jesus: similar to being possessed. That means a force, under a force, which is stronger than the individual good will. And so I used that term. Of course, I emphasized very much I don't mean it in a mythological sense — as little demons or a personal Satan running around the world — but I mean it as structures which are ambiguous, both to a certain extent creative, but ultimately destructive. This is the reason why I introduced that term. So, instead of only speaking of estranged mankind, and not using the old terminology anyhow, I had to find a term which covers the transpersonal power which takes hold of men and of society; of men in stages, let's say, of drunkenness, being a drunkard, and not being able to overcome it, or producing a society in which either class conflicts or as today in the whole world, conflicts of great ideologies, of great forms of political faiths which struggle with each other — and every step to overcome them has usually the consequence of driving the people more deeply into them. Now this is what I meant with the demonic. So I hope I made one thing clear: that I don't mean it in the old mythological sense which of course has to be demythologized.

ROGERS: . . . And certainly when I look at some of the things going on in the world from the power point of view and so on, I can see why you might think in terms of demonic structures.

I'd like to talk a little bit about the way I see this matter of alienation and estrangement. It seems to me that the infant is not estranged from himself. To me it seems that the infant is a whole and integrated organism, gradually individual, and that the estrangement that occurs is one that he learns — that in order to preserve the love of others, parents usually, he takes into himself as something he has experienced for himself, the judgments of his parents: just like the small boy who has been rebuked for pulling his sister's hair goes around saying, "bad boy, bad boy." Meanwhile, he is pulling her hair again. In other words, he has introjected the notion that he is bad, where actually he is enjoying the experience, and it is this estrangement between what he is experiencing and the concepts he links up with what he is experiencing that seems to me to constitute the basic estrangement. I don't know whether you want to comment on that . . .

TILLICH: Yes; because the infant is a very important problem; I call this in philosophical or, better, psychological terms, the mythological state of Adam and Eve before the Fall: dreaming innocence. It has not yet reached reality; it is still dreaming. Of course, this also is a symbol, but it is a symbol which is nearer to our psychological language than the Fall of Adam and Eve, but it means the same thing, and it means that Adam, namely men — the Hebrew "Adam" means men — that men, every man, is in the process of transition from dreaming innocence to conscious self-actualization, and in this process the estrangement also takes place, as well as the fulfillment; therefore, my concept of ambiguity. I agree with you that there is also in what the parents used to call "bad boy" or "bad girl," there is also a necessary act of self-fulfillment, but there is also something asocial in it, because it hurts his sister and so it has to be repressed, and whether we say "bad boy," or prevent it in any other way, this is equally necessary, and these experiences mean for me the slow process of transition from dreaming innocence into self-actualization on the one side and self-estrangement on the other side, and these two acts are ambiguously intermixed. Now that would be about my interpretation of the situation of the infants.

ROGERS: Well, there is much in that that I would agree with. I'd like to say a little bit about the kind of relationship in which I think man's estrangement can be healed, as I see it from my own experience. For example, when we talk about — when either of us talks about the courage to be or the tendency to become one-self, I feel that perhaps that can only be fully achieved in a relationship. Perhaps the best example of what I am talking about is that I believe that the person can only accept the unacceptable in himself when he is in a close relationship in which he experiences acceptance. This, I think, is a large share of what constitutes psychotherapy — that the individual finds that the feelings he has been ashamed of or that he has been unable to admit into his awareness, that those can be accepted by another person, so then he becomes able to accept them as a part of himself. I don't know too much of your thinking about interpersonal relationships, but I wonder how that sounds to you.

TILLICH: I believe that you are absolutely right in saying that the man-to-man experience of forgiveness, or better, acceptance of the unacceptable, is a very necessary precondition for self-affirmation. And you cannot forgive yourself, you cannot accept yourself. If you look in the spiritual mirror, then you are much more prone to hate yourself and to be disgusted with yourself. So I believe that all forms of confessional in the churches and the confessions between friends and married people — and now the sacroanalytic confession of one's deeper levels which are opened up by the analyst — that without these things, there is no possibility of experiencing something which belongs ultimately to another dimension: the dimension of the ultimate, let me call it preliminarily. But I would say, with you, only the right acceptance is the medium through which it is necessary men have to go — from men to men — before the dimension of the ultimate is possible. I may add here that I have not used often anymore the word "forgiveness," because this often produces a bad superiority in him who forgives and the humiliation of him who is forgiven. Therefore, I prefer the concept of acceptance. If you accept this acceptance, then I think I can confess that I have learned it from psychoanalysis. I have learned to translate an ideological concept which doesn't communicate any longer and replaced it by the way in which the psychoanalyst accepts his patients: not judging him, not telling him first he should be good, otherwise I cannot accept you, but accepting him just because he is not good, but he has something within himself that wants to be good.

ROGERS: Certainly in my own experience, the potency of acceptance of another person has been demonstrated time and time again, when an individual feels that he is both fully accepted in all that he has been able to express and yet prized as a person. This has a very potent influence on his life and on his behavior.

TILLICH: Yes, now I believe that this is really the center of what we call the "good news" in the Christian message.

[*Intermission.*]

TILLICH: The minister, who represents the ultimate meaning of life, can have much skill unconsciously, although he is unskilled, but even then he should not establish himself as a secondrate psychotherapist. Now that seems to me a very important rule. Otherwise, cooperation would soon end in little catastrophes and would come to an end altogether.

ROGERS: Well, that sort of sets off in me a somewhat deeper question. I realize very well that I and many other therapists are interested in the kind of issues that involve the religious worker and the theologian, and yet, for myself, I prefer to put my thinking on those issues in humanistic terms, or to attack those issues through the channels of scientific investigation. I guess I have some real sympathy for the modern view that is sort of symbolized in the phrase that "God is dead"; that is, that religion no longer *does* speak to people in the modern world, and I would be interested in knowing why you tend to put your thinking — which certainly is very congenial to that of a number of psychologists these days — why you tend to put your thinking in religious terminology and theological language.

TILLICH: Now, I think that is a very large question . . .

ROGERS: Yes, it is . . .

TILLICH: . . . and it could take all our time, so I want to confine myself to a few points. First: now the fundamental point is that I believe, metaphorically speaking, man lives not only in the horizontal dimension, namely the relationship of himself as a finite being to other finite beings, observing them and managing them, but he also has in himself something which I call, metaphorically, the vertical line; the line not to a heaven with God and other beings in it, but what I mean with the vertical line is towards something which is not transitory and finite; something which is infinite, unconditional, ultimate — I usually say that. Man has an experience in himself that he is more than a piece of finite objects which come and go. He experiences something beyond time and space. I don't speak here — I must emphasize this in speeches again and again — in terms of life after death, or in other symbols which cannot be used in this way anymore, but I speak of the immediate experience of the temporal, of the eternal in the temporal, or of the temporal invaded by the eternal in some moments of our life and of the life together with other people and of the group life. Now, that is for me the reason why I try to continue to interpret the great traditional religious symbols as relevant for us: because I know, and that was the other point you made, that they have become largely irrelevant, and that we cannot use them in the way in which they are used still very much in preaching, religious teaching, and liturgies, for people who can live in them, who are not by critical analysis estranged from them, but for those large amounts of people whom you call humanists, we need a translation and interpretation of this symbol, but not, as you seem to indicate, a replacement. I don't believe that scientific language is able to express the vertical dimension adequately, because it is bound to the relationship of finite things to each other, even in psychology and certainly in all physical sciences. This is the reason why I think we need another language, and this language is the language of symbols and myths; it is a religious language. But we poor theologians, in contrast to you happy psychologists, are in the bad situation that we know the symbols with which we deal have to be reinterpreted and even *radically* reinterpreted. But I have taken this heavy yoke upon myself and I have decided long ago I will continue to the end with it.

ROGERS: Well, I realized as you were talking, I have a sort of a fantasy of this vertical dimension for me, not going up, but going down. What I mean is this: I feel at times when I'm really being helpful to a client of mine, in those sort of rare moments when there is something approximating an I-Thou relationship between us, and when I feel that something significant is happening, then I feel as though I am somehow in tune with the forces in the universe or that forces are operating through me in regard to this helping relationship that — well, I guess I feel somewhat the way the scientist does when he is able to bring about the splitting of the atom. He didn't create it with his own little hands, but he nevertheless put himself in line with the significant forces of the universe and thereby was able to trigger off a significant event, and I feel much the same way, I think, oftentimes, in dealing with a client when I really am being helpful.

TILLICH: I am very grateful about what you say. Now, the first words were especially interesting to me, when you said a vertical line has always an up and a down. And you will be interested to hear from me that I am accused very often by my theological colleagues that I speak much too much of down, instead of up, and that is true; when I want to give a name to that with which I am ultimately concerned, then I call it the "ground of being" and ground is, of course, down and not up — so I go with you down. Now the question is, *where* do we go? Here again I had the feeling I could go far away with you when you use the term "universe," forces of the universe, but when I speak of "ground of being," I don't understand this depth of the universe in terms of an addition of all elements in the universe, of all single things, but, as many philosophers and theologians did, the creative ground of the universe, that out of which all these forms and elements come: and I call it the creative ground. And this was the second point in which I was glad. This creative ground can be experienced in everything which is rooted in the creative ground. For instance, in a person-to-person encounter — and I had without being an analyst, but in many forms of encounters with human beings, very similar experiences to those you had — there is something present which transcends the limited reality of the Thou and the Ego of the other one and of myself, and I sometimes called it at special moments the presence of the holy, in a nonreligious conversation. That I can experience and have experienced, and I agree with you.

Then finally, there was your third point about the scientists, and I often told my scientist friends that they follow strictly the principle formulated classically by Thomas Aquinas, the great medieval theologian: If you know something, then you know something about God. And I would agree with this statement — and therefore these men also have an experience of what I like to call the vertical line, down and perhaps also up, although what they do in splitting atoms is discovering and managing finite relations to each other.

ROGERS: I'd like to shift to another topic that has been of interest to me and I suspect may be of interest to you. This is the question of what constitutes the optimal person. In other words, what is it that we're working toward, whether in therapy or in the area of religion? For myself, I have a rather simple definition, yet one which I think has a good many implications. I feel that I'm quite pleased in my work as a therapist if I find that my client and I, too, are — if we are both moving toward what I think of as greater openness to experience. If the individual is becoming more able to listen to what's going on within himself, more sensitive to the reactions he's having to a given situation, if he's more accurately perceptive of the world around him — both the world of reality and the world of relationships — then I think my feeling is I will be pleased. That's the direction I would hope we would move, because then he will be in the process — first of all, he will be in the process all the time. This isn't a static kind of a goal for an individual, and he will be in the process of becoming more fully himself. He'll also be realistic, in the best sense, in that he's realistic about what is going on within himself, as well as realistic about the world, and I think he will also be in the process of becoming more social simply because one of the elements which he can't help but actualize in himself is the need and desire for closer human relationships; so for me, this concept of openness to experience describes a good deal of what I would hope to see in the more optimal person, whether we're talking about the person who emerges from therapy, or the development of a good citizen, or whatever. I wonder if you would have any comments on that or on your own point of view in that area.

TILLICH: Yes, there are two questions in this. The one is the way — namely the openness — and the other is the aim. It is, of course, not a static aim, not a dynamic aim, but it's an aim. Let me speak to both points: the openness is a word which is very familiar to myself because there are many questions a theologian is asked, and which can be answered only by the concept of openness, or opening up. I will give you two examples. The one example is the function of classical symbols and symbols generally. I always used to answer: "Symbols open up, they open up reality and they open up something in us." If this word were not forbidden in the university today, I would call it something in our *soul*, but you know as a psychologist, as somebody who deals with the soul, that the word "soul" is forbidden in academic contexts. But that's what symbols do, and they do it not only to individuals, but they do it also to groups and usually only through groups to individuals — so that's the one thing where I use the word "open." This seems to me one of the main functions, perhaps *the* main function of symbols — namely to open up. Then another use of the word "open" is that I am asked, "Now what can I do to experience God or to get the Divine Spirit?" or things like that. My answer is, "The only thing you can do is keep yourselves open. You cannot force God down, you cannot produce the Divine Spirit in yourselves, but what you can do is open yourselves, to keep yourselves open for It." This is, of course, in your terminology, a particular experience, but we must keep open for all experiences. So I would agree very much with the way which you have described. I would even believe that in all experiences, there is a possibility of having an ultimate experience.

Then, the aim: now, the aim is the many folds we discussed. Perhaps we could agree about realization of our true self, bringing into actuality what is essentially given to us; or, when I speak in religious symbolism, I could say: "To become the way in which God sees us, in all our potentialities." And what that now practically is, is the next and very important question. You also indicated something of this: namely, to become social. I think this is a part of a larger concept. I would call it love, in the sense of the Greek word *agape*, which is a particular word in the New Testament, and which means that love which is described by Paul in I Corinthians 13, and which accepts the other as a person and then tries to reunite with him and to overcome the separation, the existential separation, which exists between men and men. Now, with this aim, I would agree; but I would add, of course, since I speak also in terms of the vertical dimension, that it is the keeping *to* that dimension to maintain in the faith into an ultimate meaning of life, and the absolute and unconditional seriousness of this direction of this ultimate aim of life. So when I shall speak now in popular terms, which is very dangerous always, I would say: faith and love are the two concepts which are necessary, but faith not in the sense of beliefs but in the sense of being related to the ultimate, and love not in the sense of any sentimentality, but in a sense of affirming the other person and *even* one's own person, because I believe with Augustine, Erich Fromm, and others, that there is a justified self-affirmation and self-acceptance. I wouldn't use the term "self-love" — that's too difficult — but self-affirmation and self-acceptance, one of the most difficult things to reach.

ROGERS: Well, I find that I like it best when you become concrete; that is, when you put it in terms of faith and love. Those can be very abstract concepts which can have all kinds of different meanings, but putting it in the concrete — yes, I do feel that the person does have to gain a real appreciation of or liking of himself, if he is going to affirm himself in a healthy and useful fashion. There's one other corollary to this notion of being open to experience that we might explore a bit, too. To me, the individual who is reasonably open to his experience is involved in a continuous valuing process; that is, I think that — I realize that I've sort of dropped the notion of values in the conventional sense of there being certain values which you could list, and that kind of thing — but it does seem to me that the individual who is open to his experience is continually valuing each moment and valuing his behavior in each moment, as to whether it is related to his own self-fulfillment, his own actualization, and that it's that kind of valuing process that to me makes sense in the mature person. It also makes sense in a world where the whole situation is changing so rapidly that I feel that ordinary lists of values are probably not as appropriate or meaningful as they were in periods gone by.

TILLICH: Yes. Now I am an outspoken critic of the philosophy of values, so I certainly agree with you. I replace this thing by my concept of *agape*, or love — namely, love which is listening.

I call it listening love, which doesn't follow abstract valuations, but which is related to the concrete situation, and out of its listening to this very moment gains its decision for action and its inner feeling of satisfaction and even joy or dissatisfaction and bad conscience.

ROGERS: I like that phrase because I think it could be a listening within, a listening to oneself, as well as a listening love for the other individual . . .

TILLICH: Yes, when I say listening to the situation, I mean the situation is constituted out of everything around me and myself; so, listening love is always listening to both sides.

ROGERS: I feel we're not very far apart in our thinking about this value approach; I thought we might be further apart than we seem to be. But, one other instance: I feel that the small infant is a good example of the valuing process that is going on continuously. He isn't troubled by the concepts and standards that have been built up for adults, and he's continually valuing his experience as either making for his enhancement or being opposed to that actualization.

TILLICH: Now, this valuation, of course, would be not an intellectual valuation, but an evaluation with his whole being . . .

ROGERS: I think of it as an organismic valuing process.

TILLICH: That means a reaction of his whole being, and I certainly believe that it is an adequate description.

5
B. F. Skinner

Burrhus Frederic Skinner was born March 20, 1904, in Susquehanna, in northeastern Pennsylvania. His parents were William, a lawyer, and Grace Burrhus Skinner. In what has been described as a warm and stable environment, Skinner was an industrious and inquisitive child, immensely fascinated by mechanical things, and "always building something."

He also developed a love of reading and writing, and went on to major in literature at Hamilton College in Clinton, New York. Between his junior and senior year he attended the Breadloaf writers' workshop in Middlebury, Vermont, where Robert Frost encouraged the young writer. After winning the Hawley Greek Prize and graduating Phi Beta Kappa, he spent the next year writing fiction and "discovered the unhappy fact that I had nothing to say." Although he abandoned his fiction writing, he maintained his interest in human behavior.

In 1928, intrigued by the writings of Bertrand Russell and John B. Watson, he decided to do graduate work in psychology at Harvard University, where he received his Ph.D. in 1931. He remained at Harvard for five more years, conducting research in experimental psychology. He married Yvonne Blue in 1936. The couple had two daughters.

Skinner taught at the University of Minnesota from 1936 to 1945, followed by almost three years as professor of psychology and department chairman at the University of Indiana at Bloomington. In 1947 he was invited to return to Harvard to be William James Lecturer, and was subsequently appointed a faculty professor in 1948. He remained at Harvard until his retirement in 1974 and continued thereafter as professor emeritus.

A rigorous scientist, Skinner in his experiments focused on the spontaneous behavior of an organism in response to its environment. He called this "operant" behavior, and when the behavior was reinforced — either positively, to encourage more of it, or negatively, to discourage the behavior — he termed it "operant conditioning." During World War II, Skinner experimented with pigeons, believing that operant conditioning could be used to train the pigeons to perform such tasks as guiding missiles, bombs, or torpedos to intercept and destroy enemy aircraft. Although the plan proved to be feasible, it was never implemented.

It was after the war, in 1945, that Skinner first came to national attention, when he published an article in the *Ladies' Home Journal* in which he described the "air-crib" he had designed and built for his younger daughter. A crib-sized, air-conditioned, soundproof box with a sliding window of safety glass, it was designed to provide an optimum environment for the baby. Though it excited much interest, several prominent pediatricians and child psychologists expressed reservations, and it was never widely manufactured. Skinner defended it, saying, "The whole idea was to provide the child with a very comfortable, stimulating environment."

Believing that there could be a science of behavior independent of neurology or physiology or psychology, with its concepts such as "mind" or "thinking" or "goals" or "feeling," Skinner focused all his work on the reinforcement of observable behavior. Through decades of research, teaching, and writing, he became the leading figure in the school of behavioral psychology. Not only are the principles of behavioral psychology and operant conditioning taught in colleges and universities across the United States and much of the world, these principles have exerted a dramatic influence on many fields. Programmed instruction, behavior therapy, family systems theory, biofeedback, linguistics, and education are only some of the areas that have been significantly influenced or even created as a result of the behaviorist school of thought.

Among Skinner's major works are *Science and Human Behavior* (1953), *Verbal Behavior* (1957), *Schedules of Reinforcement* (1957), *The Analysis of Behavior: A Program for Self-Instruction* (1961), *The*

Technology of Teaching (1968), *Beyond Freedom and Dignity* (1971), *About Behaviorism* (1974), and the first part of his autobiography, *Particulars of My Life* (1976). In his controversial book *Walden Two* (1948), which has sold well over a million copies, Skinner extrapolated behaviorist principles to the organization of society and attempted to solve major problems inherent in the control of human behavior, with a focus on solutions to contemporary social issues.

Along with many other honors, Skinner received the National Medal of Science (1968) and the Gold Medal of the American Psychological Association (1971). He has been a fellow of the Royal Society of Arts, a member of the National Academy of Sciences, the American Philosophical Society, the American Academy of Arts and Sciences, the American Psychological Association, and professional societies abroad.

With the behaviorist and humanist movements in psychology developing simultaneously, it was inevitable that the leaders of both schools of thought would eventually come to know of each other's work. Especially so, since Skinner and Rogers were tending to generalize the findings from their own laboratories to a variety of wider settings. Had they remained focused on the specific scientific problems presented by their separate work, they might never have clashed publicly. However, as they began to write with conviction about child rearing, education, and society, the contrast between their viewpoints became increasingly evident. So when they finally spoke directly to one another on the issues of their disagreement, the "Rogers-Skinner debate" soon became the most widely popularized discussion of the differences between behaviorist and humanistic psychology.

As stated in the Introduction, the first Rogers-Skinner encounter, their 1956 symposium on "Some Issues Concerning the Control of Human Behavior," has been printed and reprinted in countless journals and anthologies. While an important event, this relatively short exchange can hardly be called a dialogue. After reading one another's papers prior to the conference, Skinner began the symposium by reading his paper, Rogers read his own paper, including his reactions to Skinner's remarks, and finally, Skinner gave a brief, prepared rebuttal. A second, even shorter encounter between the two occurred at a small meeting of prominent psychologists organized by the American Academy of Arts and Sciences in December 1960. Again, prepared papers were delivered, and the proceedings were never published.

Recognizing that the 1956 Rogers-Skinner exchange was just a beginning, Gerald Gladstein and his colleagues at the University of Minnesota at Duluth succeeded in bringing the two men together for an extended meeting on June 11 and 12, 1962. Before an audience of more than five hundred people, Rogers and Skinner, for the first time, were able to truly dialogue with each other on issues concerning "Education and the Control of Human Behavior." While they sometimes resorted to prepared remarks or familiar expositions of their thought, at other times they really talked to and listened to each other and, as the moderator of another Rogers dialogue put it, said things they had never said before. It was a historic occasion.

Surprisingly, the transcript of this "Dialogue on Education and the Control of Human Behavior" was never published, although Gladstein and Jeffrey Norton Publishers did produce a six-cassette album of the proceedings (see reference in the Introduction). But because the recorded version had very limited circulation, the 1962 meeting has been virtually unknown. We are pleased to present this important meeting here for the first time in published form.

ROGERS: It's good to be here, to see Fred Skinner again, and to have an opportunity to pursue in depth some of our common interests and differences. I also look out over this audience, which I expected to be a very small one, and am tempted to say, "Who are you?"; but I trust that we will learn that as we begin to get questions and contributions from you. I'd like to summarize very briefly what seem to me to be some of the important elements which underlie our dialogue.

I think there is a fresh current in our culture, a fresh breeze blowing through the world, that is showing itself in many ways and speaking through many voices. It is expressed in a growing interest in existentialism and in the existentialist point of view. It is evident in ways that may seem odd to some, such as the interest in Zen Buddhism. It is evident in the concern with the self in psychology, and in the interest in a phenomenological approach to psychological problems. Even on the political scene it can be seen in the upsurge of one new country after another, rising out of a colonial past. It is exhibited in what Maslow termed the "third force" in American psychology: the development of self theories, the concern with the existential person, the discussions of being and becoming as against the two older forces, that is, the positivistic behaviorism point of view and the Freudian point of view. As I endeavor to understand this vigorous new cultural trend, it seems to me to be the voice of subjective man speaking up loudly for himself. Man has long felt himself to be a puppet in life, molded by world forces, by economic forces. He has been enslaved by persons, by institutions, and, more recently, by aspects of modern science. But he is firmly setting forth a new declaration of independence. He is discarding the alibis of "unfreedom." He is choosing himself, endeavoring to become himself: not a puppet, not a slave, not a copy of some model, but his own unique individual self. He is saying, in no uncertain terms, "I am. I exist. I choose myself in life. I choose the meaning of death."

I find myself very sympathetic to this trend because it is so deeply in line with the experience I have had in working with clients in therapy. One therapist has said that the essence of therapy is the client's movement from feeling unfree and controlled by others toward the frightening but rewarding sense of freedom to map out and choose his new personality. I have described therapeutic development as "a self-initiated process of learning to be free." This learning is composed of movement from, as well as movement toward. Clients move away from being driven by inner forces they do not understand, away from fear and distrust of these deep feelings and of themselves, and away from living by values they have taken from others. They move toward acceptance and enjoyment of their own feelings, toward valuing and trusting the deeper layers of their nature, finding strength in their own uniqueness, and living by values based in their own experience. This learning, this movement, enables them to live as more individuated, more creative, more responsive, and more responsible persons. Clients are often sharply aware of such directions in themselves, even as they move with apprehension toward being freely themselves.

But how can I talk about freedom when, as a behavioral scientist, I conduct research on the assumption that the sequences of cause and effect operate quite as much in the psychological as in the physical world? What possible definition of freedom can there be in a modern world?

Let me try to tell you what it means to me:

In the first place, the freedom which my clients experience is essentially an inner thing, something which exists in the living person quite aside from any outward choice of alternatives which we so often think of as constituting freedom. I am speaking of the kind of freedom which Viktor Frankl vividly describes in his experience of the concentration camp, when everything — possessions, identity, choice of alternatives — was taken from the prisoners. Months and even years in such an environment showed only that "Everything can be taken from a man but one thing: the last of the human freedoms, to choose one's own attitude in any given set of circumstances, to choose one's own way." It is this inner, subjective, existential freedom which I have observed. It is the realization in my clients that "I can live myself here and now by my own choice." It is the quality of courage which enables a person to step into the uncertainty of the unknown as he chooses himself. It is the discovery of meaning from within, which comes from listening sensitively and openly to the complexities of what one is experiencing. It is the burden of being responsible for the self one chooses to be. It is the recognition that the person is an emerging process, not a static end product. The individual who is thus deeply and courageously thinking his own thoughts, becoming his own uniqueness, responsibly choosing himself, may be fortunate in having hundreds of objective alternatives from which to choose, or he may be unfortunate in having none, but his freedom exists nevertheless. So we are first of all speaking of something which exists *within* the individual, of something phenomenological rather than objective, but nonetheless to be prized.

A second point in defining this experience of freedom is that it exists not as a contradiction to the picture of the psychological universe as a sequence of cause and effect, but as a complement to such a universe. Freedom, rightly understood, is a fulfillment by the person of the ordered sequence of his life. As Martin Buber puts it, "The free man believes in destiny, and believes that it stands in need of him." He moves out voluntarily, freely, responsibly, to play his significant part in a world whose determined events move through him and through his spontaneous choice and will.

This is the experience of the client as he moves in therapy toward an acceptance of the realities of the world outside and inside himself and moves, too, toward becoming a responsible agent in this real world. As I have indicated, this significant human freedom exists alongside the complete determinism of modern science as a paradox. It exists in our human experience with as much reality as do the facts of science, and we cannot wisely disregard it. It is one of the great contributions of our century that we are beginning to realize that man's moods, attitudes, actions, his adaptations as well as his maladaptations, can be understood in the same lawful terms as the events of the physical world. Viewed from this objective perspective, it seems probable that we will be able increasingly to understand man's actions in terms of laws that are similar to those discovered in the natural sciences. It is this that leads to the possibility of being able to control human behavior. It is this that leads to the issue of this discussion.

There seems no doubt that the behavioral sciences will move steadily in the direction of making man an object to himself, a complex sequence of events no different in kind from the complex chain of equations by which various chemical substances interact to form new substances or to release energy. But no matter how completely man comes to understand himself as a determined phenomenon, the product of past elements and forces and the determined cause of future events and behaviors, he can never live as an object. He can live only subjectively. Some of the most pathetic individuals I know are those who continually attempt to understand and predict their behavior objectively. Each action is meaningful to them only as the predetermined effect of preceding causes, and their whole life becomes an unhappy caricature of the centipede self-consciously watching his feet. In my experience, some of the failures in psychoanalytic therapy exhibit this overintellectualized objectivity.

The person who is developing his full potential, however, is able to accept the subjective aspect of himself and to live subjectively. When he is angry, he is angry, not merely an exhibition of the effects of adrenaline. When he loves, he is loving and not merely cathected toward a love object. He moves in self-selected directions. He chooses responsibly. He is a person who thinks and feels and experiences. He is not merely an object in whom these events occur. We cannot, without great peril, deny this subjective element in ourselves. It precedes our scientific activities. It is more encompassing than scientific knowledge. It is an essential part of being human, of being a person. No present or future development of the behavioral sciences can ever contradict this basic fact.

Yet I am well aware that the experimentalist-positivist-behaviorist stream of thought in psychology, and Dr. Skinner as a most able proponent of that trend, hold very different views. For example, here are some of the words and concepts that I have used which are almost totally without meaning in the behaviorist frame of reference: freedom is a term with no meaning; choice, in the sense that I have used it, has no meaning; subjectivity is, I believe, regarded as of very little importance; purpose, self-direction, value or value choice — none of these has any meaning; personal responsibility as a concept has no meaning. The democratic philosophy of human nature, Dr. Skinner has pointed out, has been a useful resource of the revolutionist in the past, but is now very probably out of date. So it is clear that some of the most basic concepts of this new third force in psychology have no meaning at all for the behaviorist group. I trust that this dialogue may help us to clear up any misunderstandings of such differences, and also to clarify our real differences, where they do exist.

In summary: to the extent that a behaviorist point of view in psychology is leading us toward a disregard of the person, toward treating persons primarily as manipulable objects, toward control of the person by shaping his behavior without his participant choice, or toward minimizing the significance of the subjective —to that extent I question it very deeply. My experience leads me to say that such a point of view is going against one of the strongest undercurrents of modern life, and is taking us down a pathway with destructive consequences.

SKINNER: I always make the same mistake. In debating with Carl Rogers I assume that he will make no effort to influence the audience. Then I have to follow him and speak, as I do now, to a group of people who are very far from free to accept my views. In fact, I was just reminded of a story that I once heard about Carl Rogers and I will tell it now, hoping to have him confirm or deny it. I suppose it is apocryphal. At least I am sure it has grown in this dimension. The story as I heard it is as follows: Carl Rogers was never much of a duck hunter, but he was persuaded upon one occasion to go duck hunting. He and some friends went to a blind and sat through a dreary cold early dawn. No ducks arrived until the very end of the time that shooting was possible. Finally, one lone duck came in and Rogers's friends allowed him to shoot, and he did. At the same time, along the shore a few hundred yards away, another man shot at the same duck. The duck fell. *Plop!* Rogers got out of the blind and started toward the duck. The other man got out of his blind and started toward the same duck. They arrived simultaneously. Rogers turned to the man and said, "You feel that this is your duck." I was reminded of that story because the end of it is that Rogers brought the duck home. I shall do my best to prevent a similar outcome. (*Skinner laughs.*)

We do agree on a good many things, and I like to feel that perhaps I have had some influence on Carl Rogers, because from time to time he has conceded certain things. He has agreed that human behavior has been controlled and is probably coming to be controlled with greater and greater success as the science of behavior evolves. The controllability of behavior is an old story, of course. Historians have always been delighted when they could prove the influence of some kind of biographical event on a hero. Biographers take the same line. The social sciences have certainly brought further evidence of a statistical nature, and an experimental analysis of the behavior of an individual organism has now essentially clinched the point. I don't believe it could be proved that all the behavior of a human organism is controlled, but I think the assumption is more and more plausible, at least as a working assumption for a science and also for human affairs in general.

Now Carl Rogers, in conceding this much, has tended to narrow the notion of control. He cites as examples of recent advances in controlling behavior the evidence that under certain social conditions a man may be led to make judgments which are contrary to the evidence of his senses. In other experiments it has been shown that a person may change his opinion without being aware of what has influenced him to do so. He has cited satisfying electrical stimulation as an all-compelling kind of gratification that might very well be used to control behavior, and of course the effects of drugs in producing vivid hallucinations, changes in disposition or personality, would also be cited by him.

But control to me means much more than this. These particular examples are examples of surreptitious control, control where the controllee is not aware that he is being controlled. They are specific examples of powerful control. What I am talking about, when I say "the control of human behavior," is any contribution which is made toward determining a man's action. It does not need to be surreptitious. It does not mean that the man may not be fully aware of what's being done to him. And it does not mean that it would be one hundred percent successful. I am talking about such control as is achieved in economics with various wage systems, the ordinary rather ineffective ones or special incentive wages and so on. And one has only to examine other nations, other cultures, to appreciate the extent to which, in the United States, our economic system does energize people — makes them productive and enterprising in undertaking new kinds of things. I mean by "control" the various police and military forces which governments use to keep people working within certain legal frameworks. I mean by "control" the various techniques which are used in education to bring about what we call the acquisition of knowledge or traits of character, and so on.

Now the fact that occasionally an employee doesn't go to work for the day, or a man becomes a hobo and stops working altogether, or a student plays hooky, or someone breaks a law or escapes from jail, these do not mean that the influences are not powerful and controlling. The exceptions are to be expected, because in no one of these cases are the variables which are manipulated the *only* variables, and hence control is not one hundred percent. So when we are talking here about "control," I hope we will speak more generally, and not limit the discussion to concealed control, although I agree there are specific problems involved there. I also hope to deal not only with control that is one hundred percent effective. I wanted to state this in these early remarks. I think it will come up again in the discussions.

Another issue has to do with the implications of the notion that human behavior is controlled. Let's, for the moment, talk just about complete control. Another of my valued opponents in this line of thinking is Joseph Wood Krutch, whose book *The Measure of Man* is largely an attack on *Walden Two*, my utopian novel, and also on other works of mine. He has recently returned to the attack in an article in *Saturday Review of Literature*, in which suddenly I find myself classed with the existentialists, being cited by Krutch as symbolizing what he calls the dead end of the tendency represented by Darwin and Marx. He cites me as denying categorically and absolutely that man has any control over his destiny, or that he has any power to choose or determine. He goes on to document this by saying that I write in my book, *Science and Human Behavior*, "The inner man who is held responsible for the behavior of the external biological organism is only a prescientific substitute for the kinds of causes which are discovered in the course of a scientific analysis, and all of these causes lie outside the individual."

Now let us assume for the moment that man is completely controlled by his genetic and environmental history. This does not in any sense mean that he cannot control his own destiny. He has been doing this both in the field of genetics and in the field of the environment. From the very beginning of civilization or culture or man as we know him, man has been working upon the genetic and environmental forces which are responsible for his existence. The geneticists today talk quite openly about the possibility of improvements in man through genetic intervention. There is a current view that favors sperm banks or special donor fathership. This could mean that in the world of the future a father will be proud not that a child is of his own blood but that the child has the best blood money can buy. Environmental control is already here and has been for thousands of years. Man is largely responsible for the environment in which men live. We live more and more in a man-made world, and it is a world which man has worked out largely because of its effect upon his behavior. It has reduced a need to escape from extremes of temperature and so on. We tend to be reasonably comfortable and well-fed, and can devote ourselves to things which are of more importance. This is a contribution of physical technology.

But the social technology, the cultural technology which has gone along with this, is even more important. Man has created a world in which he is governed, in which he is employed or can hire, in which he can gain wealth through borrowing or stealing. In this sense he has controlled himself. If human behavior is one hundred percent a product of genetic and environmental history, nevertheless man has created and can modify that genetic and environmental history and in that sense can control himself. I am not playing on words. Very often the man who builds the environment, whether the physical or cultural world, is not the man who is controlled by it, but often that *is* the case. The techniques of self-control, which can be extracted from religious, ethical, and moral works of the past, can be analyzed in terms of manipulation of environment. The man who has thus manipulated the environment will behave in a way which will cause him less trouble or will gain him greater achievements. So, even in a world in which human behavior is totally controlled, we *do* control ourselves, because we modify that behavior. This may seem logically impossible, but the point is that we do this not because we step outside any causal stream or outside the stream of history, but because it happens to be in man's nature to take steps of this sort.

This brings me to a third theme which we will certainly be dealing with again and again in this debate: the so-called choice of values. Why do we, in controlling man, control him in one direction and not in another? How do we decide in advance how we want to control? This comes up in the case of education. Suppose you have a very powerful educational technique. What will you teach? Your psychology can tell you the techniques. Can it tell you what ought to be taught? This is the field of value judgment but is not necessarily outside the realm of science. As far as I am concerned there is only science. There is only one way of knowing. It may be in the hands of scientists or of others, but it comes to the same thing. I know of no special wisdom available when science must stop and turn over to others the choice of values. The question of values concerns some characteristics of human behavior which have led to various explorations in the design of culture.

Some activities of man, as in the case of physical technology, can be explained by appealing to the immediate results. Early peoples hunted and fished because in hunting and fishing you are reinforced immediately with something edible. Later culture developed methods of storing food: drying, preserving, freezing. Methods of agriculture were developed where something was done in early spring in order to eat in late summer. Slowly a culture builds the capacity to do things with consequences that are more and more remote. This is also true in the case of cultural technology. A man who is able to whip anyone else in battle may steal, may take from others, and may force them to labor for him. This is a primitive kind of governmental structure. It can be explained in terms of the immediate reinforcement of the strong. Later, government which becomes more sensible in its understanding of long-term consequences will work out ways of controlling which do not resort to brute force, and will have greater survival in the long run, because such government makes better use of the people governed. As is true in physical technology, the growing importance of more and more remote consequences can also be seen in cultural technology, and this, I believe, brings us to the crucial issue.

Now Dr. Rogers has suggested that there are three ways of looking at human behavior: the Freudian; the positivistic behaviorist; or that which emphasizes the selfhood of the individual, an interest in the self as a source of wisdom and strength in altering conduct. My colleague David McClellan has written a book on psychoanalysis and religion which has taken the same theme. McClellan has noted that the Protestant Reformation, the Jewish Hasidic mystical movement, and Freud in his psychoanalysis all exemplified a kind of revolt against external control. This is an example of the conflict between psychoanalysis and governmental operations. It is the general turning to the individual to find salvation. This is the theme for the Protestant Reformation: that one can seek one's God within oneself. Freud carries this on by hoping to find within the individual the source of a pattern of life which is not imposed from outside.

I don't believe that is a correct way of stating the case. I think it can be modified in a way which fits my purposes very well. The change is not from external control of the individual to internal control. It is a change from coercive, punitive control to other techniques of control, which are related, ultimately, to positive reinforcement. There are ways to control people that influence what they want to do. And there are ways to control them that force them to do what they do not want to do. A shift from a legalistic coercive system to individual freedom, the whole theory of democracy, appears to take the good behavior of the citizen out of the hands of the police and turn it over to the individual himself. I suggest that the inner control which is then discovered is nothing but the product of another kind of external control which has been concerned with getting individuals to want to behave in certain ways, rather than coercing them to behave in those ways because of an external threat.

I see the evolution of culture moving away from the immediate punitive ways of controlling people, to more remote techniques, based upon a knowledge of human behavior, which require a sensitive understanding of these techniques, and which in the long run exert a more powerful control. I believe this kind of control is more likely to build a stronger group because, and here I would agree with Dr. Rogers, it releases resources of the individual which are quite lost under aversive control.

Those are the three things I wanted to mention. We agree that behavior is controlled, but I want to interpret that broadly. We agree, I hope, that even on an assumption of complete determinism man is and has been free to determine his destiny by the design of the world which determines him. And the slow evolution of cultural practices could very well be working toward releasing the potentialities of the individual without necessarily leaving it to the individual to determine his own behavior.

ROGERS: I think first I'd like to clear up the duck story. There is a great deal of truth in it, except for the punch line. Instead of my saying, "You feel that you shot the duck," we resorted instead to a procedure very highly regarded in scientific circles: we flipped a coin, and that proved that I had shot the duck.

As I listened, I felt as I often have when I have read his material: there is so much on which we are in real agreement. It is puzzling to know why five hundred people would turn out to see what the differences are. Nevertheless, I take it seriously that although we do seem to be in agreement on many scores, yet there are some real differences. There is something more at stake here than semantics. I am not sure that I can pin down those differences. One feeling I had, as he spoke, is that the scientific view is the whole world for Skinner. It isn't that it is one very useful way in which to perceive the world: it is the whole world. I noticed he had no comment on the paradox that to me has considerable meaning. I hope he will comment on that. For more than a year now I have wanted to ask Dr. Skinner something. We were both at a conference in Boston. He had given his paper on the design of cultures and then had commented on that. After hearing his comments, I directed these remarks to him. I said, "From what I understood Dr. Skinner to say, it is his understanding that though he might have thought he chose to come to this meeting, might have thought he had a purpose in giving this speech, such thoughts are really illusory. He actually made certain marks on paper and emitted certain sounds here simply because his genetic makeup and his past environment had operantly conditioned his behavior in such a way that it was rewarding to make these sounds, and that he as a person doesn't enter into this. In fact, if I got his thinking correctly from his strictly scientific point of view, he as a person perhaps doesn't exist." I thought I would draw him out on the subjective side of why he was there, but to my amazement he said he wouldn't go into the question of whether he had any choice in the matter, and added, "I do accept your characterization of my own presence here." I've wondered ever since. I would like you to comment further on that, because I think that gets close to the heart of some of the difference between us.

SKINNER: I think it does. I think it's very close. There is this strange feeling that if you deny the individual freedom or deny an interpretation of the individual based upon freedom and personal responsibility that somehow or other the individual vanishes. This is not at all the conclusion one could arrive at. I think you can make the assumption that each person is completely determined to do what he is now doing and is going to do by his own genetic and environmental history. I say this to my class at the end of the term. I give a course in human behavior with a fairly large number of students, and many of them become very anxious about this. In fact just this year I have learned two strange things about my course at Harvard: one, that it sends more students to courses in the divinity school than any other undergraduate course; and also that it sends more to the health service. There is a recognizable syndrome that turns up.

Now I try to reassure my students by pointing out to them that each of them is an absolutely unique locus through which certain lines of force pass. Each one of you represents an absolutely unique genetic combination of factors in the evolution of the human race. Each of you represents an absolutely unique combination of environmental forces: your family, your childhood, the school you passed through, the books you read, the various governmental and economic forces under which you lived, and so on. Now I can visualize the growth of a more and more successful human being as a biological organism, and a more and more successful culture or society as a cultural organization, or an organism emerging from the ordinary principles of evolution and selection as a more powerful version when diversity appears. This gives me a reasonable sense of my own individuality and good reason for telling anyone else that he is an individual and may have very important contributions to make. I do not do this to exhort my students. That would be quite inconsistent of me except insofar as I can prove that my own history has suggested that I exhort in order to produce certain effects. I don't believe in exhorting. I don't believe in the notion of personal responsibility in a legal sense. I think it disappears when you resort to nonaversive techniques of control. When people are held responsible for their acts, the consequences of which they foresaw, then there is meaning to the notion of responsibility, in the sense that they can be justly punished. But when people have been induced to behave in particular ways, without aversive consequences entering into the picture, there is no meaning to the conception of personal responsibility. There is never any question of the uniqueness of the individual, however, or of his possible importance in the evolution of a future culture. Nothing we have now is by any means the last word.

ROGERS: I'd like to come back to the first part of that. One of the things I have thought about is what meaning it would have to a Freedom Rider, for example, to tell him that he is the locus of a number of unique forces which have predetermined him to move southward and to sit in certain illegal places; that he has been operantly conditioned to behave in ways which bring him into conflict with the law; that he finds it rewarding to emit certain sounds when he is beaten, et cetera. I recognize the picture of behavior that you are giving as a picture that seems to be in general line with our current knowledge of people as viewed from the outside. However, I notice you steer very clear of even taking a look at the person from the inside. And when I think of trying to explain to a Freedom Rider his actions in those terms, I not only believe he would not accept it, but that it makes meaningless something which has meaning socially. Does this make any sense to you at all?

SKINNER: I have two points here. Suppose I could convince this Freedom Rider that I was right. Would he then stop being a Freedom Rider? You're getting at that, aren't you? That he has a conception of himself as someone who can do something to bring about an important change for which he will then be able to take a modest credit, and that people, certain people at least, will admire him for having done this. Now I think he does this because of a heritage which has come to him from his own culture, undertaking a certain kind of martyrdom and undergoing punitive treatment in order to bring about some other state of affairs. If he has been through a culture which goes in for this, he will do it. There are many cultures which would never produce Freedom Riders at all.

Apart from whether he would then stop, there is another issue: whether it is correct to say that he is doing this for reasons which are important to him beyond his training. The converse of this is the delinquent or the alcoholic, when he has seized upon this justification, who will say, "Well, I'm sorry, I know I'm an old drunk, but I really am ill. You shouldn't complain. You shouldn't criticize me. I need treatment." Now up to a certain point society has controlled drunkenness by shaming the town drunk, by teaching children either to laugh at or to blame these people, to point out how their families suffer. This is an effort to control through punishment.

Our modern view of this is that it just doesn't work, and the better way is to try to find other ways of treating an alcoholic. The alcoholic, then, may seize upon this to escape from the censure and blame. Well, he is more or less entitled to do that in the sense that you have left yourself open to this. When you shift from one technique of control, from punishment, to another — which might be medical or it could be positive educational measures — when you shift, there is a transitional period in which people seem to be at loose ends. They are lost: the old system isn't working, the new system hasn't taken control. In both cases you have a form of control, but in the long run you have a better one if you work out a positive educational treatment for alcoholism. This involves a great deal of cultural engineering and is very difficult. I think that any government worth its salt should prohibit advertising which makes the consumption of alcoholic beverages attractive or honorable or distinguished. I am not saying that people ought to be kept from buying alcoholic beverages. That didn't work. But I think advertisers should not be allowed to make the drinking of alcoholic beverages look beautiful or glamorous. This is a kind of design fault of the culture and if we could eliminate all of that with a positive educational program, we could treat the alcoholic without his having to be shamed, thrown into jail, punished, threatened with damnation, or whatever the aversive control is. And I would prefer a culture which works that way. Not only because of my own preference for nonaversive techniques, but because in the long run such a culture would be more effective. In such a culture there would be no moral struggle, there would be no need for exerting one's personal responsibility.

ROGERS: As I listen, the message I get, and I'd be glad to be corrected, is that you are saying, "I'll talk at any length about how one influences or controls behavior from the outside, but any comments on whether man's subjective view of himself has any importance whatsoever, that I don't wish to get into." And what I tried to indicate, when I talked about the Freedom Rider, is that if we take only the objective external perspective on man, if this is a kind of modern Calvinism where the clock was wound up originally and now runs inevitably to its conclusion, and if we say, "That's the total picture of man," then there is nothing more to be said about this Freedom Rider or any other person other than that he is inevitably doing exactly what he was conditioned to do and that he as a person has no part in it. If that is given as our total picture of man, to me it is insufficient, inadequate, and gives a picture of man as meaningless. I think it gives a picture of the universe, too, as meaningless.

The reason I feel strongly about this is that it doesn't check at all with what I learned with people from the inside. In other words, I find myself in ninety percent agreement with all you say about people when you are talking about them from the outside, but I notice you are not willing to get at them from the inside.

SKINNER: This could be a point at which we will simply go on disagreeing. I don't question the reality of the evidence that you are pointing to, and I surprise many people talking about my own feelings. I feel I do that.

ROGERS: That really relieves me.

SKINNER: Who knows what *you're* going to reveal. Yet falling back on my experience as a scientist, too, I always come back to the discovery that when I give up trying to account for something with an inner entity of some sort and try, very awkwardly at first, to deal with external entities which might be responsible for it, in the long run it comes out. I went a long time using the concept of drive, for example, in talking about behavior. It was, I think, the last of the fictions that I dispossessed myself of in my history as a theoretician. And it was awfully awkward, instead of saying a rat has a "high hunger drive," to say, "This rat is at eighty percent of his body weight," or "He has been deprived of food for twenty-four or forty-eight hours," or something like that. It seems so simple. There is something called hunger and there it is. Actually, in practice, it is extremely valuable to insist upon the conditions which generate this drive. This is positivism, of course, but I think it is a highly valuable practice. If I could just give you another example on this. I think we're both trying to understand each other.

ROGERS: Yes.

SKINNER: At present I'm doing a book on the technology of teaching, in which there will not be a long disposition on teaching machines, but an analysis of the processes of instruction from this point of view. There are certain chapters which I think would be of interest because they represent a search for the external correlates of the kinds of character traits that we have always assigned to the inner man. We can dispose, I think, of knowledge and skills. Those are fictions. Knowledge of something is only evident when you can talk intelligently about it. I prefer to talk about the behavior of talking about things rather than about knowledge. Take such things as the enjoyment of literature, for example, or an interest in what you are doing, or a dedication or industry or perseveration against the fatigue of excessive work, or courage, doing something in the face of aversive consequences. These things are very easily assigned to personality traits which seem to come with the baby. People who have them can do these things and people who don't have them don't do them. The dedicated scientist who is in his laboratory fifteen hours a day seems to have something: zeal, a dedication which many people don't have. We assume that a great many people could never be absorbed in a subject to that extent.

There is reasonable certainty, on the basis of evidence available now, that the extent to which a person enjoys music or art or literature, or the extent to which a person continues to work with a high level of interest in a given field — these things can be traced to lucky histories of reinforcement. For example, take the enjoyment of books. A school wants to boast of the level of its students, and so they make students read books long before they ought to read them. No one has made a reasonable effort to schedule a set of books so that having got a successful result from reading one page and then another page and so on, the reader continues to read and get periodic satisfactions which keep him going. Now if that were done properly I am sure we could build in any individual an extraordinary capacity for enjoying books, and the same is true of music, and so on.

In the case of scientific zeal, teaching someone to want to be a scientist is quite different from teaching him how to use apparatus in a laboratory. You want to schedule discovery so that he has the experience of making a discovery the first day, when he first tries it. Two or three days later he should make another and then ten days later another, and we know how to stretch this schedule out. Eventually you've got either a pigeon that bats against a key ten thousand times a day for several years, or a scientist who bats his brains out on the walls of his laboratory sixteen hours a day for years.

If you've ever seen a room full of women playing bingo (*Rogers laughs*), I don't know why it is that women play bingo, but they have terrific dedication, of the sort which American industry would love to be able to command with ordinary wage systems. The variable ratio schedule in the bingo game is enough to build this. They'll sit for hours with four or five cards, listening to numbers, and looking very keenly. Is this something they are born with? No, it is something in them because of their history of reinforcement, and I would take words such as "enjoyment," or "courage," as examples of what you would find *in* the individual that I am trying to find outside.

ROGERS: That's a very good statement. I, too, think of the possibilities and potentialities of human control that all of us will face and the consequences of which we all will face. I have two comments on what you've just said. In your talking about the external causes of behavior, you spoke as though for every external cause we can find, then you can drop a previous erroneous internal cause which you formerly posited. I want to make it clear, that is not what I am talking about at all. I think that is a part of the advance of science. Behaviors that were formerly dealt with as though they were caused by little homunculi within the individual, or various internal causes, are now seen to have other types of causation. Yet man lives a subjective life as well as being a sequence of cause and effect. It seems to me this has an importance which you don't acknowledge.

When you said you often spoke about your feelings, I wondered, Why? Perhaps you haven't yet found the cause of them. But it seems to me that there are other reasons for speaking of our feelings. Man's subjective life has significance as a perspective on life which stands quite separately and paradoxically in relationship to our view of him as one molecule in the vast chain of cause and effect. And one might say, "Well, but that's just a different way of looking at it. It really makes no difference." No, that's not true at all. When the subjective life does seem to have significance, then we adopt different courses of action from those we adopt if we regard it as having no significance at all.

Now I'd like to turn to your remarks about "learning machines." I think that's what they ought to be called rather than teaching machines, don't you?

SKINNER: If I may interrupt, the computer people talk about a machine which learns . . .

ROGERS: Hmmm, I see, and that's a "learning machine."

SKINNER: . . . a machine which modifies itself because of its own experience, and I think that they have the right then to call it a learning machine.

ROGERS: Okay.

SKINNER: In French, you can use the same word for learn and teach, but you can't in English.

ROGERS: Okay, we'll call them "teaching machines." It seems to me that, depending on whether we give subjectivity any significance, we might use programmed learning in quite different ways. A student's mathematics is inadequate. If he could go to a program of mathematics at that point, to learn what he needs to know, this would be optimal. If he needs to know about optics and there are programs along that line, he can take another program and learn that. All of it coming at a time when his interest and need are maximal. The learning would be quick and would be efficient. It can lead to the very best of what I think of as student-centered teaching and learning. Now let's select some slightly more debatable examples. Suppose the student wishes to improve his appreciation of art. He could easily take a program in art appreciation which would lead him to understand the principles of representational art. He could also take a program which would lead him to understand and appreciate some of the things that abstract painters are trying to achieve. This would be excellent because he would be faced with his own values, his own decisions, his own personal appreciation, and where he stood. Even in the political field I can think of nothing more educational than if there were a good programmed learning sequence on the principles and benefits of the Communist way of life and a good program on the principles and benefits of a more democratic approach. If a student had to take both, he would be faced with an internal subjective concern, conflict, difference, which he would have to straighten out within himself. That's the kind of thing I mean when I say that placing importance on the subjective leads to an approach different from simply shaping a person's behavior.

SKINNER: Perhaps I ought to take some time to state how one views experience and this inner life, from the point of view of a behavioral science. I don't deny for a moment that each person has enclosed within his skin a small part of the universe with which he has especially good connections. You can have your toothache but I can't have it, and this goes for a great many other physiological conditions. Now, in spite of a libel often urged against me, I don't think the organism is empty. (*Rogers laughs.*) I am sure that all sorts of things go on inside, but I am concerned with not having to wait until the physiologists have cleared all of that up to move forward, and I believe you would take the same line.

But what is the nature of self-observation in that case? If there are things that go on inside you with which you have special connection, you might say those are things that you will know that no one else can know about you. But will you know them? I have analyzed this problem. I can teach a child color, if he has color vision, by getting him to say red, blue, green, and so on at appropriate times when I am holding up red, blue, and green, assuming that I have color vision also or have these labeled, or I can analyze them with a spectrograph or something. In any case, I know something about the stimulus, and I can say to him, "Right," or "Wrong," as he learns the names of the colors. But I can't teach him the names of his emotions in the same way. I can't say, "Now there, you see, that's diffidence, and this is embarrassment." I may guess correctly that he's feeling diffident and use the word diffident, and he may then use it, but is it the way *I* use it? It is very difficult to set up any common vocabulary for the description of inner events, and this includes not only emotional but sensory events, experiential events, the observation of your own behavioral tendencies, the probability that you will behave in a given way today or tomorrow, and what you have done in the past, as well as reporting on your behavior.

So although people *do* come to watch things going on inside them while they are being stimulated and while they are acting in various ways, this always *follows* the action or the stimulation. It is always something ex post facto. And I would argue that the inner events which seem so important to us are not essential to action and probably do not, in any important case, precede action. When I talk about these inner things as fiction, you used the word "erroneous." I wouldn't call them errors: I think they are dispensable verbal tools that we could get rid of and profit by being rid of them.

But when I talk about these, people say, "Yes, but I can feel my hunger, I can feel my anxiety, I can feel my timidity," and so on. Well, can you? Freud, I think, made an important contribution in the notion of the unconscious. I am not bothered by that notion of the unconscious. So far as I'm concerned, conscious and unconscious behavior are all the same, the only distinction being that in the case of conscious behavior you know what you're doing or why you are doing it. In the case of unconscious, you don't. In other words, this ex post facto thing can happen in the case of conscious acts, but does not happen in the case of unconscious. Freud, I think, showed clearly that the kinds of variables which influence conscious behavior can also be proved to have been responsible for unconscious behavior. He freed the causal nature of experience from the need for observation. That is, what happens to you will affect your behavior whether you know it or not. When you do know it, we say it is conscious. When you don't know it, we say it is not conscious. Freud's evidence isn't conclusive to everyone, but we accept the general principle that there are things we do that we don't know we're doing, or we don't know we've done, or we don't know we are going to do. There are reasons for acting that we don't know about. There are others we do know. Now, if this is the case, then experience will always be something which follows action, or at least a disposition to act, and will not have any causal status. And I would look beyond experience to whatever it is which gives rise to the experience.

Your references to education take the line, of course, which Rousseau first portrayed so beautifully in that marvelous book *Emile*, which John Dewey and William James and others were advocating at the end of the last century, that you want the student to be interested. If you can make him interested, then he will learn. You suggest that if someone wanted to build a telescope, he would then turn to the proper program to learn about optics. I am concerned with his wanting to build the telescope. If it means to you there is something inside him moving him to build a telescope, then the teaching machine would only apply to showing him how to do this. But I want to trace the wanting to build a telescope back to earlier events outside him, in which he came into contact with telescopes, or pictures of telescopes, or books about them, and so on. As to the student who wants to learn more about art, you say it's all right to use programmed instruction to teach the student what he wants to know. But I want to teach him to want to know more about art, and I believe it can be done. This is not something arising spontaneously within him; it comes from his own past history.

ROGERS: I have many thoughts about what you are saying, but it strikes me that perhaps I could communicate best by a story that I think is quite relevant to this discussion. A short time ago, one of my clients was trying to tell me how he had always been able to cope with authority and all kinds of difficult situations by drawing into a nothingness. It was a new learning for him to realize that he just pulled in and became blank whenever anyone made too many demands on him. As I listened to all that he was saying (it was much more confused than I have put it), I said to him, "The way I hear that is that you had a kind of private joke against the world. No one could possibly defeat you. You could just pull in and this was your little joke." He listened and thought a moment and then began to chuckle. Then he broke into really uncontrollable laughter, and he was embarrassed, because he wanted to stop. Both of us realized that for the first time he was openly enjoying a joke he had been playing on the world for many years.

Now, where does this fit in? Well, for me it fits in a number of ways. To be sure, when I speak about that incident with him, I am talking about behavior which had its roots in the past — no question about that. I am talking about your saying that we couldn't teach a person what to call a feeling. In a sense, that's partly what therapy is, and this is a fairly vivid example of it. He certainly had never thought of himself as playing a joke on life or a joke on the people who tried to control him. Yet when it was put in those terms, suddenly all kinds of inner bells were rung and he realized, That is it, and he broke out laughing at the joke he had always pulled on life.

Perhaps by telling a small incident of this kind I can also communicate that an explanation of it solely from the outside is not a complete picture of the inner learning which took place. I am sure we are both being influenced by our own past experience in this, where probably you have not had the opportunity to know what goes on inside the pigeon and rat in the same way that I have had a chance to know what goes on within the human being.

I think, because of that difference in past experience, you stress one dimension only and to me both dimensions are significant.

SKINNER: Well, let me report my reactions to that story. The phenomenon of escaping from would-be controllers is, of course, characteristic. The student plays truant. Education has its own word for this — "truancy" — which, incidentally, comes from an old word meaning wretched. Religion has its apostasy. Government has its escapees (its own version of apostasy). Economics has strikes, where people refuse to work, although paid, or consumer strikes, where they refuse to buy goods at prices deemed to be too high, and so on. These are reactions to an effort to control, which is done not only with respect to the organized controllers, but to the general ethical control in the sense of control exerted by the group of which you are a member. The hermit is an escapee from social life. A beatnik is a different type of escapee. The inner, drawn-in, withdrawn kind of person is that too.

Now, evidently you are working with a person who has resorted to this kind of reaction to control. If he, himself, used the words "pulled in and became blank" without any direction, it would indicate to me that he was characterizing his behavior in a rather metaphorical way. Perhaps you don't want this to be a metaphor, but I do. I think: "Pulling in? I don't know what that means to you. You're still as large as you were before. But you may be becoming hysterically blind to the environment, or just not going to notice things. You are certainly pulling into your world in that you are cutting off reactions to it." So the first step in this person's history is that he reacted this way, and presumably it got him into trouble. That's why he came to see you. Then, perhaps for the first time, you indicated to him, or in talking with you he indicated to himself, that he was using this gesture to avoid being controlled. He might never have seen this on his own. The hermit might not realize that the reason he likes the life of a hermit is that nobody is criticizing him, or some other reason of the sort. But now he gets an insight, if you like, into the negative reinforcement which is leading him to behave in this way. That would be the second step. First, the actual escape from control. Second, the recognition that it is escape. He may very well escape without knowing that he's doing it. Now he sees he's doing it.

I can't account for his laughter. It might be the suddenness of the realization, but I can't account for laughter anyway, so it doesn't bother me. In this case it occurred, but I do not suppose it would inevitably occur in someone who suddenly realized that he was retreating from society and escaping from its influences. Some of this might have been known to him before he came to see you. I am sure that as he talked with you he saw more of what he was doing and the reasons that he was doing it. That, to me, is the human substance of the game of self-understanding in such a case.

ROGERS: Well, I don't know whether this gets anywhere in the intellectual discussion. Your not wishing to understand any human experience except in highly structured, intellectualistic terms really fascinates me, and I was particularly intrigued by your reaction to his phrase "pulling in." You remark that in actuality he was as large after he pulled in as he had been before. This is certainly true, and yet very different from the kind of things that have been meaningful in my own experience. When a client begins to talk in terms of analogies and fantasies, I realize he is beginning to get somewhere. The person who is able to speak in fantasy or metaphorical terms, terms not related to the strict structure of everyday life, is thinking and feeling significantly about the deeper meanings of his own life. I am sure both "pulling in" and the "blankness" that he described could be shown to be behaviorally meaningless terms, but as terms descriptive of his own subjective orientation to life, they are extremely meaningful.

Somehow in your last remarks I felt more keenly than before what the difference between us may be. It seems to me you are saying that all of life, or any particular incident from life, can be neatly packaged or analyzed in strictly intellectual terms which have nothing to do with meaning and which are straight descriptions of outward events. That's great if you can do it, but I don't believe it. That narrow a point of view runs the same risk as some students we used to see at Chicago, who had committed their whole lives to the belief that "I don't have to feel. I don't have to choose. Everything can be worked out rationally. My life is going to be lived on a completely rational basis." That's fine except it just doesn't work.

SKINNER: I thought I had agreed as to the existence of these experiences. What I object to is the assumption of causal efficacy.

I know that you shouldn't be held responsible for Freudian psychology . . .

ROGERS: No, I really shouldn't.

SKINNER: . . . but I'd like to give an example. The thing I want
to point out is clearer with Freud because of the elaborate metaphor which he used to deal with the relation between inner mental events and the external authority which he claimed to achieve
(and I've talked with good analysts who agree on this) — that
no evidence is available to establish the temporal sequence between being cured and recalling a traumatic experience. It may
be, as the Freudians would have it, on the analogy of excising a
tumor, that getting the traumatic experience out of the unconscious works the cure. But it could also be that the cure permits
the patient to recognize and recall a traumatic experience. So that
it cannot be certain that you have excised a cause of trouble and
brought about therapy.

Now, as I say, I am not burdening you with that, but I do think
that you want to order events in such a way that an understanding
of one's inner experience comes before the overt consequences of
this. You said that when a client begins to talk in terms of analogies, or to start reporting fantasies, he begins to get somewhere. I
assume that this "getting somewhere" means that he now begins
to understand himself, perhaps even working out better ways of
dealing with the world. If you will permit me to suppose that "getting somewhere" is capable of a rational description, I think the
issue between us is whether or not one's rational understanding
of where he stands in the world follows from irrational or fantasy glimpses of his own experience, or whether the experiences
come after some glimpse of the rational fact. My example of the
"pulling in" took that line. I suggested the first thing that happened to this client was to understand that in drawing into himself, as he put it, he was indeed escaping from unpleasant aspects
of the world around him. He might have done this withdrawing
and been able to see that he was doing it without knowing the primary consequence was that he was freeing himself from aversive
stimulation. Then I would have said that any metaphor he might
use, in connection with a joke perhaps (which in this case was
suggested to him), would come after rather than before the actual understanding of external events. By external events I mean

behavior in relation to controlling variables. He saw that he was turning away from important things in the environment because in doing so he reduced the net aversive stimulation in his life. We are going to have to either agree to disagree on this point or try to clear it up further. I am raising the question of the relative importance of these experiences, not their existence.

ROGERS: All right. I don't believe we differ in any fundamental way about the approach one would take in trying to resolve a scientific question. For example, I am much interested in what does produce change in psychotherapy. I have played with all kinds of hypotheses — including the possibility of psychotherapy being operant conditioning. We both agree, I believe, that studies could be set up which would gradually throw light on what the causes of change might be. I don't think we differ as to the kind of approach required in order to get a scientific answer to a particular puzzle. But my own hypothesis is that experience precedes insight, and I gather you were saying the opposite. I think when this person burst out in uncontrollable laughter, he was appreciating and experiencing the satisfactions of tricking his controllers, to use your terminology, and eventually, as a consequence of that experience, he would be able to put that kind of insight into words. Again, that's an empirical fact that could be the other way around.

One other comment I would like to make is that it seems you still believe that when I speak of subjective experiences, inner experiences and so on, that I am talking about them as a cause of something external. In other words, I have brought in some outside force to operate. That is not the meaning I give to it. The subjective experiencing of man, in my estimation, is a preceding dimension — it is a dimension which precedes our scientific desires, scientific activities, scientific behavior. It is a more primitive fact than our scientific behavior. I don't bring it in as a little gadget to produce causal explanations. I think of this as a significant dimension of life: more primitive, more basic, the aspect of life to which we turn to see whether we regard one approach to science as better than another. As a part of our subjective life and experience, we have gradually developed a most marvelously complex set of rules against deceiving ourselves, and we call that science. I have a great deal of respect for that, and I think we move significantly along scientific lines, but it will be unfortunate if that narrower perspective of science blinds us to the fact that we are also and most basically subjective beings.

SKINNER: Well I think this is going to remain a difference.

ROGERS: I suspect it will.

SKINNER: You have some very powerful and important authorities on your side. There has been considerable revival of interest in the personal aspects of science. Professor Bridgman, before he died, used to argue this. I spent many an hour trying to explain to him how one might deal with the question of whether the green he sees is not the red I see, and so on, and he went to his grave not knowing the answer and very much worried about it. I think this is the wrong tack. I don't think science is the experience of scientists at all. It is a corpus of procedures and practices. I should hate to think that physics is in any sense what goes on in the mind of a physicist. It is what physicists have done and what they can do. It is a series of marks that belong to conventional languages which permit other people to do things, including to talk about them quantitatively.

If experience seems very immediate and valuable and important, I think it is another consequence of the fact that each of us has a bit of the universe inside his skin and is in touch with it. If I want to teach a child the meaning of the word "toothache," I have to know when the child has a toothache. If I am a dentist and I am probing around and the child jumps, I say, "Now there you are, that's a toothache." Or if the child comes in and his jaw is swollen, I say, "Well, you have a toothache." The evidence of the dentist is the sight of a tooth with a cavity and a bit of steel striking it. The sight of a swollen jaw or a hand against a jaw is another kind of evidence. Those are the mediating stimuli that enable me to teach the child the meaning of the word "toothache." But the child is getting a very powerful stimulus from the tooth itself, and forever after that is what the child means by "toothache." This is much more important than the external criteria the community has used to teach him this term.

Where there are powerful stimuli of that sort, they naturally take control of the word, and what the word describes to the child is the actual painful stimulus, not a hand to the jaw. In the case of human behavior and in the case of many other things where we work with a variety of external stimuli without strong internal counterparts, the terms continue to refer to what is evident to the community. This is generally true of the language which describes our own behavior. We learn this when it is overt and broad enough in scope so that we can say, "Yes, you are now lifting your hand. You are now saying the word 'Now,' " and so on. But later, you can lift your hand without moving a muscle, and you can say a word to yourself, moving only very small muscles or perhaps none at all. You say, "Yes, just a moment ago I said something to myself." I close my eyes and see this room reasonably well, and am perfectly frank in telling you I am doing that. Something is going on which was going on when my eyes were open, and I can report on it.

In general, while those who deal with experience are likely to make a great deal of the inner stimulation, those of us who deal with behavior are much more likely to talk about the common elements available to the verbal community as well as the individual. Naturally I want to minimize the ache in the toothache and deal with an operational definition of "toothache." (*Rogers chuckles.*) Now that may be awfully silly, because we know about toothaches and they are very important and powerful. But operational definitions describing one's own behavior and moods are quite different, and in general I prefer to remain at the level of behavior, without denying at all that when I am angry with someone something is occurring which I can react to as I react to a toothache, although I would still define anger in terms of the damage committed upon others. I want a behavioral definition of anger, though in many cases a reasonable consistency would be obtained by asking one to describe bright and dull pressures in the chest, as was done in the past.

ROGERS: But that desire for a behavioral description of anger would scarcely apply when you are angry.

SKINNER: It would not have when I was young. Now, as a scientist, it would very much. When I was a child I would not have known how to describe the behavior, and I would have picked up the word "anger" and would have tied it to the marked but not too consistent stimuli generated by my autonomic nervous system, among other things. Now I want to define anger in a way that describes my angry acts. If I have said anything today because it would hurt you and have not seen this, I lack scientific insight, not knowledge of my feelings. I confess that I have not felt angry toward you at any time today, but if someone could prove to me that I have used an example or a figure of speech as a dig, now that would be an objective behavioral definition of anger, and I would put more faith in someone else's proof that I had been angry toward you than I would in evidence from my own inner feelings.

ROGERS: Well, that's exceedingly interesting. I am not quite sure whether you are saying, when you experience anger, "I am having some autonomic reactions directed toward so-and-so." Is it really that intellectual?

SKINNER: No. In general, certain kinds of behavior patterns are accompanied by autonomic discharge. It's not always emotional. Strong exercise is too.

ROGERS: Sure.

SKINNER: This thing we call anger, which I would want to define behaviorally as a predisposition to harm or to damage — it's a behavioral definition — is often accompanied by stimulation which is relatively consistent, so that without moving at all and without being aware of any actual impulse to act in any way, I might report that I feel angry. One thing Freud has done is to make us examine our acts. Not to discover our feelings, because they were unconscious, but to discover the consequences which were influential in determining our behavior. This I take to be a behavioral analysis of an emotion. All unconscious behavior has got to be that, by definition.

ROGERS: I'll have to mull this over. I am trying very hard to find out whether you are aware of living subjectively, and you have said things on both sides of that, and I don't feel quite sure. For your sake I hope so, but . . .

SKINNER: Well, I would hope so, if you mean by this that I have learned to observe certain states of my own body and to discuss them with some consistency in connection with my behaviors. I can report to you that I enjoy listening to Wagner and what I am doing when I am listening to it, and so on. I live a very emotional life, I suppose, in that sense. But that is not the thing that interests me about my emotions. I expect to go on enjoying life that

way. What interests me is my emotion in the sense of my disposition to act this way or that with respect to a variety of situations.
Many times I have gone back and looked at something I wrote
and been shocked to discover the emotionally loaded words. I was
not aware then and I can't believe now that I felt that way about
anybody, and by feeling that, all I mean is that I was inclined to
damage people this way. This is a discovery of any stimulation in
here (*gestures toward his body*) or wherever it is. I think it's a very
trivial thing for me to discover that I am angry in that sense. I
think it is very important to me to discover whether or not my
behavior with respect to people at large is angry behavior, and
that it seems to be practically unconnected with what's going on
inside me. Now I can enjoy being angry at someone, and I can
enjoy other, better emotions than anger. I hope to go on doing
so. In this sense I live a life of experience, of course.

ROGERS: I share that with you, because I, too, live a life of feelings. Sometimes I regret them and often I enjoy them, and so on.
Part of what I have been trying to say is that the subjective feeling
of life itself is an exceedingly important part of being human. I
see no reason for being apologetic in regard to it. It gives dimension and perspective to our more objective views.

Before we get completely beyond it, I'd like to go back to some
of your comments about science which interested me a great deal.
If I understood correctly, you really do see scientific knowledge
as a corpus of external fact which exists regardless of you, me,
the physicist, or anyone else, sort of out here in semantic space.
I think that one of the efforts of science is to achieve such a body
of truth, separate from any individual, and yet the actual pursuit
of science is a highly personal thing, governed by subjective decision in which subjective choices determine many things: what we
will study; the methods we will use; the kind of meaning we will
draw from it. When enough people draw similar meanings from
similar experiences we say, "That seems to be a pretty well veri-
fied scientific fact." But still it rests on a subjective base.

I don't think I have ever tried to put it into words, and I am
not quite sure how this will come out, but as I watch clients who
move a good deal in therapy, as they approach a better adjustment, it seems they have learned in a sense to live a subjective
science. Perhaps this will seem like a complete contradiction in

terms, but as the person becomes more open to what is going on within himself he has better data on which to act. His hypotheses are more likely to be confirmed by his experience. He is, in a curious way, living out the very best of science on an internal subjective basis with regard to the events going on within, the hypotheses he draws from those events, and the consequent behaviors upon which he acts. That has always intrigued me.

SKINNER: Well, we were getting along famously for a minute or two. I was admitting that I enjoyed my experiences and you were enjoying yours. That was fine until you started making them responsible for choices and decisions, and there you start making them do something, and they don't do anything. They are the result of doing something. When a person is making a decision, he is undoubtedly working on himself, but through the environment, or through an internalization of action which was first learned in the environment. Afterward he will feel the rightness of a choice or decision perhaps, but this is something which follows.

If I were to teach someone how to make decisions, I would not try to teach him this inner life. I would teach him the external, mathematical, statistical procedures to go through to arrive at the most likely decision in a given set of circumstances. Now, what is happening when you make a lightning decision? I don't think you or I know that. Neither has inner or external data. The thing happens too fast to follow. I insist on the distinction of causal efficacy. I don't mean that a person who has arrived at a decision about his own life doesn't then feel the decision. He feels it is right. He feels what he is now going to do, and so on. But I would go as far as possible in asking whether the essential ingredients here were not the environment and his self-controlling, self-managing manipulations of the environment.

ROGERS: I feel various responses to that, but you were kind enough to give me the first statement this afternoon, and I see by the clock our time is really up, so I will give you the last word in our discussion today.

SKINNER: Dr. Rogers has kindly offered to let me start first this time, since I let him do that yesterday. I hope this is symbolic of a continuing effort to deal fairly with each other in this protracted interview. I want to make two points in my opening remarks this morning. One, I want to respond to the moderator's hint that we ought to start talking about education pretty soon. I want also to try to make progress in coming to some understanding with Dr. Rogers about the techniques which we espouse in arriving at what I am sure are very similar goals. The main issue which developed yesterday concerned the question of inner experience and its place in human behavior. I am going to try to state my case as clearly as I can and hope we can attempt to see whether there is a basic disagreement or whether we are in some sense talking about the same thing.

I want to examine three cases from the analysis of education which have to do with supposed inner events relevant to what is necessarily an external process of instruction. I don't hold Dr. Rogers responsible for any one of these, but I have to regard him as a fellow traveler in the sense that the points I am going to bring up seem to me to exemplify an effort to account for behavior by isolating the originating event as something to do with inner experience. I want to take the three educational problems of teaching knowledge (verbal knowledge or skill), teaching thinking, and teaching some of the personality traits which I mentioned in passing yesterday.

The first of these has to do with the meaning of verbal behavior. I have written a rather long and, I am told, very difficult book which attempts to account for verbal behavior on the part of the speaker and responses to verbal stimuli on the part of the listener, without invoking, one, the notion of meaning, two, the earlier notion of idea or proposition, or three, the more recent notion of information. These three terms all make a fundamental mistake in supposing that there is some kind of cognitive activity which is not itself verbal, which happens before verbal behavior, and that verbal behavior becomes simply the symptom or symbol. Words actually mean the inner activity.

Now to take a nonverbal example first, there was the old joke of the difference between a man racing for a train and a man training for a race. Physiologically they are both doing the same thing. How do they differ? If you believe in meaning as something which characterizes behavior, then you would have to suppose that their behaviors are not identical. They may be the same physiologically, but one of them is possessing the meaning of catching a train, and the other is possessing the meaning of improving himself for a future race. I look for that difference — not in the behavior, which I think is or could be the same in both cases, but in the variables responsible for the behavior. In each case there is a different history, and what could be called a different purpose. Now purpose is another inner thing which Dr. Rogers mentioned as something which had no meaning for a behavioristic analysis. I think it has great meaning, and I have tried to suggest that reinforcement is nothing more than another way of talking about purpose. The only difference is that it identifies the characteristic moment at which an event is important.

In the evolution of behavior, if you say a spider is building a web in order to catch flies so that the spider will survive and perpetuate its kind, it looks as if the future catching of flies in the web had something to do with the building of the web. Actually, I think a biologist would agree that that is the wrong order of events, and that the purpose of the web lies in the past. That is, spiders in the past that have built effective webs have found a supply of food. This has meant that they have survived with their behavior, and I believe it is an inherited behavior pattern that was responsible for the supply of food. So that in the biological evolutionary scheme of things, what seems to be the future purpose of an event is actually a reference to past instances.

This is true in the case of operant behavior also, because what I am doing now in order to have an effect on you can hardly be determined by the effect which I have not yet had. It is determined by effects I have had in the past which have shaped my verbal behavior in various ways, and you, of course, are going to shape my behavior in the next five or ten minutes. I willingly accept the point of the joke about the rat who points out that he has me well controlled. Any science is eventually shaped as a human activity by its subject matter. The man designing a cyclotron designs it precisely so that certain events will happen in it in a given way. If he doesn't do that, his cyclotron will be discarded and someone else's will survive. So the feelings you have that the meaning of what you are doing — the purpose of what you are doing — is very important are genuine enough. If I ask someone, "What are you running for?" and he says, "I am running to catch a train," this doesn't mean he is aware of his purpose, except in the sense that he is aware of the conditions under which he is running and the condition which will bring that running to an end. He observes this as a purpose in his past.

In analyzing the teaching of verbal knowledge, I think it is very important to understand that it is always concerned with the teaching of behavior, and not the ideas expressed in the behavior. Logically, there is no such thing as a proposition apart from all the ways in which the proposition can be expressed. That's a fairly logical statement, but doesn't make much sense. What you do to teach a given idea in depth is teach it in many ways of speaking. That is the closest you will ever get to an idea apart from verbal behavior; some set of conditions that are responsible for a cluster of verbal responses. The difference between rote learning and teaching insightfully is often just that: you teach the thing not as a memorized single verbal response, but as a cluster of responses related to the same variables.

Now the second example has to do with seeking something inside the student in order to explain his behavior. To my mind this misinterprets the object of education. There is an example of that. There is a scene from Plato in which Socrates pretends to teach the slave boy Pythagoras' Golden Theorem. Now, Plato was a devotee of the inner life and felt that the soul knows the truth and that learning is merely remembering or recollecting. Perhaps it is recollecting in the sense of reassembling, suggesting that the process of education is only bringing out something which is latent in the student. This is still a prevalent attitude in education today.

Let's examine that case. Socrates wants to prove the point that any human organism knows a very difficult proposition, the doubling of a square. He calls the slave boy in and goes through a ritualistic procedure which is highly Socratic in essence. First he constructs a square and then says to the boy, "This is a square, isn't it?" The boy says, "Yes." He says, "If I do this it divides into two parts, doesn't it?" The boy says, "Yes," and he goes on this way. This example is still cited today as proof of a way of teaching the insightful understanding of a mathematical theorem with the general pattern of drawing the solution out of a student. I once went to the trouble of having the boy's comments copied out of that passage, and when put together they run exactly one minute. The set of the boy's responses goes something like this: "Yes." "Certainly, Socrates." "Quite right, Socrates." "No, of course not, Socrates." "Yes, you are undoubtedly right, Socrates," and so on. When he gets through, there is no effort made to show whether the boy can go through it again. I am sure he could not. He had done nothing but agree with Socrates. This is one of the great frauds of educational literature, and it is still cited as an example of how one can draw truth from the inside experience of the student.

This is the theory behind many current mathematics curricular programs: that you must get the student excited; you must get him to discover for himself. The implication is that you don't know until you have discovered for yourself, and that something you have discovered for yourself, you will remember better. I have no doubt that in the hands of a good teacher, this kind of Socratic technique can stimulate interest, curiosity, and perhaps even industry on the part of the student. But when you analyze what is happening, it comes back to behavioral manipulation. There has never been any demonstration that we all possess Euclid internally in some latent form, and that we can be led to discover it for ourselves. Men discovered geometry. Euclid, I suppose, brought together a long history of discovery and put it into a book. It was a difficult thing, and to suppose that we must do it all over again before we know geometry is, I think, an inefficient way to approach education. I have seen a seventh-grade teacher trying to teach grammar in this way. Now, the Greeks discovered grammar as well as geometry. It was a great discovery and must have taken a great deal of time. Why a seventh-grade class must go through all of that again on its own, I don't know. This teacher had a sentence written on the board and was trying to get the students to say, "That's a 'thing' word and that's an 'action' word." The students who spoke up and said "noun" and "verb" were shushed and told not to use those words — "Let's find out about this for ourselves." So for a long class period, the students struggled toward the recognition of two types of words which eventually turn out to be called "nouns" and "verbs." Well this may have some motivating effect, but I could think of much better ways to motivate children.

My third example has to do with some of the character traits that I talked about yesterday as examples of behavior which we like to attribute to something inside the organism. I mentioned the enjoyment of art, music, literature, one's interest in what one does. Someone brought up the question of emotional conditioning, and I'll give an example. There are children who can take punishment without crying. They seem to be particularly brave and can take novel experiences without panicking. Now how is this brought about? Is there something called courage born into some of us and not into others, or could anyone be given these traits of character? In the book *Emile*, a remarkable treatise on human behavior, which, though probably fundamentally wrong, was nevertheless a most ingenious book for its time, Rousseau suggests ways in which children can be taught to take strongly aversive stimuli without emotional reaction. He begins with the idea of cold bathwater, which will make a baby cry. He suggests that you begin on the first day with water at body temperature, and then reduce the temperature every day. He recommends the use of a thermometer to be scientific about this. You bring the temperature down one degree every day. Eventually you are plopping the baby into ice water, and the baby takes it perfectly well, is not disturbed at all. Now, you may not call it an emotion, but it is the ability to take something which an ordinary child, one who has not been through that course in history, would not be able to take, and who might be timid or cowardly all his life.

Rousseau also took the case of a more emotional example. He tells the story of Hector and Andrometer and the baby who was frightened by his father's war helmet as he says farewell to him. He raises the question of why it is that small children can be frightened by ugly masks or faces. He suggests you construct a series of masks, running the gamut from a very pleasant face to a terrifying face, by very small steps. You work with the baby one day with the pleasant face on, then gradually move toward the frightening mask. The result is that he is never again disturbed by the frightening spectacle. Now, I believe we have seriously neglected emotional training in our educational systems. People object violently to the scene in *Walden Two* in which the children are to wear lollipops around their necks but are not to touch them with their tongues during the day. But I would like to see a little more moral and ethical self-control taught. This can be done, I believe, so that everyone will be a brave man or brave woman, will be able to take necessary painful stimuli without flinching, and will not be disturbed by what would otherwise be terribly emotional circumstances. This could include periods of failure, or of frustration.

I have taken these three examples: the meaning of a verbal proposition, the thinking through of a problem in mathematics, and a character trait. These are all areas in which the national tendency is to suppose that the individual who is marked by this possesses something inside himself which is very important. The person who knows it has got it in here. He can talk about it, but when he isn't talking about it, it's in here. Well, I'm sure it's in here, too, in some physiological condition. I am sure, too, that very often the person knows whether it's in there or not. But it is in there because it's been put in. Knowledge has been implanted, not drawn out. Many people misunderstand the meaning of the word "educate." *Educare*: drawing something out from inside the student. Knowledge is implanted, and our job as educators is to implant or shape behavior — to build it up and to strengthen it, rather than to find it already in the student and draw it out. I don't deny for a moment the existence of things which one can see when one looks at and reports on oneself — whether he is afraid or not, whether he is getting the point of this problem or not, whether he sees the point of an explanation of a theorem and so on. I am sure this goes on. The question between us is not one of the existence of the inner events, but their status as explanatory, efficacious causes of the overt behavior which it is the business of education to set up.

One other quick point. When you put a student into a difficult situation, one which might frighten him but doesn't, because he is able to control himself; one which might puzzle him but doesn't, because he solves the problem; one which might show him to be ignorant but doesn't, because he comes through with the answer; when you do this sink-or-swim technique of creating a situation in which a child or a student must be knowledgeable, insightful, and brave, you leave it up to the individual to solve his own instructional problems, and that has been the trend in education. On the other hand, when he does solve them in rare cases, you admire him. You admire Abraham Lincoln for getting an education, although no one taught him. You don't admire Franklin Roosevelt for getting an education at Harvard because Harvard taught him. (*Rogers laughs.*) There is nothing to admire if the educational system is powerful enough to produce these results in everyone. The only point of admiring is to make up for the deficiencies of your education. I would prefer a world in which everyone got an education without trying very hard. If we don't have that world, I will share in your admiration for a person who gets an education against great odds. The difference is that in an effective world, the reasons for admiring will disappear. We'll miss that, but it's something we've got to learn to get along without.

ROGERS: Dr. Skinner told me that he got up early this morning — I didn't know he got up *that* early. I feel in regard to all that he has been saying: I am not quite sure who it is he is talking to, but somehow he is not talking to me. I mean that quite seriously. As so often happens where differences are quite real and quite deep, it's difficult to prevent communication from sliding off-center. I have no particular response to what he has just said, because I don't feel he is talking to the kind of issues I feel. Instead I feel compelled to give a speech of my own. The real reconciliation, the making of this into a real dialogue, may come later in this hour, or perhaps it can only occur in you [the audience], I am not sure. We'll have to see.

When I thought about yesterday's session, I felt that, since the topic was control of behavior, my own remarks tended to be critical and "anti-." That's not characteristic of me. I am a person who affirms more than criticizes, and so I felt a little unhappy about that. Perhaps to offset that, I'd like to make a few remarks about the design of a culture, to use Dr. Skinner's good phrase. I will also bring in the matter of education, but I'd like to do so within that context. Part of my purpose in doing this is to indicate that when one designs a culture one takes different directions if one values the subjective aspects of experience. The thing that got me to thinking about this specifically was Wendel Johnson's challenge to us last night that we should point up the differences between pigeons and persons. That had real meaning to me.

Persons *do* have a capacity for awareness. We have a rich capacity for symbolization, which I believe is synonymous with awareness. We have the capacity for a rich subjective living. We have the capacity for an organismic valuing process. That is, we are able to test objects and events in terms of our own experiencing and can gauge the values they have for enhancing us or for being destructive in our experience. Those are a few of the capacities which persons have. Most of those pigeons have relatively little capacity for anything except the last, and on that it's possible we could learn from them. I'd like to talk about designing a culture which would maximize truly human qualities, to build a culture for persons, not for pigeons.

I will start by basing my remarks on some research in psychotherapy, because I am to some degree a scientist, though I was amused last night to think of myself only as an overwhelmed practitioner. However, I have had some experience with the scientific side as well. Some of the studies completed in psychotherapy indicate the kind of psychological climate which would promote and maximize the most truly human qualities, and have begun to specify some of the elements of that psychological climate. We know that when a person is prized as a person, valued as a person, it is helpful. We know that when the personal meanings which a person finds within his own experience are deeply understood by another, so that they are confirmed in him, this, too, is a quality of the psychological climate which can release constructive human qualities. We know that when a person comes into genuine subjective encounter with other real persons, this is also a releasing element.

In the kind of culture I would be in favor of designing, parents, teachers, and others could be helped to establish such conditions in the life situations of the persons with whom they deal. Now, I would hope and expect to discover more elements which would have that kind of releasing quality. Our goal in such studies and in such research would be to find the conditions which would increase the capacity for personal choice, for self-direction, for spontaneity and creativity, for independence, for flexibility. Such conditions would increase the tendency described so well in the panel discussion last night as being toward personal scientific locus; that is, living in terms of scientific principles within one's own personal and subjective life. In short, by establishing these conditions, we would tend to bring about the likelihood that individuals could not be shaped by controllers.

Now, a word or two about the application of those ideas to the educational situation. I have, on a number of occasions, endeavored to establish those conditions as a learning climate for students. I haven't always been successful. There is a good deal we do not know about the kinds of conditions that really do release freedom in people. And yet when one has been able to set the psychological climate which enables individuals to become more free in choosing, more self-directing toward their goals, so that they tend to feel a greater reliance on their own initiative, the results are sufficiently compelling that one cannot resist trying to advance that field further. I am talking here of something which can be empirically measured and studied. It is the kind of educational climate which I would hope for in a culture we might design for persons. It would, I believe, enhance and promote self-directed learning. It doesn't mean going back to struggle step by step through all that the Greeks learned centuries ago. Rather it means a following through of one's current focuses, using all the modern resources available, and doing so on a self-chosen, self-directed, self-initiated basis. That kind of an education would not achieve static goals which could be defined in advance. It would achieve the development of changing persons, persons with a greater degree of self-confidence in directing themselves.

This is something the modern world needs very badly. As I see it, the whole philosophy of democracy and its stress upon self-determination has thus far made very slight progress in the world. It has been established a little bit in the political realm and has begun to show slight pervasiveness in other areas. But I am talking about extending the philosophy of democracy down to individual life, individual learning, group and family living. Not only the worth of the individual, but his capacity and right for self-determination and choice would be important. Obviously the kind of thing I am describing would not produce a closed society. No one could possibly plan this in advance as a closed book. It would produce an open, changing kind of society. Change and the process of change would be built into it. This, I think, is valuable. By developing a society in which parents and teachers and all of those in positions of leadership, whether governmental or otherwise, were skilled in providing the conditions which make for personal growth, we would have a society in which variability and individual self-actualization would be present. We would have individuals developing uniquely, with a sense of personal freedom, freely seeking solutions to the problems that were real to them, and at the same time seeking solutions to the problems of society. In this kind of a culture, every citizen would be a responsible planner. We would have initiated a process of continuing and self-directed change, not a community of static goals established by one person, or established by an elite. The likelihood of society being a living, changing flow of intelligent encounter with the problems faced in the world would be greatly enhanced.

To me, the most important task of the behavioral sciences is to discover and to endeavor to establish the conditions which release variability, release creative behavior and self-directedness, thus making the individual less predictable and less likely to be controlled. This is just as feasible a goal for the behavioral sciences as to establish a planned control. Well, end of speech.

(A short gap followed while tape was being changed.)

ROGERS: One story I have heard — I don't know whether it's true; if it isn't, it should or could be — is that one of the early people investigating the operant conditioning of verbal behavior made a very convincing presentation to his students on the research which showed that you could condition the verbal behavior of individuals. Some of his students thought that it would be fun to operantly condition him. He had a certain gesture that he tended to use, and they all agreed to nod or smile or look especially attentive whenever he used that gesture — to "reward" him for that behavior and to condition his behavior to increase the gesture. So they did that, and it worked. More and more he began to use the gesture they were rewarding. When they felt they had him sufficiently conditioned, they told him about the experiment and all had a good laugh together.

Now the point that is crucial to me is that once the instructor realized that he was being manipulated by the rewards, they would no longer operate as rewards. It is clear that though all of the external behaviors might remain exactly the same — the students might continue to operantly condition this gesture, but the rewards would no longer be effective. Why? Because of a change in the subjective perception of the instructor as to what constitutes a reward. No longer would the head-nodding and smiling be perceived as a reward. It's that kind of thing that I think we need to include in our world of science.

SKINNER: First, let me clear up that anecdote. There are actually two cases blended together here. In one of them, I shaped the behavior of a psychiatrist who was participating in a roundtable and who was, I thought, talking a little too much for good communication. I passed a slip of paper down the table to a friend of mine, saying, "Watch Dr. X's left hand. I am going to shape a chopping response." It just so happened that Dr. X was across the table from me and looked mainly at me. And he tended to gesture a great deal. So I simply looked to one side, and out of the corner of my eye I could see his general posture fairly well. Whenever his left arm was up, I looked at him with deadpan. And whenever his left hand went down, I nodded. Within five minutes he was holding on to his wristwatch. The note came back. "Let's see you extinguish it." And, I must confess, I wasn't able to.

The other story, which I think is part of this apocryphal story you have just heard, is that some time ago I gave a series of lectures at a midwestern college, and a professor at the college was enraged that I had been asked to speak. He opened the week that I was in residence there by telling his class that I was a menace, and that so long as I stayed in an ivory tower all would be well, but if I ever showed any signs of having a practical effect, he would be in favor of calling out the firing squad. (*Rogers laughs.*) Well, the students in his class resented this a little, and did plan this particular trick. They agreed that first of all they would reinforce him for coming over and standing on the right-hand corner of the platform, and, when they had achieved that, they would then reinforce him for going back and facing the blackboard. They all did this by being very deadpan until he moved in that direction and then they began to smile and agree with him, and very soon he was teetering on the corner of the platform. Then the signal went out that that was enough of that, and he teetered a while, but they were all deadpan. When he faced back toward the board and turned to look at the class they all nodded again. I wasn't there, but they tell me that he finished the lecture facing the blackboard, talking over his shoulder.

Now, in neither of these cases, to my knowledge, did the controlled person ever learn what happened, and I should not like to think of the consequences if they did, because it is certainly true that once you discover that these characteristic social reinforcers have been used for a purpose, you build your resistance against them. The backslapping Dale Carnegie fellow who is out to make you his friend and influence you doesn't get very far if you have read Dale Carnegie also. It is not true, however, that reinforcers don't work, and I don't know of anyone who has not been to some extent reinforced by flattery even though he knew of the ulterior purposes of the flatterer. The pathological gambler may know all too well why he is gambling if he has studied books on schedules of reinforcement. He is the victim of a variable ratio schedule. For that reason he cannot stop it. The social reinforcement of approval, a smile for instance, can be destroyed if you discover that the person who uses it is out to control, because that devalues the reinforcer. But when the reinforcer has a stability, as money has, you may know very well that it's being used to control you and still suffer control.

ROGERS: Could I comment on that? It's extremely interesting to think through this issue. A theory of human behavior which is effective only when the operation of that theory can be concealed from those on whom it is operating seems to me to be a relatively unsatisfactory theory of human behavior. If for example, the persons in *Walden Two* became aware of the planning that had gone into it and if, to that extent, it would destroy the effectiveness of many of the reinforcers, then that is not a complete or effective theory of behavior. This has been one of the things that has perplexed me, and I am interested that Dr. Skinner agrees.

Similarly there are some theories of psychotherapy which operate effectively only if the client is quite unaware of the theory that the therapist is acting upon and the principles he is trying to promote. In the kind of therapeutic approach that makes sense to me, the more the individual knows of the climate I want to create, and of the principles that I believe to be operative, the more intelligently he can participate in the experience of therapy. It also seems to me the same would be true in the culture that I was trying to describe. The more the individual realized the basic principles we were after, or the more he realized the theory of what was happening, the more intelligent and probably the more enthusiastic would be his participation in that culture. For me, that is one reason for feeling that it is a more potent or widely useable theory: that it is not destroyed by people becoming aware of what is happening.

SKINNER: I'm afraid I didn't make my point. The reason that discovering that someone is flattering you insincerely leads to a countercontrolling action on your part is not that there is anything wrong with the notion of reinforcement, but that the particular reinforcer has been devalued.

ROGERS: Subjectively, would you say?

SKINNER: No, I wouldn't, actually. A piece of money, a dollar bill, has reinforcing effects, power, value, because it is exchangeable for immediately reinforcing goods of one kind or another. If the money devalues, if that bill becomes worthless, it will no longer reinforce. But that doesn't negate its reinforcing effects when it had this particular value, and the thing which devalues it is that it is no longer exchangeable for our primary reinforcers. I don't know of any case in which knowledge of the process of reinforcement does destroy its effect. If someone is insincere in his compliments, the effect is destroyed just as the effect of money as a reinforcer is destroyed in an excessive inflation. I myself work for a living, although I know perfectly well that I am being reinforced with money. I came out here because I am getting reinforced. Knowing that, I still came, and in fact am very delighted to be here. If you are trying to reduce or control your weight, you are highly aware of the reinforcing effects of various foodstuffs, and although you may be successful in countercontrolling on this, you don't deny that these are reinforcing, and if you don't watch it they will strengthen behaviors of ingestion to the point that you will be damaged. It is a common misunderstanding that if you know you are being worked on, it won't work. If you know that the money being used to pay you is bad money, it won't work, but that comes about by an extinction of the conditioning process which made it a conditioned reinforcer in the first place.

ROGERS: I am interested in your statement that to the extent the individual realizes that the reinforcer is offered insincerely, it would change in value for him. This brings me to something that is a very real feeling reaction that I would like to express. I have a high respect for your sincerity. You seem to me to be a genuinely sincere person. Yet as I hear your theories described practically, I get a very different feeling. I was perplexed last night to sense the way I was reacting to the reading of the excerpt from *Walden Two*. It's been quite a while since I read *Walden Two*, so it came to me as a fresh thing, and I was genuinely surprised at the revulsion I felt. Afterward I tried to puzzle out why, because what was being described were group therapy and devotional-type exercises, which certainly seemed innocuous enough in themselves.

I think the reason I had the reaction I did was that it seemed that in the world as you would like to see it, nothing is really genuine. Everything has a "pseudo" quality to it. Because of your devaluation of the subjective, everything real is something different from what it seems to be. For example, for the people in the devotional-type exercises, expressions of loyalty to the code would be experienced subjectively as a real devotion. But Frazier [the planner of the society] knows and knew that they were planned that way, that these were not real, that they were nothing but a piece of human engineering designed to keep people in line with the code. I realized that if an individual in *Walden Two* ever knew that, the least he would do would be to stop going to those exercises. So, as I understood it, the whole society was based on the notion of surreptitious control. It made me wonder how long a real Walden Two would last. This is no idle question, because I have heard that you are trying to get funds to establish an actual Walden Two. So, in spite of your sincerity, which I really trust, it seems to me that the hypothetical worlds which you construct are basically insincere. They are not what they seem to be. They are not genuine.

SKINNER: I am glad that you have given me an opportunity to answer last night's comments on *Walden Two*, though they were not designed to warm the cockles of an author's heart. (*Rogers laughs.*) But actually I planned it that way. (*Rogers laughs again.*) There are two things about that book which have to be taken into account in discussing Frazier. The question was raised of the difficulty a critic has in identifying the author with a particular character. One thing you can do is to ask the author. Now, I am here to say that when I wrote the book, I was in grave doubts about Frazier. I think the book is mainly a struggle between two aspects of my own personality, which were represented by Burris and Frazier. But when I had given Frazier, as a fictional character, the chance to say things I didn't dare say myself, it all seemed to me to make sense, and I am now a confirmed Frazerian.

This, however, does not make that particular passage a strong passage, for two reasons. In the first place, Frazier makes this point. I have deliberately made him an unpleasant person, and there is a scene in which this whole question is argued out. The whole point here is, as Frazier says, that a person may, through a scientific analysis, work out a better way of life, and yet may not, himself, be able to lead that life. He himself may not be the kind of admirable person that particular culture can now produce, because he is not a product of it. Frazier said things to the contrary: one can arrive at good cultural practices without being able to absorb them oneself. Frazier has what you might call negative charisma. All great leaders have had charisma. Jesus had charisma. St. Paul had charisma. Other leaders have had a less admirable charisma. They were effective as people, but Frazier is not effective as a person. No one knows who he is, and no one knows his part in founding the community. He tries to get a couple of architects to come and explain something to a small group and they go off swimming instead, and so on. He is not a leader in the current sense at all, and this was deliberately put into the book.

So his description of the Sunday services was meant to be cynical, meant to arouse the reader to a critical attitude. Then, too, I wrote the book to alert people to the possibilities of a utopia. The main problem, as somebody has pointed out, goes back quite a long time in critical thinking about utopias. The problem today is not whether they are possible, but how to prevent them. (*Rogers laughs.*) This can be serious. As Dr. Rogers has said, I am sincere about this. I am very much concerned about the possible misuse of a behavior technology.

The other reason that passage is weak is that, as interpreted last night, it brought in the various values, which Frazier lists. I wanted to write a book describing an experiment, and I had to guess at the result of that ten-year run. The point of the book is that all cultures are experimental — or should be. They are experimental whether they are designed to be or not, because if they are not strong, they will eventually disappear. A properly designed culture should design itself as an experiment, so that it can be tested and can change as occasion dictates. I had to guess at the values which would have emerged at the end of ten years. And they turn out to be middle-class values. I am perfectly aware of that. I am aware of my middle-class status and middle-class training, and, naturally, I go for things like health, wisdom, wealth, comfort, productivity, creativity, and so on.

But the passage in which those are discussed directly, I think, presents them in better light. To begin with, you have to settle on some plan for a community. As Frazier said, "To begin with, I prefer health to illness. I prefer wisdom to ignorance." And so on. I think we could all agree on that while not overlooking the fact that there may be times when one must decide whether to value health above wisdom, and so on. You start a design based upon some of these principles. They are not really values in the philosophical sense. You have to design for something you plan for something, and to begin with, you would choose what seems best in our way of life. Under the conditions of an experimental community, though, you might very well find these things changing. I worry that we will be too successful not in regimenting people, but in making them too rambunctious and hard to handle.

I am not sure that I will ever start an experimental community, but if I should, one of the things which would be most challenging would be the total ecological control of the child from birth for the first five or six years. Those are the great wasted years in our present culture. These sensitive organisms during that period are capable of fantastic achievements, and all arrive at the age of five or six badly messed up. Now that can be done in a different way. It can be done with total control at the beginning on the part of the environment, and will engender techniques of self-management and self-control so that, as the child grows, the

environment can relax and the child will be on its own. I quite
agree with Dr. Rogers that we need to release the inner freedom of the individual, meaning by that, freedom from explicit
and, particularly, aversive external controls. I want to teach the
person to talk to himself, go over plans, review himself as an individual, and so on.

Techniques of self-management can and should be taught at
a tender age. There is no reason why a child at the age of six
cannot have arrived at a very effective system of ethical self-
management. It is not too early. We don't know what is too
early. The whole notion of readiness is one of the awful things
about these inner forces that I am certain Dr. Rogers would de-
cry as rapidly as I. "The child can't learn to read until he is ready
to read" is one of the worst of the inhibiting, inner experiential, fictional, hypothetical limitations on human behavior. Yale
University has three-and-a-half-year-old children typing complete sentences on electric typewriters, using correct fingering.
These are not routine rote-learned patterns at all. They are verbal responses to projected sentences on the screen. Three and a
half years old! They are middle-class children from New Haven.
They are not geniuses at all. We have no idea at all what this very
intricate human organism is capable of.

I want to give Dr. Rogers time to answer before we stop, but I
hope, before the morning is over, that I can also raise the question of how pigeons differ from people.

ROGERS: Okay. One of the really basic things on which Dr.
Skinner and I agree is in our view of the vast untapped potentialities of the human organism that have never been fully
released or fully developed. Though we might take somewhat
different pathways to it, I think we are in real agreement on
that. I haven't been sure how much influence — he would call
it control, I would call it influence — I might have had on Dr.
Skinner. I was intrigued by his statement that if you are going
to design a culture or a society, you have to choose certain
values to start with. I don't know what he means in his terminology by having to choose certain values. Because it was my
whole understanding that it was on precisely that point that
he felt this was not feasible. I heartily agree, though, with his
statement that we *do* have to choose certain values and that

those choices precede our attempt to redesign a culture. I also hope that we would choose values which incorporate the whole process of change. I have never been fond of the rather static type of values, whether middle class or otherwise, which are incorporated in *Walden Two* or in other of Dr. Skinner's writings.

Now I'd like to change the topic just a bit, to bring in one other issue that we haven't touched on. This is the feeling that we are likely to settle for much too narrow a view of the behavioral sciences. This, I think, is one of the real differences between us. I'd like to read very quickly two statements, one from a psychiatrist and one from a psychologist. The psychiatrist says, "Unfortunately, those who make a fetish of scientific method tend to exclude subjectivity from their data because it is not 'scientific.' For my part, I cannot believe that any study of man which excludes the subjective can be a science at all. At best it is only a partial science. I should think that a science must include all the data of experience. And when life problems are the subject matter, then the data of subjectivity must bulk exceedingly large." A psychologist in California puts it in terms that are a little too drastic to suit my taste, but still they are meaningful. He says, "The behaviorists have shown us the true nature of neurosis, not in what they have taught, but in how they have redefined man to avoid the real danger of adopting much too narrow a perspective when we turn the tools of our science toward the study of man." I hope that as we try to design cultures, as we endeavor to improve education and to release these potentialities in the individual, we can have a science which takes a look at the whole range of data and at the wholeness of the human being.

SKINNER: I want to make just one remark before we break. I do not, I believe, exclude anything from my considerations. I thought that I had acknowledged several times the existence of events within the individual with which that individual has an especially intimate contact. I confessed to my having feelings and so on. I confessed to their importance in my life. As a scientist, I raise the question of whether they are something which precede and determine my action, or whether they are an observation of my own behavior after the fact — or possibly before the fact, if what I am actually observing are the conditions which are to be responsible for my behavior in the future.

I think we are arriving at two fairly satisfactory conditions here. We have identified some basic differences. On the other hand, I have profited greatly from this. You asked to whom I was talking, and felt that I was not talking to you in my opening remarks. You and I ought to be able to analyze verbal behavior better than that, it seems to me. You have been interested, more than anyone else, I think, in the nature of verbal contact. I have written a book about it and have been interested in it, too. I don't believe any more than you do in the communication of ideas back and forth, the implanting of opinions or attitudes. These are not effective ways of talking about verbal behavior. I didn't come out here to tell you anything in the ordinary sense of communicating, or to be told anything in that sense. I came to participate in a certain amount of verbal behavior as I might have come out here to play football or something like that, but I would hope to go away changed from this, and I think I am changed, although I may not know to what extent. There is a story about Gertrude Stein which is relevant here. Gertrude Stein and Alice B. Toklas, her companion, were having dinner one night with Robert Hutchins when he was president of University of Chicago. Mortimer Adler was there and other intellects, and there was a very lively discussion. And when the evening came to a close, Alice B. Toklas went up to Mortimer Adler and said, "Gertrude Stein has said things here tonight it will take her months to understand." I look forward to a very good month following this conference.

ROGERS: Let's take a break.

MODERATOR: During this next hour, we hope to help you resolve some of the questions facing you. For the first half hour, we will deal with some written questions which were given to us last evening as a result of the group meetings. Out of hundreds, we have synthesized these into about twenty. Out of the twenty, we have tried to select ten (*Rogers laughs*); let's hope we get beyond five. I shall indicate the question. Dr. Skinner and Dr. Rogers each has a copy of the list. The person to whom the question was directed will be invited to respond. If the other person wants to respond, he may do so also. The first question is

directed to Dr. Rogers: Is a subjective feeling of freedom sufficient evidence that this freedom is real, and that man is not
subject to the control of his genetic and environmental conditions?

ROGERS: I think that indicates some misunderstanding of the
point of view I have presented because, as I have said, I am
in thorough agreement with Dr. Skinner that, viewed from the
external, scientific, objective perspective, man is determined by
genetic and cultural influences. I have also said that in an entirely different dimension, such things as freedom and choice
are extremely real. I would remind you of the example I gave
of Viktor Frankl in the concentration camp. It would have been
interesting to try to tell him that a freedom of choice, which he
felt remained to himself, was completely unreal. He knew it was
real because he saw people who did not exercise that, and who
felt they really were completely controlled, die like flies. The
ones who had the best chance of survival were those who re-
tained the concept that "I am a person, I choose." So, for me,
this is an entirely different dimension and is not easily reconcilable to the deterministic point of view. I see it as being similar to
the situation in physics where you can prove that the wave theory of light is supported by evidence, as is the corpuscular theory,
though the two of them appear to be contradictory. They are not,
at the present state of knowledge, reconcilable, but one would be
narrowing his perception of physics to deny one or the other. It is
in this same sense that I regard both of these dimensions as real,
although they exist in paradoxical relationship.

MODERATOR: Dr. Skinner, do you have a response?

SKINNER: Yes. There are areas in the world where people have
very little of this conception of self or of personal worth, and it is
difficult for us, coming from our culture, to deal with them and
to understand what is involved or why they are not more active
in their own behalf. I trace this not to a genetic difference or as
having to do with the basic structure of the organisms, but rather
to what we call literature of democracy. When you are trying to
overthrow the despotic control of a ruler, your only strength is
likely to be found in the people themselves. Now, the literature
of democracy has provided a history in which the individual has
been assured that he is the ultimate source of power and that he

himself can rise against someone who would control him; that he can, by organizing with others who have similar inclinations, become a powerful force, and that, in some sense, he can rule himself. At least he can consent to being ruled by someone who rules in line with his own interests. Now, that was, as I see it, a discovery. It was a discovery of a theory of democracy, and I don't mean Greek or Roman democracy, which was that of an elite. This was a discovery of the importance of the common man. It illuminated the fact that he could be converted into a person able to take political, and sometimes revolutionary or military activity and overthrow other kinds of control. We have this in our own culture. We teach our children that they themselves are the final measure, that life is designed for them, and that if they are not getting what they want they can do something about it.

This carried over rather feebly, it would seem, to concentration camps and to prisoner-of-war camps, for example, in Korea or in China. There is evidence that the democratic way of life is suffering. It is not being transmitted well by our culture, and the reason for this, I think, is that it is in conflict with certain scientific facts about personal freedom and initiative. And I am interested in trying to work out a philosophy which will do just as much for the individual, but which will not take on the expression of freedom and inner-initiated activity which have served their purpose and I think are now outmoded.

MODERATOR: The second question, directed mainly to Dr. Skinner: You spoke of your preference for studying observable behaviors rather than less observable areas such as personality traits. Do you regard the study and measurement of these behaviors as sufficient for the science of human behavior, or do you feel you must then move up the abstraction ladder and somehow relate observable behaviors to broader concepts such as personality?

SKINNER: Well, I'm aware of the oversimplification of the operant situation as an experimental situation. All early science is oversimplified, because you can't do anything until you develop techniques which permit you to handle simple relations. Then, once you have those, you can handle the more complex. Currently in the field of operant conditioning, we deal with elaborate samples or segments of behavior, and we could, I think, set up a reasonable analogy to some of the elements we have been discussing at this conference. However, I will withhold my remarks on the difference between pigeons and people until later.

The question about personality is not whether it is an area to be studied, but whether it is a useful concept. It is one of these inner terms, and it has been a dangerous one. If you say that a juvenile delinquent is suffering from a disordered personality, and then want to explain the disordered personality, you have to go back to the individual's earlier history and perhaps genetic factors, and, even more likely, to his cultural conditioning. Then, once you've gone back there, you can use those facts to explain the juvenile delinquency itself, rather than going through the middle term of personality. As I see it, personality is an explanatory fiction which, at times, seems to offer the chance of talking about broader patterns of behavior — greater constellations of behavior than are conveniently handled in terms of behavior itself — and it may serve some heuristic purpose at this stage in our knowledge. However, the person interested in personality must eventually get back to what it is that expresses a personality, and once this is analyzed effectively, you will come up with an alternative way of dealing with these problems which will be much more satisfactory. Problem behavior should be related to the various conditions which influence behavior, without calling it the expression of a problem-ridden personality. I see no advantage in the term, except a temporary one in that it permits you to talk about important issues in a not-too-awkward way. I think the avoidance of awkwardness comes at a very high price, however.

MODERATOR: Dr. Rogers, do you want to respond to that?

ROGERS: I'd like to comment briefly. Every time a question has to do with scientific procedure, Dr. Skinner and I find ourselves in agreement. From the perspective of science it is observable behavior that interests us both. For example, in studying the process of change as it occurs in psychotherapy, we have been spending a great deal of time trying to tease out the observable behaviors which are indicative of change and to study those observable behaviors. Insofar as theory is concerned, as our science matures, more and more theories will be the reconciliation and integration of large bodies of observed data, rather than being constructions of fantasy.

MODERATOR: The next question is directed to both: Is this just another philosophical discussion about free will versus determinism? If not, how does it differ?

SKINNER: It is not just another philosophical discussion, because we are both concerned with important practical consequences. I am concerned with arriving at a conception of the individual which is one we accept, find useful, find dignified and worthwhile, yet which is compatible with the approach of a natural or social science of human behavior. The time has come when this issue must be taken out of the realm of philosophical discussion and deliberately faced. If we are (as we are in political science, in literary criticism, and in many areas dealing with human behavior) still likely to be dealing with a conception of man which allows a great deal of leeway for caprice, for individual spontaneous changes, and so on, we are going to get into trouble. We must make palatable and worthwhile a different kind of picture of man. And while the issue of determinism is certainly raised, I hope that what we have said here goes well beyond what is usually said in late-evening discussions of that topic in dormitories.

ROGERS: I certainly agree that this does not seem to be a philosophical discussion about free will versus determinism. For one thing, both of us agree that when viewed from a scientific perspective, man's behavior does appear to be determined, and that the whole realm of the behavioral sciences is interested in studying those sequences of cause and effect. I have tried to indicate that our science should be broad enough to include a concern with and an interest in the subjective, as well as the purely external behaviors. I have also indicated that we need to recognize the fact that a scientific perspective is not all of life, and is not a sufficient basis for a total philosophy of life or of persons. That, to me, is what the discussion has been about.

MODERATOR: The next question is more practical, and, I assume, primarily for Dr. Rogers: Can a high school counselor use both conditioning principles and Rogerian psychotherapy with equal effectiveness?

ROGERS: A high school counselor, or any counselor, is obligated to be searching continually for what is effective in producing constructive personality change. Fortunately, this question is one that in the long run will yield itself to empirical investigation. So far there have been few investigations along that line, none that I know of with high school students. One that is remotely related was a study by two men who endeavored to use three different types of therapy with alcoholics in an institution. One was a learning-theory type of approach (not an operant conditioning approach but a learning-theory type of approach); another was an analytic approach; the third was a client-centered type of approach. The results were studied objectively in terms of tests, in terms of return to the hospital for alcoholism, and so on. It is a research that has been of a good deal of interest to me because the groups carrying it on started out with the personal bias — it's almost impossible in such a situation to escape some personal bias — that it would be the learning-theory approach that would be most helpful. As it turned out, that was the least helpful. In fact, this approach showed objective evidence of having done some damage to these individuals. The one that turned out to be most effective was the client-centered approach. I don't, however, adopt that as a final conclusion or anything of the sort. That was one study. We need to have many studies of what actually is effective in producing constructive change.

SKINNER: I am not at all surprised that a learning-theory approach could go wrong, because I have seen so many of them so badly designed that I wouldn't recognize them. (*Rogers laughs.*) I would want to know the details before I would confess to any anxiety about this particular case.

ROGERS: If it would make you less anxious, this was Mowrer's learning theory, and he did serve as consultant on it, so it was within terms that were realistic as far as he was concerned.

SKINNER: Yes, well, that still doesn't reassure me. The word "counseling" here bothers me. Obviously I am not the authority at this table in that field, and I am not at all happy about trying to conjure up some use of operant conditioning principles with respect to a student on one side of the table and the counselor on the other. I would guess that a lot needs to be done before a counselor could safely work simply in the field of reinforcement in helping people. I would say that the counselor who was interested in the so-called mental health of his school system might better spend his time not at that table at all. Rather, he should be looking into how the children are handled in the school; how they come to school; how their schedules are arranged; what things they get out of school; what problems arise because of the teachers with whom they are matched up, and so on. I would take a more preventive therapy approach, in this case, and I am sure that Dr. Rogers is as interested in that as I am. I don't feel that these problems must wait for a confrontation across a counseling table, and certainly not on the counseling couch. The application to education of the principles that I find productive and useful would be much more concerned with this puzzling design of the educational system than dealing with its special effects on individual students.

MODERATOR: The following question is directed to both: What is the role of a "code of conduct" or "religion" in a culture, as you view it?

ROGERS: I have given a good deal of thought to the question of the way in which people arrive at their values. I am afraid "code of conduct" is a phrase that would not have much meaning to me in the kind of culture I was trying to describe this morning. On the other hand, the kind of a valuing process which seems to be characteristic of psychologically mature people in our culture would, I hope, be characteristic of individuals in the sort of culture I would like to see established. I am not sure that I can describe it briefly, but I will try. The person who is psychologically mature tends to be open to the various aspects of his experience. He is open to the external aspects: the demands of society, the likelihood of smooth or turbulent interpersonal relationships, the legal demands, the demands of the physical environment, and so on. He is also open and sensitive to the feeling reactions and personal meanings which exist in his own experiencing and that have grown out of his own past learnings. Out of that, every new object, every new event, is evaluated by him in his own experiencing as either making for his own welfare or not making for his own welfare. That is, the most sensitive valuing process in the world exists, I believe, in the psychologically mature person. When he is engaged in this valuing process — in the interaction with his environment, and so on — this is not a selfish kind of valuing, though to be sure he values things as to whether they make for his own actualization or not. It is essentially, however, a social kind of valuing process, simply because the nature of the human animal turns out to be highly social. So I would not be inclined to discuss a code of conduct, nor would I be inclined to discuss a religion in this society, in this culture I was trying to describe. However, I would be much concerned that individuals be able sensitively and openly to be their own evaluators of the experiences and events in which they were involved.

SKINNER: I see the question as bearing on the whole issue of the evolution of cultural practices. When a group of people start living together they begin to affect each other, they are part of the environments of each other. A strong man may, for example, despoil all the others because of his own personal strength, but the others quickly, at least quickly in terms of evolutionary time, may very well countercontrol by organizing and by calling it wrong to use force. Later, perhaps, someone becomes clever and uses his wits and deceives other people, deceives even the strong man. This is Br'er Rabbit deceiving Br'er Wolf and Br'er Fox. Br'er Fox also comes into it on the side of the sharpie. But then it is decided that it is wrong to misrepresent, wrong to deceive. Now, I don't mean it's decided in the sense that anybody sits down and comes to that conclusion. You just start punishing people who use force or deceive others. That can all go on without codification. I am sure that the Jews practiced the principles in the Ten Commandments before they were codified. The value of the codification is that it clarifies the practices of the group, makes it possible for the individual to conform more readily. It's an instructional kind of thing.

You see this if you turn away from cultural technology to physical technology. Early physical techniques, such as had to be taught by an artisan to an apprentice, were often put in the form of rules, maxims, or proverbs. For example, in the Middle Ages, the blacksmith, bringing a boy in to operate the bellows which kept his forge going, taught the boy a little poem, which goes as follows: "Up high, down low, up fast, down slow, and that's the way to blow." Now what is actually involved here is the proper operation of a bellows. You must take the full excursion, up high, down low. On the way up nothing is happening, so it's up fast, down slow; otherwise, you will blow the fire apart. After you have learned the little poem, you have become an expert bellows boy. Early scientific law is probably of this sort: they are statements of effective behavior, or they guide effective behavior. There is no mystery to the fact that the great codifiers, the great lawgivers, have always been highly honored. The Romans played a great role in civilization in codifying laws which undoubtedly were practiced before they were ever codified. And there is something to be gained from codification: you can teach precept instead of practice. We gave up a great deal when we decided that we have to teach ethical and moral principles by practice only, and not by precept. Since we teach science by precept, I see no reason why we can't teach ethics by precept too. And you can do it if you can control the motivation of the student, and generally this turning to practice instead of precept has been a search for motivation for the student, rather than for effective instruction.

The difference between a moral code of that sort and a religion is simply a difference in the implied or expressed sanctions involved. If you say that if you behave in this way people will like you and everyone will be better off, that is a naturalistic religion. It is pointing to the consequences which make a cultural practice worthwhile. On the other hand, if you say that the code has been revealed by a prophet and is the word of God — if the sanctions lie in another world, and if you follow the code you will be rewarded by that epitome of all rewards, heaven, but if you don't, you will be punished by that epitome of all negative reinforcement, hell — then you are working in the field of religion. Now there is no doubt that these have been effective sanctions, and may continue to be so. The naturalistic approach argues that man does not need that kind of supernatural sanction, and that it is possible to have a purely humanistic ethic. I think this is something which remains to be demonstrated. All of this question of the codification seems to me to be a cultural invention — a cultural design — which clarifies the controlling forces that the group exercises over the behavior of the individual.

ROGERS: I'd like to make the comment that perhaps the trouble with meetings of this sort, and with any attempt to settle issues between individuals or groups, is that we don't follow that bellows motto. We should up slowly, in order to gradually take in and really understand what is being said, but usually we up fast. We should down slow, in order to thoughtfully express ourselves, but what usually happens is we down fast, and out comes a great gush of air.

SKINNER: May I point out, however, that what goes into the fire is cold air.

ROGERS: Good point.

(Tape starts again at the end of Skinner's statement in response to a question about child rearing.)

SKINNER: . . . subscribed to Frazier's statement that home is not the place to raise children.

ROGERS: The kind of psychological climate which promotes growth and development is the same whether we are talking about therapy, or school, or the home. We are making solid scientific progress in learning the elements and attitudes which compose a psychological climate which makes for the most constructive individual and personal development. The evidence indicates that people who are real, who are not afraid of exhibiting themselves in terms of the feelings they are actually experiencing, are more constructive in human relationships than those who put up a façade. A climate in which the individual is prized — whether we are talking about a small child or a therapy client — is very likely to promote growth. When an individual finds his inner life of meanings understood by another person and recognizes that he doesn't live in existential isolation, this too is of assistance in helping him to grow and develop. When it comes to the kind of limitations that would be most helpful in the rearing of a child, so often we think in terms of what the child should or should not be permitted to do. I would like to see, as much as possible, that the very necessary limitation of behavior grow out of confrontation of feelings. The mother who is all worn out and says to her child at night, "Well, I don't think you've been getting enough sleep lately. I think it would be best if you went to bed an hour early tonight," is in for trouble. She is not being genuine, and she gets resistance. If she were honest about what she is feeling, saying, "I am simply too tired tonight to put up with you for another minute. You are going to bed; I can't stand you any longer!" — this would be a far healthier relationship. The child still will be unhappy about going to bed, but it will be for the real reason, and this can exist as a real aspect of the relationship between them. In addition, it has a reciprocal effect on the mother. Having openly expressed her feeling of "I have had it," she then realizes she has other feelings as well, and she is more likely to put the child to bed more tenderly than she would have. So my notion of the best in limitations on child behavior is when the child's feelings are in real contact with the parent's feelings, and out of that may come some realistic limitation of behavior that is, over the long run, mutually acceptable. In some instances it may be more acceptable to one than to the other, but over the long run both arrive at a realistic relationship of feelings that is mutually acceptable and which helps persons live in a human world of feelings.

MODERATOR: At this point we have come to the second part of our question period. We could not answer some of the questions that were submitted to us in writing. Perhaps some of you would be willing to raise them in person. Any questions? Yes, ma'am. . . . The question, as I understand it, is: In an ideal community, where we reduce all tensions, would we also reduce the likelihood of genius?

SKINNER: I take it that's directed at me. Freud faced the same question. After having shown that great works of genius were essentially neurotic, he then proposed to cure neuroses, which seems to indicate that he had something against genius, or works of genius. But his answer, and I think it is a perfectly good one, is that people are geniuses against whatever background they may be living in. In a world where there are many neuroses, some of these will be really fine neuroses, and we will call them works of art or works of genius. But in a world in which people live a more orderly or more successful life, there will also be works of genius because of man's capacity to do great things. They will, however, be somewhat different. It won't be art based upon neurotic tendencies, and it can't be literature that deals with personal conflicts if there are no personal conflicts. An example of this is in children's stories where a fireman is portrayed as a heroic person. It's very important, if you have buildings that are likely to burn down, to have brave firemen. But if you invent fireproof buildings and get rid of all the ones that are not fireproof, there is no longer any need for brave firemen. This means that in the world of the future, all those things we loved to read about as children would not exist and something would be missing. The same is true in a much more important way with respect to war. In the past, war has been inevitable; I hope that won't be true in the future. But we have learned to enjoy it by making heroes out of warriors, and a great part of the literature of the world has dealt with heroic warriors. But if we ever do achieve a world at peace, and it is a peace so complete that we can't even imagine a world at war, there will no longer be interest in literature having to do with heroes who kill other people in battle. And the works of, say, a Dostoyevsky, would become relatively meaningless in a world where no one had the need to confess an imagined sin or something of the kind. Personally, I would settle for that. I would sacrifice the works of Dostoyevsky to reach such a world. I don't imagine for a moment that people are going to be any less creative, any less imaginative, or exhibit any less genius because the nature of subject matter changes. There are cases of people who have been very productive artistically, without it being a question of working off neuroses. Johann Sebastian Bach had nineteen children, and we can conclude something from that about his freedom from neurosis, and yet he could not help writing music. He was still composing music on his deathbed. That's a Freudian answer, and I would use it myself. I am sure there are activities in which the genius in man will manifest itself, and if it does not have to deal with neurotic topics, so much the better.

ROGERS: I agree with that last sentence, but in general I take a slightly different approach to this question. In the kind of culture I tried to talk about briefly this morning, I hope I didn't give the impression there would be no tension. I just gave a very minute example of the kind of tension that would exist in talking about the mother and child. There are always tensions in interpersonal relations. There are tensions in all of us as we face new and more demanding tasks in life. And out of those tensions — which are not disabling and not destructive in nature — out of those constructive tensions there can be enormous creativity and genius.

MODERATOR: Question in this part of the audience? . . . As I get it, the question is: Perhaps we have not given due notice to the power of positive reinforcement, and is Rogers's concept of self-actualization tied in with this? Dr. Skinner?

SKINNER: I don't think for a moment that positive reinforcement is the only process which can be used in the design of a culture. It happens to be, I think, a very important one. But a total analysis of the various mainsprings of human action seems to me to be relevant to any phase of human behavior. And I won't say that I would improve Dr. Rogers's practices by reinterpreting what he does in my own terms, but I think I could do that. I am sure Dr. Rogers and I are both dealing with the human organism as given by the genetic human process, and, to the extent that we are successful, we have discovered important characteristics of that organism. I would like to see the human being actualize himself, reach his full potentiality, and I believe that when we get a glimpse of that, it's going to be a very surprising thing.

ROGERS: I don't know that I get this question with sufficient clarity to comment on it helpfully, but I would say that reinforcement is surely a positive tool. In developing the potential of the individual, however, we have often thought only of external reinforcements. The nature of the human organism is such that many things are discovered to be internally rewarding. For example, we do not have to reward the child for curious and exploratory behavior. That is something which he finds satisfying organismically. That would be true of a number of the life activities of the individual who is moving toward the development of his potentialities.

MODERATOR: As I understand the question: Perhaps the two sets of values of Rogers and Skinner are about the same, and in particular, for Dr. Skinner, does the way that he trains his own students differ from how one might deal in psychotherapy?

SKINNER: Well, I don't know that I am any happier about the way I train my students than I am with the way that I raise my own children, as I don't have too much control over the educational environment, although I am trying to do more about that. I believe there is something called rational behavior, usually exemplified in science, and the aim for a patient in therapy is, I suppose, to see the world about him and his own problems in rational rather than irrational terms. Perhaps Dr. Rogers would hold that there are emotional or experiential elements here that are rather different from the scientific process, but insofar as it

is helpful to respond to the world in a rational way, then education is a kind of preventive therapy, and could not be used also as
therapy after trouble has arisen. I have spent quite a lot of time
analyzing superstitious behavior and other forms of irrational
behavior. The techniques of science are designed to protect us
against some of this, and to that extent they are useful cultural
practices. I believe a therapist is doing something of the same sort
in clarifying influences which have had a deleterious effect and
bringing the individual more strictly under the control of the environment as it actually is.

ROGERS: I welcome being reminded of Dr. Skinner's very in-
spiring article in the *American Psychologist* on the processes of
science as he had experienced them in his own career. As I remember that article, Dr. Skinner gives a very vivid picture of
the scientific life as process. This is exactly the kind of thing
I have been trying to describe as the "Good Life." Far from
knowing where he was going to come out, he had to live in
process and had to let learnings emerge as they emerged, shaping his new behavior. This makes me feel a great deal about
Dr. Skinner, to realize that in his own life . . . *(Skinner laughs)*
. . . in his own life he values that emerging unpredictable process. What I have been trying to say about the kind of culture I
would want to design, and the kind of outcomes I see in therapy when therapy is successful, is that it leads to exactly that kind
of thing. The individual becomes an ongoing process of life in
which the outcome is not set. There are no static goals. You
don't even know whether you will come out happy. You are living this on a day-by-day basis, endeavoring to be open to all of
your experience. This was another aspect of that article: endeavoring to be open to all aspects of what had occurred, in order to
learn from them. This is a very good example of the personal
life being essentially the living of a scientific approach. On this
we could really get together, because this sense of life as a process — which can only be existentially lived if it is to be meaningful — makes all kinds of sense. It makes much more sense than
saying, "Here is where we should come out, and we must plan it
that way."

SKINNER: This may be a historic moment. I think I have been
changed by that argument. The point of my article was actually

to criticize the codification of science by methodologists, statisticians, design-of-experiment people who, having very little experience with science as it is practiced, try to tell you how the scientist works. It's a great mistake that we teach young psychologists science in the form of statistics, because this has very little to do with actual scientific practice. However, I am not going to concede everything, because I am interested in teaching scientific practice, and with skillful planning one could make sure that more people would be the product of lucky histories of this sort than is now the case. I am sure I have had a great deal of luck, which has not only directed me in profitable directions but has kept me going by the very lucky schedule of reinforcement I have experienced. This ought to be viewed as a very important factor in building scientific dedication, and some of it can be arranged. I quite agree, though, that you cannot foresee all of the courses it is going to take. I now begin to see what you mean by "becoming."

ROGERS: This is very meaningful to me because I quite share your feeling. I, too, would want to teach a scientific approach. I want to stress again that the kind of professional living, and the experiencing of a professional scientific life which you were describing in that article, comes very close to what I am talking about when I speak about a person in process of becoming. It is most gratifying to find that we do strike some deep similarity on that score.

MODERATOR: I think we have time for one last question in this section. . . . As I get the question, it is: On these internal factors or variables, Dr. Skinner has indicated that one can always identify external causes. What would lead one not to conclude that one could start with these as the possible originating causes?

SKINNER: I think the question is mainly concerned with the practice of science. I agree that the whole causal stream goes on back indefinitely, that there must be some reason why the environment is as it is at the moment it influences an individual, and so on. I question these things mainly because of their historical connotations of mentalism, of nonphysical mediators or manipulators of physical events, which is not a useful approach at all. If you take these inner events to be discoverable, as such, then I don't deny that if something happens to me as a child and my inability to deal openly with a colleague today reflects anxiety that results from my having been punished for fighting my brother, or something like that, something has lasted in me. Something has survived in me from punishment for sibling rivalry fifty years ago, in my inability to deal openly with a figurative brother in the group today. My objection to these inner experiential — if not mentalistic — events is that they don't adequately report what change was made in me fifty years ago, nor do they offer much help in predicting what is now happening to me as a result of that event fifty years ago.

Suppose you say, "I was punished for repeatedly striking my brother, until I reached the point where I didn't strike him, but I always felt anxious because I was on the point of striking him. That is an anxiety that has persisted to the present time, and it makes it impossible for me to be open with my friends today," or something like that. What does the word "anxiety" do here? If I have been punished for striking someone, and when I am now inclined to strike, it generates physiological changes in me which I report as anxiety, all right. But the word "anxiety" is not carrying the history of that punishment very accurately, and it certainly is not giving details to the prediction of what I cannot or can do at the present time. I do not question that something has happened in the individual which is inside him, and I do not question the fact that some day — and I think it will be the distant future — the neurologists and physiologists will tell us what that is. I am criticizing the purely verbal use of these concepts at the present time, because I think they damage our case by making us believe we know more than we do, and mischaracterize what are often important variables.

ROGERS: On this score I would find myself in general agreement with Dr. Skinner. There has been much too much use made of internal events as though we knew them descriptively, and then we use them as explanations of causes of other events. Long-range inference — where you reach a mile for an inference — has never appealed to me, and I don't believe it is a justifiable part of science. A postdoctoral fellow working with us a year or two ago wrote a couple of papers under the general title of "Toward a Science of Subjective Experience," pointing out the progress being made in determining objective cues of inner subjective events. This will bring us closer to being able to study objectively some of the internal meanings and subjective experiences which are operating in our behavior. The question is, how close can we get to them in studying them? This interest in trying to get more objective cues to the subjective aspects of experience is related to, but by no means the same as, the stress on the importance of the subjective in life, which I have emphasized earlier.

MODERATOR: . . . And now to Dr. Skinner for his closing statement first.

SKINNER: I want to take up this question of planning, and whether it injures the product planned. It is very important to keep in mind that a culture — any culture at any time — is a kind of behavioral experiment. Every child born into American life today will come under certain very powerful cultural practices. [We have yet to] have an education which makes the most of the capacities of the genetic stock of American life. If we have ethical and religious and moral practices which keep people behaving in ways that reduce their need to defend themselves against attack and worries and things of that kind, then America is strong. We will continue to develop better practices, and we will make a very important contribution to the practices of the future.

Now, these things work in a way something like biological evolution, but not entirely. In cultural evolution, someone hits upon a cultural practice: a new way of handling children in kindergarten; a new way of paying wages. There are thousands of these little cultural designs, inventions. Some survive because they contribute to the strength of the group. Others disappear because they produce trouble. In this way we advance, through codification or otherwise. We build a corpus of cultural practices which will be tested, whether we like it or not, in the crucible of survival. If Russia or China or some other culture is going to advance more rapidly, whether we like it or not, we shall then have to take second place. I don't think that for a moment. I was in Russia a year ago, and I am not at all impressed by the way in which they energize the human behavior of their people. I am not impressed by their standards of a good life or anything of that sort. But I still don't think we can rest on our laurels.

It behooves us to examine culture. Even if you hit upon a cultural invention accidentally, it may turn out to be a very good practice. Whether it's good or not has little to do with its origins. A person who is quite unintelligent might hit upon a better way of rearing his children that might be copied by others and become an established practice for a long time. The origins are not important. The survival effects are. But at some point in the history of this evolutionary process something new emerges, and this is the growth of science as a way of dealing with nature, and the eventual application of science to human behavior. When the techniques of science have been well developed, and brought to bear on the problem of human behavior, then we are in a better position to see the relation between cultural practices and the resulting strong or weak behavior of the individual who has been exposed to them. Then we can plan practices on the basis of predicted effects which are important to us, and they will be important to us in the same way in which the accidental practices are important to us. They will survive or disappear in the same way also. So that at some point, with the development of a science of behavior, man is able to accelerate the evolution of cultures by designing practices instead of allowing them to arise through happenstance.

This is also true in genetic evolution. We are now able, to some extent, to change the germ plasm. We have been able, for some time, to change genetic structures by selection of parents. We can produce mutations and are not far off from making rather specific changes in chromosomes, and so on. At that point something new will have occurred in the evolution of the organism as a biological entity. Something new has already occurred in the evolution of cultures. So we can, by using intelligence and the scientific method, improve our culture.

This can be interpreted, however, as meddling, as doing something about other people, as trying to control other people. And of course the word "control" is a value-charged word. We have all been controlled for purposes of exploitation. We have been controlled through techniques which are aversive in themselves. So we have developed a philosophy which is opposed to control and even opposed to planning. I think this is silly. If we try to insist that human cultures not be planned, we shall close the door on a remarkable opportunity which may never come to us again.

Joseph Wood Krutch has attacked *Walden Two* violently because it describes a world that is "planned."

Let me suggest the following situation to you. Mr. Krutch prefers the Southwest, and wanders around out there as an amateur naturalist. Suppose in his wanderings he comes to a mesa, climbs up and discovers a tribe of Indians living there under conditions which are exactly comparable to *Walden Two*. Their educational system prepares them for the life they are going to meet. The children are well cared for, happy, productive. They have economic practices which give them all a simple but good life. They have what they need to eat, to clothe themselves; they have artistic activities, music flourishes, and so on. Wouldn't Krutch come down out of that mountain shouting to the world, "What fools we are! This is it! Here is a way of life that is acceptable to me because it is maximizing all of the potentialities of the people who are living in it."

But then suppose some Indian following him down out of the mesa taps him on the shoulder and says, "There's just one thing I forgot to tell you. An old Indian named Skinner planned it this way." That would destroy the whole thing. The knowledge that someone had thought this out, rather than that it had been the product of an accidental evolution of cultures, would make it absolutely worthless. That old Indian would have had all sorts of despotic, tyrannical motives. Even though he is now dead, perhaps, he will have been controlling people. These people will be living a life which he planned. Now if we are so silly as to allow our reactions to past patterns of control to interfere with our free exercise of science in the design of culture, then we are going to get exactly what we are going to get. But somebody else will not be that silly, and they will be the people who will contribute to the world of the future.

ROGERS: Dr. Skinner remarked earlier that we would be discovering the learnings from this meeting for weeks and months afterward. I feel that is very true. I find it difficult to come up with any really concluding remarks. I would like to say I have acquired an increasing respect for Dr. Skinner the person, his sincerity, gentleness, his wit, his wide scholarly interests, and the honesty with which he is trying to face the implications of the directions in which the behavioral sciences are taking us. I have

learned deeply from him, both in the past and during these meetings. I have often felt and would like to say that I think he is the
one person in the behavioral stream of psychology who has had a
highly significant impact on our society and on our culture, and
I respect his work.

There do remain some profound differences between us —
though I think definitely less than when these discussions com-
menced — and I suspect that the deeper differences will not be
reconciled by us. They will be reconciled by you and by other people. I don't know whether Dr. Skinner is aware of this,
but a former student of his and a former student of mine are
working together on developing a programmed instruction for
the improvement of interpersonal relationships. Are you aware
of that? (*Skinner laughs.*) So that in a sort of second generation, it is possible that there will be significant working toward
a reconciliation.

I see large areas of agreement between us, though I won't try to
specify all of them. One is the fact that many of the remarks Dr.
Skinner has made point toward a behavioral science eventually
having a significant part in designing our culture. The profound
question remains: what kind of part will it play? We certainly
have agreement on the rules of science, and with regard to the
human being when looked at from a scientific perspective. From
this perspective we both see behavior as determined, and we both
see the possibility of establishing preconditions which lead to de-
sired effects, and which, in essence, lead to the basis for a design
of culture.

But there is a difference in the way science is viewed by us.
As I understand it, Skinner sees himself and the world, and the
individual in his *Walden Two*, as automated figures moving inexorably in preordained paths. I hold this perspective as a fruitful
one in my work as a scientist, but not as a total world view, and
find it inadequate as a viewpoint toward all of man.

It has been obvious throughout our discussions that one of
our sharpest differences is in regard to the place of the subjective. To me, words like "freedom" have deep experiential
meaning and reality and significance. I hope I have helped to
indicate that when we believe in individual freedom and choice
as a paradoxical reality in a determined world, we take different

directions and have a different kind of regard for the human individual than we do if we do not hold that view. I believe this is one point on which we differ, although I have been surprised at several of the things I have heard Dr. Skinner say and am now a little unsure just where he does stand. At one point yesterday he said with real conviction, "I believe . . ." I was so shaken by this I have forgotten just what it was he believed. He mentioned, too, that if we were to design a culture, it would be necessary to choose the values which we wished to establish. Then, this morning, he spoke of working out a philosophy which would be appropriate. To me, a philosophy is the meaning of experience. That seems to be contradictory to some of the other things he has said. So I am not sure. At any rate, it has come through clearly that he has and lives a subjective life in which belief and freedom operate. It also seems to me, however, that he attaches secondary or little importance to the subjective life for others, and doesn't consider it very seriously in his design of a culture. In this respect, I do differ rather deeply.

Another difference is that I believe Dr. Skinner doesn't discriminate between control and influence. To me those seem quite discrete. It is important whether the person with whom we are dealing has a participative choice. If I understand Dr. Skinner correctly, this is secondary and not of particular importance. The thing I prize about this meeting is that you, the audience, are free to choose subjectively what you wish to accept or reject. One of the things I would value, not only for this meeting, but for any kind of culture I would have a part in designing, is that it would be full of experiences like this. People would be faced with the difficulty and reality of choice — exposed to differing facts, viewpoints, opinions, and so on — and would have to choose the stance to take in regard to such issues. One of the essential bases for maximizing the human potential is to make continually available the opportunity and the necessity of choice.

Another point on which perhaps we differ — and here again I am a bit puzzled — is in regard to the value of genuineness. I have come to feel, particularly in my work in therapy, that one of the most important values in human relationships is the quality of genuineness, of one person being in real and genuine contact with another: an individual being — as completely as he is able — the feelings which he is experiencing at that moment. In a culture that I might design, I would hope for leaders who could be transparent: they would not be concealing; they would be people willing to expose their views, attitudes, feelings to the individuals with whom they were working so that encounters between individuals would be real and based on the existent inner realities. There is no question in my mind about the personal genuineness of Dr. Skinner. I get puzzled, however, when he talks about designing cultures, because there it seems as though — to oversimplify and perhaps be a little extreme — it seems as though nothing is "for real." That is, the behaviors which are induced are for other purposes, not for themselves. I believe he feels that since all human relationships are simply manipulations whether we know it or not, the quality of genuineness doesn't have significance. I can understand that, but it doesn't square with my experience.

Then another difference that I recognize is over our willingness to control. Here again, the difference between control and influence comes up. I would hope to be able, both in dealing with individuals and with groups, to establish conditions which free and release and make for spontaneity — to establish preconditions which bring about certain consequences. My experiences in doing that have given me a great deal of confidence in the basic characteristics of the human individual when he is free. So my whole aim would be to provide conditions for optimal release and growth, rather than being primarily aimed at control.

There is one helpful, hopeful, and ironic thing: for a man who believes that the words "value" and "choice" and "purpose" retain very little of their ordinary meaning in a scientific world, there is just no question that Dr. Skinner's work has stirred up, and will continue to stir up, enormous controversy over choice of values, and purpose, and the directions that we choose to go. In this sense I feel we are really on the same side, because that's exactly what I would like to do, too. That's the way I see the purpose of this meeting. We have tried to expose various points of view, various possible purposes, various values in regard to education, in regard to the design of a future culture; and the choice of those values is something we all will be working on over the years to come.

6
Michael Polanyi

Michael Polanyi was born in Budapest, Hungary, on March 12, 1891, to an intellectual and scholarly family. He was the son of Michael, a civil engineer, and Cecile Wohl Polanyi. Educated in Budapest, Polanyi received his Doctor of Medicine degree from the University of Budapest in 1915, followed by the Doctor of Science degree from the University of Berlin in 1919. In 1921 he married Magda Kemeny, a chemical engineer, with whom he raised two sons.

Initially, Polanyi's professional career was firmly rooted in the "hard" sciences. He was lecturer in physical chemistry at Technical University, Karlsruhe, Germany, and became assistant professor at the University of Berlin in 1923, the same year he was promoted to full membership at the Kaiser Wilhelm Institute in Berlin. Although the next decade spent there was creative and satisfying professionally, Polanyi resigned in 1933 as a protest against the growing influence and policies of Hitler. At the same time he was invited to become professor of physical chemistry at the University of Manchester, England, a position he held until 1948, when he became professor of social sciences at the same institution until 1958. From 1958 to 1961, he was senior research fellow in philosophy at Merton College, Oxford University.

Magda Polanyi once stated that the turning point for her husband — when he turned from an exclusively scientific focus to the study of philosophy — occurred as the result of an invitation to give the Gifford Lectures at the University of Aberdeen in Scotland in the early 1950s. From that point on, Polanyi's primary interests and pursuits were philosophical. When he received the Lecomte du Nouy Award in 1959, Polanyi said, "I have often been asked why I gave up my work in chemistry in favor of economics, sociology, philosophy and the like. The answer is really quite simple: a desire to go back to normal. We all started with being interested in the whole world; it's the only genuine interest we can have."

Six years after the Gifford Lectures, what is considered his magnum opus was published: *Personal Knowledge: Towards a Post-Critical Philosophy* (University of Chicago Press, 1958). This is a comprehensive presentation of Polanyi's theory and is aimed at illuminating the significance of the personal as a crucial element of knowledge. He states in his preface:

> This is primarily an enquiry into the nature and justification of scientific knowledge. But my reconsideration of scientific knowledge leads on to a wide range of questions outside science.
> I start by rejecting the ideal of scientific detachment. In the exact sciences, this false ideal is perhaps harmless, for it is in fact disregarded there by scientists. But we shall see that it exercises a destructive influence in biology, psychology, and sociology, and falsifies our whole outlook far beyond the domain of science. I want to establish an alternative ideal of knowledge quite generally.

A sample of Polanyi's writings includes *Atomic Reactions* (1932), *The Rights and Duties of Science* (1939), *Science, Faith and Society* (1946), *Beauty, Elegance and Reality in Science* (1957), *The Tacit Dimension* (1966), *Knowing and Being* (1969), and *Meaning* (1975).

Considered by many to be the premier scientist-philosopher of this century, Polanyi was the recipient of many honors prior to his death in February of 1976. His work was interdisciplinary, drawing upon data from nearly every major department of knowledge. Richard Gelwick has written that "political theorists, sociologists, economists, psychologists, historians, artists, and educators, as well as lawyers, theologians, philosophers, engineers and scientists, have found large areas of his work relevant to their special tasks." H. Richard Niebuhr saw in Polanyi a "moral philosopher" who illuminated the role of faith in science and society.

Polanyi and Rogers met while both were at Stanford University's Center for Advanced Study in the Behavioral Sciences for a nine-month period from 1962 to 1963. They struck up a friendship that endured until Polanyi's death. Rogers enthusiastically welcomed Polanyi's contribution toward the development of a human science that affirmed the importance of the affective side of science as well as the objective, cognitive side. Polanyi in turn wrote of "my internal struggle between my deep friendship curiously combined with a slight personal knowledge. The fact is I love Carl Rogers, but really know very little about his many years of decisively effective work. I love his temper, so beneficent with the overhacked domain of modern mental efforts, but I really know only the way he thinks and helps by his purity. I think I disagree with its particulars, but this does not affect my joy of his person" (Kirschenbaum, H., *On Becoming Carl Rogers*, Delacorte, 1979).

The dialogue between Polanyi and Rogers took place at San Diego State University in July of 1966. This televised exchange was part of a five-day conference on "Man and the Science of Man" organized by William Coulson and Carl Rogers and sponsored by Western Behavioral Sciences Institute. Both the Polanyi-Rogers dialogue and the excerpts from the discussion which followed are reprinted here just as they appeared in Coulson and Rogers's book from the conference, *Man and the Science of Man* (Charles Merrill, 1968).

ROGERS: The social sciences today can do things for people, but they also do things *to* people, in a way. Take as a very simple example, studies of delinquency. We could say with some assurance that a boy who comes from a broken home, who lives in a slum area, who's been rejected by his parents, and so on and so on — that that boy has a high probability of becoming a delinquent. Now, we tend to think about that almost as though the boy were an object. In much the same fashion, we would say, well, a steel ball rolling down a slope will proceed at a certain speed and at a certain acceleration; and I've engaged in research of that sort myself. I feel it has real usefulness. Yet, it troubles me very deeply that we leave out the boy; we leave out the *person*. I think that the rolling of the ball down the slope is perhaps inevitable, but the question of whether the boy becomes a delinquent — that's *not* an inevitable process. There's something in his subjective state — apart from these various external circumstances — that has to do with the question. In other words, I'm concerned that the behavioral sciences are tending to depersonalize the individual, and I think often tending to cause people to feel that they are robots, rather than individuals with spontaneity and possibility of responsible action, and so on. And I wonder — I wonder for myself what the answer is to that dilemma. I certainly would be interested in your reaction to that aspect of what science seems to be doing to people.*

POLANYI: Well, this is, of course, a most exciting question. I don't think we can elucidate it in this conversation, but at least I think I can bring in something which is burning in me at this moment which has a bearing on it — and also I think, the seriousness of it. I have just written, in the last few hours I should say, an introduction to a book which will commemorate the tenth anniversary of the Hungarian Revolution, and I realized when I tried to describe what happened, how little is known of what was the actual starting point of it. It was a meeting of writers, of Communist writers. One can't repeat that often enough. These were Party members: *Communist* writers. And in that meeting there occurred a rebellion against the official leadership in which these people claimed, "We are the Party, and we reject the view which you are imposing on us." Now, what was that view? The view was that the minds of people, the thoughts of people, are superstructures of the economic process; and since the Party controls the socialistic economic process, the thoughts are under the necessary control of the Party; and what the audience — these formerly fanatical, young writers claimed was that this is not true: that the truth, and the thought which elucidates the truth has intrinsic power and intrinsic justification and must be an independent factor in public life; not a servant of the government.

*From Coulson, W. and Rogers, C. R., *Man and the Science of Man*. Columbus, Ohio: Charles E. Merrill, 1968. Pp. 193–210, 135–139, 154–163.

Now, what did *we* do about that? That is my point. These people proclaimed this. It was written up; I remember writing about it at that time as the "revolution of truth," but I was not an official voice. Neither am I at this moment, I am sure; but I picked up a journal published two years ago — one of the most distinguished journals in the English language — in which one of the most authoritative voices of the academic life in America concerned with the study of Soviet affairs gave an account of, in the first place, an article which he had written in 1950: four years earlier. In this article, he had said that the events in the Soviet Union are largely a rebellion in favor of the truth — a fighting for the truth. But when he showed the manuscript to his friends in the great university where he is functioning, they advised him against it. They said, "This is a naive and unscientific way of looking at things." And so, he crossed it out. Now he says he regrets it. There is something in it. He thinks that there was. And then he explains — and we'll not go into that — why, for the Soviet writers, it was justified to talk about the truth, and so on and so forth, which is a very complicated business.

But, what actually it amounts to, is that all during these ten years, and in fact all along, the revival of free thought in the Soviet Union as we have interpreted it in our universities, in our press, in broadcasting, and on broadcast interviews — this event is due to changes in the industrial structure; in the fact that a more complicated economic system had been set up which required different values, and so on, so forth. Now, instead of welcoming this liberation of the human mind — this liberation which really is a confirmation of our ideas — we did our best to play it down; to interpret it in the same kind of mechanistic terms against which they rebelled there; from which they liberated themselves. That is the situation in which we are, because this is a very characteristic event.

ROGERS: Well, it certainly fascinates me to think of it in terms of the Soviet Union as well as our own culture, and I guess I feel that certainly in our own culture there is gradually growing a revolt at some deep inner level. The individual is disturbed at seeing himself as purely the product, whether of strictly determined psychological forces, or economic forces, or cultural forces, or whatnot. I think that men in various ways are rebelling against that and saying, "I exist as a person; I do make a difference." In some way, we've got to incorporate this newer view into our view of *science*. At least that's the way it seems to me.

POLANYI: Yes, of course. Now first of all, let me state that I am delighted to hear what you say, because for the first time somebody supports me in the view that what is happening in the Soviet Union today — the great changes which have been taking place there for, let's say, at least ten years and more — are similar to the changes which are taking place here for similar reasons. For the unsatisfactory nature of the same mechanistic conception of man eliminates the responsibility of man, doesn't know the place for it, and has no place for the autonomous, intrinsic powers of thought in general — not only responsibility, but also the whole of our actions as having meaning. Individuals have no place in the scope of mechanistic interpretation. And I think that, as to science, I again think that we must first of all have a pretty good and new idea about knowledge in general, and then we can come to science and put it right. But in the first place, I think we must have a clear mechanism, and that is, at any rate, what I was trying to establish. A mechanism which, without obscurity and without forcing the issue or the conclusions, brings us a way of seeing — a necessary and adequate way of seeing — which does not reduce man to an aggregate of atoms or even to a mechanism, but gives us, straight away, an access to him as a person; and when we have that, we can, I think, move on a fairly large scale from man to other things, and also to history.

ROGERS: I'm particularly impressed with the distinction you draw between knowledge, as the larger field, and science. It perhaps bears on one item that has been a very real puzzle to me. As you know, I'm a therapist, a counselor, and the majority of my life has been given over to working with individuals who are in some sort of personal or psychological distress. I certainly feel I have been able to be of help to some of them, and if I ask myself what has been the real element which has been helpful, it would seem to be the intimate, close, mutual, subjective relationship — something similar to what Buber describes as "I-Thou" relationship. It's that personal experience of relationship that seems to be the element that brings about change, and yet, when trying to do research in psychotherapy, you can study the way in which the verbal behavior changes, you can study the changes in the person's way of perceiving himself, you can study the way his friends perceive him, the changes in such perceptions — you can study all kinds of external cues, and yet, so far as I can see, you can never get to the really essential experience which brought about change. Now, I relate that to what you're saying by thinking that, perhaps, it must remain a part of our knowledge but cannot be a part of our science. I don't know.

POLANYI: I think something of that kind, yes. Perhaps I should make it even clearer. I know how unusual this view is, but I have expressed it, oh, just about ten years ago, actually. I published in *Science* a piece which was actually the text of an address, and there I suggested that we should forget about the word "scientific" for ten years. If we could only get away from that, we would see so many possibilities of appreciating knowledge — of appreciating views and explorations. If we would call them penetrating, revealing, sensitive, true. True, yes, if we would call them true; it is quite an obvious way of describing them. So let's forget about *science*. That is my suggestion. "Science" itself misdescribes it, in my opinion, very badly; and therefore, when we bring in "science," we usually don't even bring in science, but we bring the misdescription of science itself. Now, nothing could be more out of the way and less useful.

ROGERS: That is very interesting indeed: to hear someone like you, with such solid scientific training, speak of sort of laying aside the term "science" for the time being. I realize I have approached that same problem, perhaps in a somewhat different way. It has seemed to me that we must enlarge the conception of science to include all kinds of things that currently people leave out of it. For example, I think of the creative intuitions, which are usually thought of as having no part of science — and yet, to my way of thinking, they're one of the central parts of real science. And I don't know which road is better: to try to include a great deal of the subjective, intuitive, phenomenological in science, or whether, as you seem to be saying, to reserve the term "science" for the operations that people usually think of in doing science, and concentrate on knowledge as a larger sphere.

POLANYI: Yes, let us not attribute particular merit to something by saying, "This is scientific." Let's describe its value and its reliability, its penetration and so on, in other terms; and the example which you mentioned is very much to the point; namely, creativity. Now, this is one of the subjects which leads a very precarious existence because the supposed methods of science cannot deal with it. They can't do anything about it, and, therefore, the theory which science makes of itself tries to exclude it. It says, "Oh, this is just psychology or sociology or something which doesn't belong to us. It's not logic." I think that all this is unnecessary and actually misleading.

ROGERS: I wonder if it would be too large a question to ask your view of science? How do you see science as separate from this larger sphere of knowledge?

POLANYI: I think that there are some forms of science. As you probably know, I think that certain forms of science like the behaviorist psychology, are actually corrupted: impaired, to put it a little less rudely — impaired by harking back to the alleged, supposed methods of science. So this is probably fairly widespread. I think in sociology you have similar influences. You see sociologists claiming that they can describe (in fact, account for and explain) all human activities in society without being concerned with right or wrong. I think that's quite absurd, because it's quite obvious that the sociologists, themselves, probably can't explain their own actions without considering that which they thought was right or wrong. Why should it be different for others whom they are describing — whom they are explaining? And, at this moment, there are great, involved issues (and there have been for the last few years in the United States while I was visiting here); and in confronting these issues many people are moved very effectively by questions of right and wrong. So, if there were no differences between right and wrong, these would be merely elusive claims which they are making. Obviously, this is completely degrading what is going on. And so one could go on: one could speak of the description, the explanation of contemporary affairs, of which I have spoken right at the beginning, which is part of our way of writing history. It has not always been the case. In the eighteenth century people wrote history, and the great historians at that time believed that it was something which was leading to progress through enlightenment; and leading to disasters, to errors or to follies. . . . In other words, human beings, as we know them, still existed as agents in history — as responsible agents in history — responsible for the improvement of the human condition and also responsible for disasters.

ROGERS: Well, I like your bringing in the issue of right and wrong. It seems to me that many behavioral scientists today are fearful of that kind of issue. I have a pipe dream which would really revolve around an initial, ethical decision. It seems to me, for example, that there is building up in the behavioral sciences some knowledge of how to deal with interpersonal tensions, and tensions that exist between groups. It seems to me that, as behavioral scientists, we have an ethical responsibility to try to use that knowledge in ways that might be effective in helping the present racial and national and international situations. I've sometimes dreamed of sort of an interdisciplinary Manhattan Project, where the reduction of psychological tension would be the subject — where you could get together the best minds, the best knowledge in this field and begin to utilize it both ethically and, I hope, effectively in resolving some of the world tensions. Now this is a little different emphasis than what you were giving it, but it seems to me to fit in there; that unless scientists regard themselves as having an ethical responsibility, they are not likely to engage in some activities that might have social usefulness.

POLANYI: Yes, they actually missed, I think, the essence of most of the things which are important in the world by doing so. But I'm not sure that I quite follow you about first observing tension, and then dealing with it from the moral point of view. I think that the study of tensions as such is already tainted by a neutrality which is misleading, because, you see, there will be difficulties the moment you apply the reduction of tension to places. Let's say you are dealing with the revolutionary movements, or the underground against Hitler — well, you surely are not in favor of reducing tensions there, but, on the contrary, of increasing tension. So, these terms are colorless or neutral terms: they have already a tendency to mislead and to curtail our scope. And perhaps it's difficult then to bring in succession to this the moral point of view. But, of course, I'm rather skeptical about the difficulties. I see them as very great. I'm very anxious to hear more about it: what hopes you have. But I see the difficulties as very great.

ROGERS: Well, I think that I would agree with the point you've made: that just reduction of tension itself would not necessarily in all situations be even an ethical goal. And I suppose that in what we do know, we do have the kind of skills that can operate to produce more constructive harmony in groups that are very much in opposition to each other. Now, I *can* see ways in which knowledge might be used in a neutral or not very responsible fashion. I guess what you're driving me back to is the realization that at the basis of anything that a scientist undertakes is, first of all, an ethical and moral value judgment that he makes.

POLANYI: Value judgments are ubiquitous — they are ubiquitous even in the exact sciences; but one can forget about them there, perhaps, if one wants to. They need not be acknowledged every moment. But I think that the kind of things which I was talking about right at the beginning; namely, that to secure the possibility of an authentic image and interpretation of man, of living beings, of man and of the universe, is first of all to be continuously involved in value judgments. Now, this I think is something which, of course, is today frowned upon, and *that* we must break down — but it is not easy going from there on, either. It is a very big task. It is almost a task of building up, in some respects, a new culture in opposition to three hundred years of brilliant progress achieved by another method: by the method of reducing things to elements which are inadequate.

ROGERS: I've always realized that your thinking was revolutionary in its scope, but I guess I never realized quite how much that's true, because really to achieve the kind of thing you're talking about right now would mean a drastic alteration in point of view; not only on the part of scientists, but on the part of a culture which supports science.

POLANYI: I think that is true; but of course I would think that we are supported by a movement which has been going on for some time. I think it has been going on — well, Kierkegaard could be mentioned, and we could have talked about Dostoyevsky; we could have talked about a number of philosophers who, at the end of the nineteenth century, had started movements which now are becoming popular here, like the phenomenological movement. I think that all this is one great effort of the fortunate changing course in philosophy.

EXCERPTS FROM THE DISCUSSION

"Science" or *"Knowledge"*?

MILLER*: I saw a document recently about a scientific meeting which reported everything that the scientists said, and then in parentheses and italics it said "laughter" or in parentheses and italics it said "applause." Now the reason they bothered to put it both in parentheses and italics was because they didn't think it had anything to do with science. And they were rather embarrassed in a sense to put it in at all — because the rules of science say that you transmit only the cognitive information, the information you can more or less put into writing. I happen to be related to Jim McConnell who puts out the *Worm-Runner's Digest*. I will not defend the content of that journal, but I will defend his argument that perhaps humor and affect and feeling could have something to do with science. I would like to suggest that at the lower levels of science, by which I mean the simpler systems — particles and atoms and molecules, etc. — these issues are not relevant. But in very complex systems like human beings, if you're going to have a science that deals with everything, then you've got to have other forms of communication besides symbols — symbols which deal only with cognition. You have to deal with those tones of the voice that concern affect; those gestures and facial expressions, etc. that concern affect and attitude and feelings. That doesn't mean that you have to leave them in that form. Personally, I think it is important for scientists in this field to find codes that you can print, just as you write choreography and write music. I think this is probably the scientific endeavor; but, unfortunately, the rules of the strict operationism (which I think is relaxing among the intelligent people everywhere, including the original operationists) and the rules of science (as of now, what you can get into the proceedings of the National Academy of Science) rule out whole forms of data that are relevant in our particular field.

POLANYI: Yes, I think I quite agree. I think our conception of

---

*James Miller, director, Mental Health Research Institute, University of Michigan.

science should not be one which strives at the logically impossible, self-destructive ideal of completely explicit statements. I think that is very important. You see, clearly there are limitations for making something more explicit than it has been, and the mere effort of going in that direction may be destructive. The problem arises in analyzing and trying to put together explicitly a thing which has been broken into parts. The tragic thing about it is, analyzing and putting together is the most powerful way of getting truth. I mean our whole biology almost exists in analyzing and putting things together. So that we are in difficulty because nobody can tell us whether what we have split up can be put together again or not; and if we build up a culture recklessly on the assumption that only things are valid which can be broken into parts — and that putting together will take care of itself — we may be quite mistaken, and all kinds of things may follow.

ROGERS: This relates to what you're saying [*speaking to Polanyi*], and also I want to pick up what Jim [Miller] was saying. In the science of man, we are going to try to include emotions and affect, etc. Yet we operate on the absolute, unquestioned assumption that the best way of doing so will be somehow to put that in cognitive and intellectual terms. I mean, that's the whole meaning of science as it exists at the present time. I can't help but wonder whether there may not some day be a new conception of science which would involve communication of more than intellectual symbols. I know that Bronowski was hinting at that yesterday when he spoke of the fact that reading *Oedipus Rex* really communicates more scientific knowledge than reading Freud about the Oedipus complex. There may be ways of getting at knowledge and communicating knowledge which question the whole damn underlying assumption that science consists of nothing but symbols, all of which must necessarily be intellectual.

MILLER: I would like to see the word "knowledge" or something like that, or "scientia" used rather than "science" because my concept of science is that it is one of three modalities for experience — the other two being comparable to the beautiful and the good; the second one being the artistic modality of experience, and the third one being the value theory or ethical or religious approach. And that you can view anything in life — anything in the world — in these three terms, and that they are separate.

I'm afraid that often we do not accept the restricted goals of the particular game called science. Rather, we include all knowledge or all *scientia* as science. I would say that the goals of science, as they exist now, should be to attempt to take all these other forms of communications — affect communications — and put them into cognitive terms so that they can be cognitively understood. That's a big advance. But the goal of art, like *Oedipus Rex*, is to experience the same phenomena by other things which are in the artistic modality; and then you can have a religious or a value experience also. I personally want to divide these three aspects of life because I think science has been getting an inflated reputation since the 1790s when the age of reason began.

ROGERS: Perhaps what we need is much more knowledge of man and less science of man.

POLANYI: Yes, I would suggest that the word "science" is not a very useful one. Of course, nobody quite knows what science is, and so it is not necessary for scientists to know what science is, but —

MILLER: They surely know what *isn't* science when somebody asks them — (*Laughter.*)

ACADEMIC PSYCHOLOGIST: This sounds a little anti-intellectual to me, and I'm just worried that I missed something. Are you all saying something smart and I don't see it?

PHYSICAL SCIENTIST: Well, I don't understand what's wrong with this formulation: that there are several modes of apprehending truth, and we were discussing the scientific mode. And there's no reason that the scientific mode shouldn't concern itself with these questions of affect, with tacit things, with unconscious things, with primary processes, with hidden motives, with hidden emotions. That means putting it into the cognitive mode; but you also want to apprehend it in an artistic mode and in a normative mode; and the integration of all these things into a cluster is very desirable. Science is a component of culture no matter where you draw the boundary. I think everybody's in agreement on that.

ROGERS: I, at least, raise one really anti-intellectual question — that's why I said maybe we need more knowledge of man and less science of man — because we can learn lots of truth in physics or make lots of mistakes in physics and it in no way particularly affects the life of the individual. But I think that in the science of man, taking people apart as objects is already having a genuine cultural effect which I don't see as very healthy.

PHYSICAL SCIENTIST: May I suggest that scientism is the threat here, and not so much science. I'm not sure that science stands convicted of dehumanizing the study of human beings; but I can see it happening all around us as a result of various kinds of pseudo-scientific and pseudo-intellectual endeavors which amount to the following —

ACADEMIC PSYCHOLOGIST: Engineering endeavors.

PHYSICAL SCIENTIST: No. Some is the excessive deference to engineering problems like therapy, but that's not something that Carl [Rogers] would get excited about. The others are of a different kind; I think that's what you were really talking about: the excessive introduction of mathematics, logic, all sorts of disciplines that tend in excess to obfuscate the material. People want to prove they're smart by introducing huge computer programs — gigantic formulas in disproportion to the need for them. Now in every subject there comes a stage when you have to use a certain amount of mathematics, you have to use a certain amount of rigor; and it's not inappropriate. But to introduce a huge amount of complicated stuff at a stage where the data don't deserve it, tends to take the material far away from what's being studied and convert it into a kind of one-upmanship — a game that people are playing with the subject matter. When the subject matter is people, this tends to be a bad thing. The slavish imitation of other subjects like physics that don't have such complicated subject material tends to distract people's attention from the possibility that they might find interesting and even simple scientific principles in part of the study of man which does not in any way resemble physics.

WISDOM*: The plea that was made yesterday and today for a form of knowledge other than scientific — I'd be the first to accept this if anyone could ever produce it; but no one ever has. What we do want is a form of knowledge that we can authenticate and have reason to accept — not just something planted without evidence. Knowledge or guesses or theories or hunches

---

*J. O. Wisdom, professor of philosophy, University of London.

for which you have evidence is what science is. Here's the only point at which I would take issue with what you said yesterday and today about physics. I am a very strong believer in getting back to physics as a model, but not because it followed mathematics and not because it followed experiments, but because it is a very, very clearly worked-out method of inventing hypotheses and testing them. Here it is the model par excellence! And I'm quite certain in my own mind that this can be done in the social sciences. You can have hypotheses about groups, about persons, and you can test them by observational methods. I am thinking of science as a method of testing hypotheses and carrying out the procedure that you find in learned journals: hypothesis on page 1; derivations on page 2; tests on page 3; summary on page 4. Now the process of discovery never appears in the scientific paper, and no one knows anything about it except perhaps a few people like yourself [speaking to Polanyi]; and this is the unwritten chapter. We must retain science because it's the only method of authenticating; you can get to a knowledge of people by any kind of method — even by crystal gazing if you like; but it then has to be subjected to the ordinary processes of scientific authentication.

POLANYI: Well, yes, ordinary — the word "ordinary" strikes me as dubitable. You see — may I just throw this in? It has been said for a very long time that there isn't any other way — no competing possibility to what we know as science. But I think there was a great deal of knowledge accumulated — take the Chinese culture which has had no science — and this all calls our attention to the fact that they correctly arrived at almost all the fundamental conceptions of biology without any scientific inquiry. We knew about life, sickness, death — for half an hour one could tell you about fundamental conceptions which were formed before science was born.

Science, Truth, and the Community
[The argument began when Carl Rogers posed the question which initially led to the Western Behavioral Sciences Institute's project in the philosophy of the behavioral sciences and gave rise to the conference itself: "Does our understanding of science need to be modified when the subject of science is man himself?" This

question quickly led to a discussion of the nature of science and
of the relationship between science and truth.]

ROGERS: What difference is there, or what difference might
there be, in a science in which the observer is also the observed?
In which inner experience is certainly one of the primary elements that we observe as human beings? Is there any way
of involving *that* in science? Granted that the kind of methods
of confirmation that Dr. Wisdom was talking about this morning — the typical view of operationalism and all that it stands
for — granted that that's a very important part of science, is
there any next step that we can foresee? Or will the science
of the human person continue to be essentially just like physics? Now, that's an extremely vague and fuzzy issue. I have no
good resolution. But I would like, at least, to toss it out again
as a possible focus for our consideration. I feel as though most
of what we have said has hinged on that in interesting ways, but
has not really hit it very directly. Maybe there can be knowledge
of man but not a science of man. Maybe that is the answer. But
in a world where science seems so extremely important, I at least
raise the question.

POLANYI: I do want to ask this question. What more can we
hope for than knowledge and truth? I mean, what does distinguish a science which makes it preferable that it should be
pursued rather than truth and knowledge? There is a preference here which I cannot follow.

ROGERS: Well, I realize that, as I said yesterday, I share both
sides of this in myself. I feel what people think of as knowledge is often uncheckable, not replicable; really its truth value
depends largely on the maturity of the person. I use "knowledge" as a kind of all-encompassing phrase; and since there's
always dispute about the maturity of a person, it means that if *X*
supplies something which could be classified as knowledge about
man, there still remains the question of whether it is in any way
true.

POLANYI: I didn't mean that kind of knowledge which vanishes
by being examined. I only meant the kind of knowledge which
we actually possess. Now, it must also have been acquired in a
particular way in order to be qualified for our interest and appreciation. That is what seems to be troubling us.

MILLER: We could possibly delineate kinds of behavior or phenomena which we might all agree could be very probably studied with an analytical method, if you will, or by operationism; and perhaps other phenomena which we'd feel pretty skeptical about studying in that way — maybe religious faith would be of this nature, or love, or humility, or sincerity. I'd feel that we were making some progress if we could find the borderline somewhere — if we could find some kind of critical samples of behavior that would serve as test cases, so that we might determine under what conditions an analytic study of behavior would destroy something that we were after.

FAIRCHILD*: Earlier, Jim Miller suggested at least three modalities or ways of knowledge, and I thought we were going to get a nice debate between John Wisdom and himself at that point, but it never developed. As I understood Wisdom, he was asking whether there was a form of knowledge that was other than scientific; that if you had theories for which you had valid evidence, this is science. I think the question we're raising now is, What are your criteria of valid evidence? If it is replicability as a means of reproducibility, this would eliminate certain great areas that we've considered knowledge — historic knowledge, for example; even certain forms of science; and I would like to see us begin to differentiate those kinds of data for which replication is a means to establish some validity, and that type of data which is not so minimal.

POLANYI: Yes, I don't see why reproducibility should be required. Surely that is not the case. There are events which are not reproducible and yet are very manifest and important for science. For about a century, the existence, or the occurrence, of meteorites was denied by the French Academy, and all the meteorites were thrown out from all the collections throughout Europe as being quite useless and misleading. Now, of course, you can't reproduce meteorites, you see, because they just occur and that happens to be the case. Then, I think, one of the meteorites really fell right on top of an academician's head, and they changed their minds and recognized that this can happen.

---

*Roy Fairchild, professor of psychology, San Francisco Theological Seminary.

Reproducibility is desirable, and nobody enjoys it more if it's there than I do, but surely it's not intrinsic that truth must be reproducible — otherwise all the great pioneering achievements of our history would be not knowledge. That's surely not the case.

CROW*: Well, I would like to go a different line here. Isn't it true that what prospers as science or what prospers as knowledge is determined in measurable part — I'd even go so far as to say in large part — by factors that don't have to do with philosophy and have more to do with what you'd say is the sociology of knowledge — the politics of knowledge and science? It's *there*, I mean, whose view gets heard.

POLANYI: I really don't think that has anything to do with it.

ROGERS: I don't either. I don't think it has anything to do with truth. NIMH will tell you what is popular in science, but that doesn't have anything to do with what's true.

CROW: What *I'm* saying is that it doesn't have anything to do with what is true. It *does* have to do with what is knowledge. It has to do with what is taught; it has to do with what resources are made available to pursue particular lines. It has, I think, everything to do with science as a human activity. I want to insist on this point. I would like some day to see a philosophy of science that's based upon science as a *human activity* in which the analogy does not come from some structural part, but would come from these other factors. I think it's by choice that we exclude them. You see, they're not considered in talking about the philosophy or the epistemology; we do not include these factors which are very much a part of science as a human activity.

POLANYI: No, I think it's logically wrong.

CROW: I think it's logically wrong, too. You see, that's the point. You want to restrict the subject matter by dealing with it only in terms of isolating it logically. I think this rules out many of the things that are important problems for science.

POLANYI: The question of what is conducive to our acceptance of something as true or meaningful or valid in any way is a logical question. The circumstances in which that truth has come about cannot determine whether it's true or false.

ROGERS: I'd really like to understand Bud's [Crow's] notion

---

*Wayman Crow, associate director, Western Behavioral Sciences Institute.

because I respect his thinking and I don't feel that I quite get the point he's making. Are you [speaking to Crow] trying to describe what goes under the name of science in our culture, as it is? Because if you are, yes, I agree. All kinds of things affect what gets accepted, etc. But if that's what you're trying to do, are you also declaring against the possibility of anything absolute about the search for truth? I guess maybe that's the best way I can ask that question. You see, I wouldn't deny for a moment but what economic considerations, fads, all kinds of things, determine what will be believed in science as of a given date — that's certainly true —

POLANYI: I don't think it quite determines —

CROW: Well, I would say that those factors will have far more effect upon what scientists will do in the future than will what philosophers of science say. Now, I think that perhaps it's regrettable; but I think if we want to talk about what science is, what science is apt to be, how it might prosper by using different strategies, what the problem is that it confronts, I think we need to take into account sociological —

COULSON*: But what you're proposing is a sociology of science or it's simply politics — it's the art of politics. How do you survive in a competitive —

CROW: No — don't narrow it down to that point.

FAIRCHILD: I think Bud's reaching out for something quite profound here. I think he's saying that anything that has a truth claim must validate itself in a community. Aren't you saying that quite apart from the explicit tests or the explicit knowledge that we say is truth, there is tacit knowledge that actually interferes with or at least contributes to the making of decisions as to what constitutes truth?

CROW: And that's half of it, the validation; but the other part is: Carl [Rogers] says to "be open to experience," and I say the experience that's there for the person to be open to is determined in part by cultural and social factors; that what's inside the person that he should be open to is there due to a socialization process and the culture that he's in. This concept that the scientist can somehow be a wiped-clean slate is argued from the philosophical

*William Coulson, research associate, Western Behavioral Sciences Institute.

point of view; but in terms of the practical matter, he is an individual born into a community. What hunches he will get, what he will think of, what he will choose, are not processes that solely can be determined in terms of individual criteria.

POLANYI: But that's not what I said. The question is whether you think that what he says or believes to be true, or what you believe to be true, is *determined* by that. I cannot see how what you believe to be true is so because everybody says it is. Well, that's a good argument, but you couldn't define truth in terms of a poll; that is, if you have a majority here against you, you say, "Now I see that I was wrong." I wouldn't dream of doing that.

CROW: You don't as an individual — you would not do that. But as a society, and as society will be affected, it will be determined by things very similar to polls.

POLANYI: Oh, yes, but they might be one hundred percent wrong.

CROW: Well, I see the scientists as having a responsibility beyond. It's a shrinking back from ethical values to say that the only responsibility I have is to satisfy myself with regard to the truth of the statement. I see scientists as having a social responsibility to see that truth prevails.

POLANYI: What I would insist on is our responsibility for *seeking* the truth, and for *making up our minds* about it. I don't think that there's any other way of doing this — this particular business with which you are concerned.

Can Science Lead to Truth about Man?

[The discussion now turned from a consideration of scientific truth and the methods of attaining it, to the question of whether *man* was the kind of subject about which science could speak unique truths. Rogers initiated this discussion with the following question to Polanyi:]

ROGERS: Granted that what we're interested in at some more fundamental level is more truth about man. What part do you see science playing in that attempt to gain more truth? And, like the question asked earlier, What would be the boundary line where that would no longer be a profitable approach?

POLANYI: Conversationally, we could say that, as a kind of crude characteristic, something is more like science and something is different — but I think it would be a mistake to draw any sharp lines. It is a homely term to talk about "science," but not a very helpful one if one wants to make it precise.

COULSON: You seem to be sufficiently at home with the term that you don't need to use it, or don't fall into the trap of using it as a value word very often; whereas I think Carl, and perhaps most of us, have "science" used on us as a value word often and, in turn, tend to value that which is scientific.

POLANYI: Well, yes, science is so beautiful — physics, etc. — so I can appreciate that one wants to be like it. Ten years ago, in the journal *Science*, I suggested that the word "scientific" should be put out of circulation for ten years and not used as a term of appreciation, because we would discover a great number of useful and more significant appreciations such as "revealing," "sound," and if I had *Roget's*, I suppose, I could give you a whole long list.

[Polanyi then went on to "illustrate how misleading it can be to use the term 'science' in an appreciative sense." He told the story of the Harvard scholar who had written that the Eastern European subversive intelligentsia was rebelling in the name of truth; colleagues dissuaded him from publishing these words on the grounds that they were naive and "unscientific." Polanyi continued:]

POLANYI: Here we have at the very center of the most authoritative point of the university system, in a very characteristic way, the use of the term "scientific" as an appreciation of what can and what cannot be done, applied in a way which is absolutely destructive — because these people have been fighting for truth and declaring it from the word go. And if this is at all characteristic of our culture, our culture is in serious danger.

HENRY*: I rather agree with Polanyi here. But — you see I was leaving recently from my studies in Paris — it is somewhat generally agreed upon in France that when you say "science" you mean the objects are observed, described, put into laws and theories without reference to the observing subject. That does not mean that when the observing subject is concerned — for instance as it would be in faith, love, sincerity, etc. — it would

---

*Paul Henry, professor of philosophy, Catholic University of Paris and University of California at San Diego.

not mean that this is not another series of truths. But it means that there is a subject that tries to get out of the facts — and *that* would be called scientific.

MILLER: I would like to reply to your first question, Carl, in the light of this, by saying that in addition to these things, if I understand science, there is a *method* of science. And this is different from the other methods of finding truth or knowledge. Now I realize that there are many disagreements among distinguished scientists as to what the method is, and P. W. Bridgman went so far as to say that "any damn way you can get a handle on it, get it into the system," to repeat a direct quote from the gentleman. But I think that, nevertheless, there is a method; for example, you want to find that something is true and you have, under some circumstances, to evaluate it statistically; and if there is no deviation from a random probability, then you can't make a statement about it. And under some circumstances, as Carl said yesterday, there must be control. There can be lots of arguments about these things, but they have to do with some general idea about a method. So I respect — more than respect, I admire — your efforts to get these very subtle things within some form of method; and I don't think you can do much about these arguments as to whether this is the best method in the world or not. You, at the moment, as I understand you, are asking the question: Can these very important and very subtle and very subjective things be brought into a method?

ROGERS: Yes, there's one deeper aspect there that I realize this discussion has helped to bring out in me, if I can get to it. As far as I can see it, anything that I believe any of us would understand by the word science leads to a reductionistic tendency. I tried to explain this to Michael [Polanyi] the other day. If you start — if the real experience of therapy, for example, is an intense, mutual interpersonal relationship, the best you can do trying to study that scientifically is to pick out elements of it from which you can perhaps get behavioral clues and rate or study or measure. You can do everything but directly study the phenomenon that you really think is important; and so part of my conflict is that, though I have enormous admiration for what science has achieved and for the method of science, yet applied to the study of man I don't like the fact that it always leads in the direction of reductionism — to more and more minute elements which deny the overall experience which frequently is the very significant one.

HALL*: I have a feeling that you get your sense of reductionism from your experience of trying to study therapy after having been in the *experience* of therapy; and that somehow taking measures of self-concept and getting ratings of segments of tape, etc. really loses sight of what it was like.

ROGERS: I guess that probably is part of my frustration: wondering how the hell you can have a nonreductionistic approach to such an experience and yet still — because I do have some liking for the term — still have it scientific.

HOCHMANN†: I have the impression that you are identifying science with the reductionist attitude. I think this was the model of physics for a long time — for centuries. I think this is true even in physics today. But I have the feeling that science cannot really be identified with the reductionist method. This is just one of the methods of science. You describe the tension in you between the scientist and the therapist; I don't really see the tension because I see you, as a therapist, as a very valid scientist. I mean if you are open to experience, if you are congruent, if you are trying to really understand what you are doing and what's happening here, you are a scientist.

ROGERS: I think in Michael's terms, I might be adding to knowledge . . .

HOCHMANN: . . . and not to science.

POLANYI: It's not my distinction; it is, I'm afraid, yours.

ROGERS: All right. This is a good example. One certainly learns deeply from living in frequent close contact with individuals. Now how do you categorize that or what do you —

POLANYI: I feel I'm just repeating myself. I have complete confidence in the value of such a pursuit and I think that one reaches truth, and one also has some reason for believing that one reaches truth, in this way; but I wouldn't worry about whether this is science or not. It seems to me not a substantial question.

---

*Gordon Hall, postdoctoral fellow, Western Behavioral Sciences Institute.
†Jacques Hochmann, postdoctoral fellow, Western Behavioral Sciences Institute.

7
Gregory Bateson

Gregory Bateson was born May 9, 1904, in Cambridge, England. As the son of the pioneer geneticist William Bateson, he grew up in a scientific atmosphere and went on to study biology and natural history at St. John's College, Cambridge, receiving his B.A. in 1925 and M.A. in anthropology in 1930.

He went to New Guinea for his fieldwork, where he met another young anthropologist, Margaret Mead, whom he married in 1936. The couple collaborated for about ten years. One project involved taking and annotating 25,000 photographs of the Balinese people from 1936 to 1938. The resulting book, *Balinese Character* (1942), is considered an anthropological classic. Bateson and Mead remained friends throughout their lives, although they divorced in 1950. He married twice again: from 1951 to 1958 and from 1961 until his death.

In the thirties and forties, Bateson held many positions, including fellow at St. John's College, anthropological film analyst at the Museum of Modern Art in New York City, lecturer in the naval school of government and administration at Columbia University, regional specialist for the U.S. Office of Strategic Services during the final years of World War II, and Visiting Professor of Anthropology at Harvard University.

From 1949 to 1951, Bateson focused his attention on psychology and communication, working as a research associate at the Langley Porter Clinic in San Francisco, where he studied alcoholism and schizophrenia. There and for the next decade at the Veterans Administration Hospital in Palo Alto, where he served as ethnologist, he developed his "double-bind" theory of schizophrenia, which describes how children who receive contradictory messages of love and rejection from their parents may develop this disorder. This theory influenced many professionals and the later development of family systems theory in therapy. Bateson regarded the double-bind hypothesis as his most important contribution to the understanding of schizophrenia. He has been described not only as "the distinguished ethnologist, biologist and anthropologist," but also as "the first man to apply cybernetic and communications theory to such problems as cultural instability, schizophrenia, learning theory, evolution, and aesthetics."

In the next decade, he was associate director in ethnology at the Communication Research Institute and then associate director for research at the Oceanic Institute in Hawaii. Such job titles, however, give no clue to the range of Bateson's activities. He advanced the antipsychiatric movement, asserting that the medical model is not applicable to mental illness. He broke new ground in communications theory, especially in his work with dolphins. He navigated easily among diverse disciplines in the natural and social sciences, making connections — sometimes startling, sometimes esoteric — among topics that were becoming major concerns of the sixties and seventies, such as ecology, psychology, spirituality, and peace. He was influential in the "small is beautiful" movement, believing that smaller impacts were less likely to disturb larger ecological systems.

His later publications included *Communication: The Social Matrix of Psychiatry* (with J. Ruesch, 1951), *Steps To an Ecology of Mind: Collected Essays in Anthropology, Psychiatry, Evolution and Epistemology* (1972), and *Mind and Nature: A Necessary Unity* (1979). After his death, his daughter, Mary Catherine Bateson, combined an uncompleted manuscript, along with her own text, in the book *Angels Fear* (1987).

In the sixties and seventies, Bateson came to be regarded as an intellectual godfather of the Aquarian Age. Large audiences around the country and in his classes at the University of California, Santa Cruz — particularly crowds of young people — came to hear him expound on environmental and social topics. Sometimes they were barely able to follow the convolutions of his subtle arguments, yet they sensed in Bateson an intellectual foundation for many of their emerging values. Bateson, in turn, enjoyed his role as scientist and classicist among the idealistic, sometimes anti-intellectual youth.

One of Bateson's intellectual disciples was youthful Governor Jerry Brown, who appointed him in 1976 to the California Board of Regents. If his role among the young was to inject a note of scholarship and historical perspective, his role among the Regents was to shake loose the academic establishment. *Newsweek* wrote that the "brilliant, peevish Gregory Bateson . . . has let fly with stinging opinions on every aspect of university life, from the quality of the students to the competence of the Regents themselves." Just as Governor Brown intended, Bateson was "shaking up" the Board of Regents and was trying to "persuade its members to pay attention to more than the fiscal minutiae of management."

From 1978 he was a scholar-in-residence at the growth center Esalen, at Big Sur. After being hospitalized with cancer, he moved to the Zen Center in San Francisco, where he died on July 4, 1980.

Mr. Bateson's dialogue with Carl Rogers took place on May 28, 1975, at the College of Marin, in Kentfield, California. The discussion was introduced by Richard Farson, Rogers's colleague for many years.

ROGERS: I really don't know Gregory Bateson very well. I know and respect his work, but I haven't had a great deal of opportunity to get acquainted with him personally. And so for me this evening is an experiment. It's a gamble that this might turn out to be two parallel monologues. It's quite possible. Or there may be a meeting of minds and ideas, whether we disagree or agree, in which case it really would be a dialogue. Or it might even be an encounter between two persons. In any event, we'll just have to see. I'm as uncertain as to how it will come out as any of you are.

A little while ago, Gregory and I were both at a conference in Tucson and we conferred at great length — I think almost ten minutes perhaps — about this session, and we agreed that we might start off on the topic of learning, in which we're both interested. He asked me to take the first ten minutes or so. I'm going to speak from notes because I want to cram in as much as I can in that time.

I want to talk a bit about the politics of education and of learning, but first I'd better say what kind of learning I'm interested in. The kind of learning that interests me is what I think of as significant learning. That's my own private term for it. In this kind of learning the whole person, with both his feelings and his intellect, is very deeply involved. This kind of learning is self-initiated and there is a sense of discovery. There is the sensation of "Oh, that's what I've been trying to find out." In other words, there is an eagerness to grasp something new. Then, to my mind, significant learning makes a pervasive difference in the knowledge, the attitudes, and the behavior of the individual. Finally, it's something that the learner wants to learn. It has meaning for him and for his life and for his way of being. That's very condensed, but that is a brief description of the kind of learning that I am interested in.

Now, how much of this kind of learning goes on in conventional education? To my mind, not very much, and then only by accident. I think the politics of conventional education are all against it. We all know the kind of interpersonal politics that I am talking about. In conventional education, power flows from the top down: from the superintendent to the principal to the teacher and on to the student. Control is always from above, which is a significant political statement about our schools. Knowledge, too, flows downward. The instructor is the expert. He or she is the possessor of knowledge, which the instructor endeavors to pour into the theoretically receptive student. Because of this power flow, students are best governed by being kept in either an intermittent or a constant state of anxiety and fear. You all know how that's done. The tools are quizzes, exams, grades, ridicule or criticism in front of the class, poor recommendations for college or for graduate school or for jobs. All those are the tools by which students are kept in a state of anxiety. A very important part of the politics of conventional education is that democracy is ignored or scorned. The virtues of democracy are highly praised, but they are never practiced in the school system. There is no place for the whole person in this conventional education —

only a place for his intellect, for his mind, for his ideas. Facts and ideas are all there are to conventional education. I think of the traditional philosophy of education as the jug-and-mug theory. The instructor is the jug and pours knowledge into the passive receptacle which is the mug, which is the student. So in conventional education, with passive, anxious students, with no place for their feelings, with no chance to choose or initiate their own learning, it is, as I say, only by chance that the student learns anything he really wants to learn, anything that has meaning for his life. The politics of the system make significant learning almost impossible.

But more and more we are seeing alternatives to conventional education, most of which might be termed "person-centered," and I feel encouraged. So I'm going to talk a little bit about the politics of a person-centered approach to education, and how significant learning tends to come about there. I'd like to talk about some of the fundamentals of a person-centered learning situation. I think there's a precondition, and that is that there must be a leader or a "perceived" leader in the situation, who is sufficiently secure within himself and in his relationship to others that he experiences an essential trust in the capacity of others to think and to learn for themselves. If this precondition exists, a lot of things tend to follow and can be implemented. The facilitative person shares with the others, whether students or parents or community members, the responsibility for the learning process. Curricular planning, or the mode of administration, the funding, the policy making, are all a responsibility of the particular group involved. Thus a class may be responsible for its own curriculum, but the total group may be responsible for overall policy. In any case, responsibility is shared. Another characteristic is that the facilitator provides learning resources from within himself and his own experience, from books or materials or community experiences. He encourages the learners to add resources of which they have knowledge or in which they have had experience. He opens doors to resources outside the experience of the group.

Another aspect is that the student develops his own program of learning, either alone or in cooperation with others. Exploring his own interests and facing this wealth of resources, he makes the choices as to his own learning directions, and carries the responsibilities for the consequences of these choices. Then, very important in this situation, a facilitative learning climate is provided. Whether it is meetings of the class or the school as a whole, there is an atmosphere which is characterized by realness, by caring, and by understanding listening. This climate may spring primarily from the person who is the perceived leader, but as the learning process continues, that climate is created more and more by students for each other — by the learners for each other. And that characteristic becomes as important as learning from any other resource. The focus is primarily on fostering the continuing process of learning. The content of the learning, while significant, falls into a secondary place. Thus a course is successfully ended not when the student has learned all he needs to know, but when he has learned how to learn what he wants to know. Another characteristic is that the discipline necessary to reach the student's goals is self-discipline, and is recognized and accepted by the learner as being his own responsibility. Self-discipline replaces the external discipline of the conventional system. The evaluation of the extent and significance of the student's learning is made primarily by the learner himself, though his self-evaluation may be influenced and enriched by caring feedback from other students and from the facilitator. In this growth-promoting climate, the learning tends to be deeper, proceeds at a more rapid rate, and is more pervasive in the life and behavior of the student than learning acquired in the traditional classroom. This comes about because the direction is self-chosen, the learning is self-initiated, and the whole person with feelings and passions, as well as intellect, is invested in the process. Thanks to some very exhaustive research carried out over the last dozen years, I am able to make those statements with assurance. We know the kind of learning, the kind of pervasive learning, that goes on when the attitudes that I have described are present in the classroom situation.

Well, I think that's enough to give a quick look at my own view of learning and education. Gregory?

BATESON: I guess there's a biggish difference in — what shall I say — natural history between Carl and me: one sort of animal; another sort of animal. As to which is better, that's another question and I'm not really interested. I *am* interested in the difference. You see, I'm a theorist, and he believes that what you do matters. Both these sorts of people have, I understand, uses in the world. I never can quite understand the use of the action people, but they have a good time and they improve the world, I guess. And, you know, that's fine. But I'm a theorist. I'm concerned with mapping the sort of things that Carl talks about onto quite abstract sorts of matrices, networks of ideas, interlocking systems of ideas. He starts, you see, in the first two minutes, by saying there's good and evil in the world and he knows which is which, and five years later he will produce data to prove that he's right. I'm not so sure about the good and evil. I believe there is good and evil in the world. As to which they are, that's difficult.

Let's start with significant learning. I think I agree with him in the idea that's in the back of his mind when he talks about significant learning: that the French gender systems, the comparative anatomy of the insect, the sequence and dates of the kings of England, somehow are not significant learning. You know those or you don't know them and that's how it is. They can be looked up in books if you don't know them, if you know which books. But, you see, I cannot take a learning creature and have him learn the anatomy of the beetles and not also give him significant learning. Now the significant learning I give him may be of sorts that Carl would like, it may be of sorts that Carl would not like. But always and inevitably there is a significant learning that goes along with whatever it is that is being taught. And it isn't any simple function of what is being taught. That is, I can teach the comparative anatomy of the beetles in a way which will make little Hitlers out of you all, or I can teach the comparative anatomy of beetles in a way which will make you all into, what shall we say, dancers or artists ... even, perhaps, democratic citizens. There is, therefore — and I think this is probably our subject of discussion — a whole order of learning, quite different from the subjects taught, inevitably always carrying implications for character, about what sort of a world you think you're living in, about what sort of a world you think the relationship between you and the teacher springs out of, and these are going to be related, of course. So then this whole business becomes a theoretical approach to the problem of significant learning, and

I suggest to you that out of that comes a much more complicated set of values as to which patterns of significant learning will combine with which other patterns, how they fit together, what sort of ecology, as I've called it, can exist between one sort of significant learning and another, and so on. It rather rapidly becomes a matter of quite technical expertise, almost inappropriate for discussion on a hot evening.

Let me start by inviting Carl to share a tool or two and see where we go from there.

Out in the desert and horrible places, there is a lot of stuff which is true within its very narrow limits. It's called behavioral modification, it's called behaviorism, it's called Skinner, it's called by other opprobrious terms. And these matters of study that they've worked on, you know, are worth studying. Trouble begins, though, when you find, of the pigeons being put into the Skinner boxes, that first of all there is a rule in the lab that nobody but a particular lady is allowed to handle the pigeons, and secondly that the graduate students and Ph.D.s emphatically are not allowed to handle their pigeons; they just write the schedules. And then you find that the pigeons adore the lady who puts them in the boxes, that they swoon with pleasure in her hands. And this part of the story is not in general recorded in the research results. Because love, you see, is not what it is supposed to be all about. It just happens to be one of the things that it is all about. Right. There is, therefore, obviously not only a learning to peck prime numbers on discs or whatever it is, there is also a learning to peck prime numbers in a context whose shape is related to love. Stone walls do not a prison make, yes, nor iron bars a cage, but love will find a way somehow. (*Pause.*)

The word that is dominant in what I've been saying is the word *context*. Those pigeons have a context which is bigger than the immediate context that is talked about in the experimental reports, and I suggest to you that what Carl means by significant learning is that learning which is determined not by the content but by the shape of the context in which the learning occurs. Fairly commonly in the jargon of those in desert places where behavior is modified, they talk about stimulus, they talk about response, they talk about reinforcement. They don't talk, really, about the relations between those three things and the fact that those relations can be totally different from one context of learning to another.

In every human learning experiment, to begin with there are two learning contexts. There is the learning context which is described as the context as seen by the subject — the rat, the graduate student, what have you. He is supposed to learn that that buzzer means "do something and get this reinforcement" or "avoid this sting." But on the other side, out there administering the sequence, there is another organism who devised the sequence — who devised it, curiously enough, in order to learn. He said he was learning things about rats, which I suspect is a good deal of falsification. If you think of him as trying to learn things about himself and hiding that fact from his consciousness while he does it, you will begin to see that there are two sets of learning contexts in every such situation. There is what is called the context as seen by the teacher, who is learning things, if he's any good; and if he isn't, he is defending himself from learning things, and this too is significant learning — I mean how to defend yourself from significant learning, you know, is very significant learning indeed! And takes, if I may say so, a lot of practice.

We now begin to put words to contexts of learning. There are going to be people, you see, who make the interchange between "teacher" and "pupil" into some sort of a game. They may contrive it as a game in which the teacher always wins, as a game in which the student always wins, or a neutral game, but *play*, you see, is a word for a context of learning. Some contexts of learning are of that nature, some are not. But this is one of the things we mean by play. Dominance is a word. Humility is a word. And if you look at the words in the human language describing human character, you will find that they are all of them words for contexts of learning, words for the significant learning that occurs and goes along with the more specific learning in a context. It's quite a good exercise to take adjectives about people: honest, deceitful, courageous, cowardly, bully-coward, passive-aggressive, et cetera, all the adjectives around, and plan what sort of context of learning you would put the person through in order that he might acquire, become the suitable recipient, of this adjective. And that's what those words mean, and how to define them. Now that means that the whole of education — and I think that I'm talking about the same thing that Carl really is — is an enor-mously technical business of the anatomy of contexts and how they interact, how they combine. Are they beautiful, ugly, de-structive? And they may be totally murderous, they may be the most elegant things in the world. In fact, I'm inclined to think that as we talk about beauty and such things this is really what we're talking about. I think I've said enough now, so it's between us.

MODERATOR: We are about to begin the conversation part of this evening. On the way over here I was asking Gregory, "How will we know whether or not we have done our job tonight?" And he said that "if either Carl or I say something that we haven't said before, we'll know that it's a success." And he said, "The one con-dition which is very important for that is that we get a pace, that we get an audience cooperation, with a chance to do some think-ing while they are having the conversation." He said, "Sometimes it takes ten seconds or so of silence to be able to formulate one's thought." He said, "It's even a good idea sometimes to ask an audience to sit, and the conversants to sit, for three minutes and not say anything, and perhaps that will change the pace." We won't do that, but we will ask you to, if you will, try in your own minds to set a different pace for this kind of conversation, because we're not trying for a debate, or an argument, or a tour-de-force. What we're really interested in is whether or not these two people can build on each other's ideas in a real dialogue. We'll need your cooperation in that, and so we will rearrange the microphones now so that they can have a chance to remain seated and have their discussion from here.

ROGERS: Let me say a word, Gregory, about the context of the kind of significant learning that I was talking about. Because I quite agree with you that the sort of significant learning I was talking about does demand a certain type of context. I have even tried to theorize about that to some degree, as well as to do something about it. And the context that we have found — this you would regard as a limited context and not perhaps the larger context — the context that we have found most fruitful is a context, part of which you've referred to as a context of caring attitudes, part of it being a context of realness in personal inter-action, and part of it being a willingness to hear the meaning of the experience to the student instead of simply flooding him with information. So that to that degree I quite go along with some of the things you were saying about the context. Or you may want to put it in a still broader context, being somewhat more philosophically minded.

One of the things that struck me in what you were saying was that your interest was simply in mapping one point of view on a larger framework. I don't know exactly how you put it, but I noticed in your remarks about behavior modification that you, too, have your values. You may not call them good and evil, but no one would have to guess very hard as to the value you've placed on that. (*Bateson laughs.*) I want you to respond to that, because I feel that one of the things that I've come to value is not hiding our values. And I think your feelings came through quite strongly in what was worded as a quite scholarly, humorous approach to behavior mod. If there is anybody in this room who doesn't know what your feelings are about it, then they weren't listening very well.

BATESON: Yes, well, I plead guilty. I would add this, though. That this is, partly, as you say, a matter of feelings. It is also partly a matter of analysis: that is, I believe the picture which they draw to be essentially an untrue picture, or a picture which is so limited in its scope as to be an untrue picture when applied to human nature at large. Now, at this point in my intellectual analysis, you see, I'm very much interested that human beings should be that dumb; it just seems to me a very peculiar development in any human culture that there should be this funny mechanization of the concept of human beings. But when I express my value preference, I am not only saying I believe this to be, in general, bad for human beings but bad for them because I believe it is an untrue Procrustean bed on which they are being dissected. I don't know how many metaphors got mixed there, but you see what I mean.

ROGERS: Yes, I see what you mean. And of course I —

BATESON: It's not pure value. It's also the intellect creating the value, that's what I want to say.

ROGERS: All right. I couldn't agree more with your analysis of behavior modification. In fact I could give an example of human beings whom I saw being dealt with in a state hospital: schizophrenics, on an intermittent reinforcement system. I was really looking forward to trying to understand what they were doing with those people. I was amazed at what happened when the patient came in: "Oh John, I haven't seen you since last week." There was just the most caring, welcoming atmosphere as they ushered him into his little cubicle, where he did the monkey business with the machine, and when he came out he said, "I damn near got the thing licked this time!" Of course there was no way of licking it because there was no system involved, but he was sure that he was trying to solve a puzzle. But what impressed me was that if there was improvement in those patients, you couldn't possibly differentiate it from what they had done on the machines and the caring attitude with which the experimenters surrounded them. So that goes even further than your rat example.

BATESON: Yes. Point of fact: Was there improvement? Did you feel . . .

ROGERS: There was, yes, as long as they got reinforcements. When the reinforcements were shut off, often there was regression back to catatonic states. And, I might add, this seemed a horrible piece of experimentation to me, to my value system.

BATESON: Me too.

ROGERS: Then I think that perhaps one real difference between us is that, if I've got it correctly, you justify the feelings that you have about it on the basis of your analysis of whether it is true or not. Well, I happen to agree with your analysis. But I think that the feelings exist whether or not the analysis is true. And I feel it is just as valuable to be aware of feelings as it is to be aware of our intellectual processes. And that often even scholars get screwed up, if I may use a technical term, by not paying attention to their feelings, but only to the ideas that they have generated. I don't know what reaction you might have to that.

(Tape ends. Other side begins in midsentence.)

ROGERS: I'd like to clear up one point here.

BATESON: Yes?

ROGERS: About feelings: I don't just refer to the hormonal variations.

BATESON: No, I'm sure not.

ROGERS: I am referring to the emotionalized personal meanings that exist.

BATESON: Right. Meanings. *Meanings* is an awfully mentalist sort of word.

ROGERS: Get all circuits deeply surrounded with feelings.

BATESON: Sure. Sure. Sure. You see, I think we agree that the mind is the one thing that's worth feeling about. And I'm not kidding about this. Where do you live, really? As you sit on the floor listening to this verbiage, suppose I attack you in terms of your understanding of the context in which you are here tonight: your respect, your amusement, your entertainment — all this weave of contextual themes, schemata, whatever you want to call it, in which we are here tonight. Me, trying to find out how I relate to Carl, Carl trying to find out how he relates to me, Dick trying to ride two horses at the same moment, and all the rest of it. If, as participants in that dance, you suddenly find you have put your foot through the floor, this is where feelings are. This is where, if you offer respect and respect isn't the thing that was asked for: "Ugh." If you offer amusement and amusement isn't it, if you are serious and you feel I am mocking you: "Ugh." Always at this point, the moment you are not at ease in the context, then you get unpleasant feelings. And the change towards ease within the context is a very large part of pleasantness of feelings. And then beyond that, of course, there are very special contexts identifying persons and your relationship to them and the way their hair fits on their faces, and all these things which are again a weave of context of some kind. This is what I call feelings. Maybe I am wrong.

ROGERS: I don't think I can respond to that directly because it would take a good deal of time to really get accustomed to your terminology and way of thinking. But let me see if I can approach it from a little different angle and get your reaction, too. To me, the person who offers the most hope in our crazy world today, which could be wiping itself out, is the individual who is most fully aware — most fully aware of what is going on within himself: physiologically, feeling-wise, his thoughts; also aware of the external world that is impinging on him. The more fully he is aware of the whole system, or perhaps context — I am not sure whether I am using that in the same way you would — the more hope there is that he would live a balanced human life without the violence, the craziness, the deceit, the horrible things that we tend to do to each other in the modern world. I don't know whether that really touches on the kind of thing that you were talking about.

BATESON: Well, I think it does. I would like to start all over again, beginning on the other end of the nature of context. I started by building it up from the Skinnerian experiment, Pavlovian dog experiment, what have you. Let's start from the other end, because that's a brief, bits-and-pieces sort of way of doing it, and if it were really true about rats, you know, we'd all end up doing quiz programs in our educational system. But let's start by asking, How were you going to pickle the information? If learning is an acquisition of information in some sense — maybe the information about the comparative anatomy of the beetles, or the information about human love and hate and your relation to the cosmos and what sort of a thing are you, information of enormously different levels — and significant learning is then a range within that, how are you going to pickle it? We catch it, and we catch it with these flaps called ears or with our eyes or something, and what's going to happen then? Now it's beginning to look, from Karl Pribram's work and others, that an important part of catching information is not making little jots and tittles in particular slots in all this gunk up here. For one thing, you can cut out large pieces of that gunk and you don't get specific loss; you get blurring, if anything. This suggests that the information is a little bit everywhere.

ROGERS: Is a little bit what? I didn't get . . . is a little bit what?

BATESON: The information is a little bit everywhere.

ROGERS: Mmm.

BATESON: Did you know Warren McCulloch?

ROGERS: Just slightly.

BATESON: Well, he died in his seventies the other day. I think his mother is still living. He had a conference at his house on information retrieval. He's one of these cybernetic boys, you know. And Grandma, the old lady, who was sitting in on the conference, became impatient, and went off into the kitchen. McCulloch followed her there to see what was happening and she started to make coffee for the group. She was really in a temper in there.

"Those young men," she said. "They don't know about information retrieval. I know something about that. I know that you
will forget things; it's no use marking where you put them. The
thing to do is to have a little bit of everything everywhere." (*Rogers laughs.*) So, some knitting in the dining room, you see, and
some cigarettes in the kitchen, and matches in the bedroom, and
a little bit of everything everywhere. Then you can find things.
Now this is achieved by complex resonating systems, essentially
stationary wave systems, usually in networks of neurons or something of the kind. All of the time in its oscillation, it receives pieces
of information that will affect a specific place, but this place affects all other places because the whole thing is a single system
and therefore, knowing the code, you can read the information
out of anywhere in the circuit.

Now it seems to me that a piece of significant learning would
be an ability to live in a universe, how can I say, in which you
will jump from one stepping stone to another. And there's always another stepping stone under your foot. Now this is really
true of many people. It used to be true of Robert Oppenheimer.
He would go out on a limb in a lecture and you would think, "Oh
my God, where is he going to go next? (*Bateson laughs.*) And there
was always another place for his foot. Now this, I think, is something to do with a complete person: not only in here do you have
resonating systems and the information is a little bit everywhere,
but also out there.

ROGERS: Yes. I have heard you speak about that and I hope you
will say more in a minute, but I want to respond just a bit to your
initial question: How do you pickle the learning? To me the comments you made about that really showed that there is no way of
pickling the learning, that it is a continuing multifaceted process
which probably extends not only through different portions of
the brain but throughout the whole organic system.

BATESON: The word *pickle* was precisely the inappropriate
word.

ROGERS: That's right.

BATESON: Correct.

ROGERS: And the thing that I draw from that, and from my
own experience more than from that, I suppose, is that there
is such a thing as learning by the whole person. And that it's

something that educationally we know very little about. We may know something about brain function and neuron function in minute detail, but how to bring about the kind of learning the old lady had in mind, where in the whole system we have valuable learnings, which are not only bits of information but often bits of self-knowledge as well, so that the whole person can learn and act as a unified organism rather than as a purely intellectual system . . . I keep coming back to that, as you see. But I hope you will pursue this notion of the resonating systems, not only within but also outside. That's an intriguing idea.

BATESON: I think the word *intellect* has to be dealt with.

ROGERS: Right.

BATESON: It's a word which we would wisely reverse for a special, narrow sort of focus. You can learn to be intellectual, and this is significant learning, of course. It may be rather undesirable, but significant learning. Having learned it, the conclusions don't seem to travel. I find this all the time with students. I will tell them, "Look, the only thing that can enter your knowledge through your sense organs is news of difference." They sort of gape at me. The notion that this might be significant, and would bear upon what they think about their girlfriends, what they think about politics, what they think about the whole world, this does not occur to them. Because the whole thing was done in a classroom. There was a context label on it that it was "only" education. I think the word *intellectual* should be used for that learning which is under a context marker, or a context box even: a semipermeable or impermeable box, so that what's learned from that box is nontransferable anywhere. Otherwise I think the mind's a fine thing.

ROGERS: (*Chuckles.*) One real difference that I sense in our approach to thinking about some of these issues is that you make it clear by a number of your statements that you are primarily a teacher, and for myself I have come to value placing primary trust in the student as learner. And that really makes for a different kind of situation in the whole educational context.

BATESON: Do you —

ROGERS: And your illustrations and all indicate to me that you are passing information to others and that often they don't appreciate it or don't understand how to use it. It doesn't really have meaning for them.

BATESON: I *am* setting a situation for them to discover, but still I am in an active role. I think that's true. Do you feel that your —

ROGERS: I don't take a passive role. You say you take an active role. My role is active too, but it is active in trying to bring about the conditions in the classroom which will encourage and facilitate the student in choosing his own goals and getting excited about his own learning, and then he finds that he does apply that to his thinking about his girlfriend or about politics or about the government or whatnot. That's been my experience.

BATESON: Yes, I think there's a difference between us as educators. I use the word *teacher*.

ROGERS: Yes.

BATESON: But I think my role is sort of, a little funny.

ROGERS: Is sort of what?

BATESON: Sort of a little funny.

ROGERS: (*Laughs.*) So is mine.

BATESON: No, that's not quite it. Yes, I think your point is well taken: that on the whole I am either communicating information or setting the stage for discovery of something or other, or indeed, looking out and trying to learn myself. But I think I am halfway aware of this, of your criticism of the contrast, and I tend to try to pull my punches in a way, by being somewhat of a clown. Now the things I say, you know, laughingly, are not less serious than the things —

ROGERS: I know.

BATESON: — I would say seriously, and perhaps often the reverse. Never an untrue word spoken in jest. (*Rogers laughs.*)

ROGERS: I have heard that about your classes. (*Bateson laughs.*) Not so much the clown aspect, but the fact that by puzzling students and by raising riddles and so on, you try to get them to think, and that I quite go along with. But I wonder whether we have a slightly different emphasis in that perhaps we have a different goal for the student. I get the feeling that perhaps you do know some of the points you want the student to reach. I only know that I want to help him start on his own self-initiated path. And perhaps that makes the difference.

BATESON: I think we have a different degree of faith in the intellect. (*Both laugh.*) My faith, creed, whatever you want to call it, is that it is in general possible to think with very sharp rigor about things that we have been talking about tonight and many other things. Human relations. My belief is that the conventional language in which people talk about those things is mainly a blinding and misleading language, that the metaphors used are in general inappropriate. Now I think you, Carl, are more willing to use the familiar forms of speech than I am. You think you can get away with them and it'll be all right, whereas I sort of drag myself into either joking, clowning, or something, or into being rather a bore, you see, in insisting on being pedantic.

ROGERS: Well, you see you probably talk more than I do, which gives you —

BATESON: I do an awful lot of talking, yes.

ROGERS: — more of a chance to show any of those things. (*Both laugh.*) But one point we're getting awfully close to here: I was really impressed when you were talking about where your faith lay. I suppose it's my experience in working with people in psychotherapy that has gradually given me more and more trust in the human individual, and so it becomes inevitable for me that I endeavor to implement that in the educational situation as well. In other words, you were speaking at the very first about the fact — an analogy that I thought was very meaningful — that you could teach about the anatomy of beetles in such a way as to turn students into Hitlers.

BATESON: Yes.

ROGERS: I quite agree, that's true.

BATESON: Or into artists.

ROGERS: Sure. And I feel . . . I don't know quite how to put this . . . I feel there is a danger in that which I endeavor to get around, or to resolve for myself, by a pluralism — by initiating the learning in each of X number of students, in which case, if they do want to learn about the anatomy of the beetle, some of them might learn about it in ways in which they would become Hitlers, but the majority probably would not. I am not making that very clear, am I?

BATESON: I missed a sentence. You said there's a danger in that, and I am not sure what the *that* was.

ROGERS: A danger in having one person in a position of authority, namely the instructor, who has the perceived status and also the very real ability to mold a whole group of people. Yes, I guess I regard that as dangerous. I grant that there are some people who —

BATESON: Uh huh. I'm sure it's dangerous, I grant that . . .

ROGERS: — have molded people in marvelous ways, and there are those people who have molded people in horribly conforming ways, and there are those who have molded people in very destructive ways. I would rather put my trust in the individuals out there than in the individual who is here. Does that make any sense?

BATESON: Makes perfectly good sense. Well, I find myself impatient, I guess, and uncommonly impatient, at the molding which has been done by others before they ever came anywhere near me.

ROGERS: Yes, me too. (*Laughs.*)

BATESON: And molding which was never done by others and ought to have been done: very simple sorts of general ideas that have not been given, and which the school system for some reason omits to mention. That there is a difference between a "number" and a "quantity," for example. This is quite a simple little epigrammatic matter. But if you get confused between numbers and quantities, God help you for the rest of your life. That the name of the thing is not the thing named. This should have been drilled or practiced or indicated or experienced in elementary school. If I ask the White Knight what the song is, the White Knight says, "The name of the song is called Haddock's Eyes." And Alice says, "Well that's a strange name." "No," says the White Knight, "that's not the name of the song, that's what the name is called." (*Rogers laughs, then Bateson laughs.*) And so on. Now I don't know in your educational system, granting its ideals for significant learning for character, where you are going to get correction of that sort of erroneous and vicious thought, that the name of the song was Haddock's Eyes.

ROGERS: Well, I think that you have more confidence for yourself than I have for myself . . .

BATESON: Yes.

ROGERS: . . . that you know some of the things that students must and should know. I don't have that degree of confidence. I don't think I do know what they should know. And I am perfectly sure that they will pick up erroneous ideas in courses they might take with me as well as in courses they might have with others. But if they are directing their own learning, it will be corrected in the same way that my learning and yours is corrected. We no longer go to teachers, we get corrected by our life experiences. And I —

BATESON: I go to teachers.

ROGERS: Mmm?

BATESON: I go to teachers. Many of them are inside books, but . . .

ROGERS: Yes. No, you don't go to teachers. Let me challenge you on that. (*Bateson laughs.*) I think that you pick up a book or you go to a person because you want to learn something, which is quite different from teaching in the ordinary sense. I don't want us to get all tied up on semantics here, but teaching usually does mean the imparting of information, which is quite different from seeking what you want to learn, and —

BATESON: From being visited by a seeker.

ROGERS: Yes, it is different from being visited by a seeker. For example, sometimes in courses I've said, "I'll even give a lecture if you want me to." Well, I can tell you it's a very different experience to be asked by a class to lecture on some given topic that they think I'm expert on, than it is to be pouring that same lecture onto them when they haven't asked for it. So I do favor —

BATESON: Yes, I agree.

ROGERS: I favor much more being visited by seekers . . .

BATESON: I've been through both those situations, yes.

ROGERS: I favor much more being visited by seekers than seeking to put something across.

BATESON: How many students are seekers, I wonder?

ROGERS: I assume on the basis of experience that they are seekers until they have gradually been squelched by our educational system. The best evidence of that, I think, is the four-year-old or five-year-old child. Is he a seeker? I'll say he is! He's just soaking up everything he can, in every area. He's learning to sense people's feelings toward him; he's gathering information about his world; he's a very eager learner. And I think that it is the context of our educational system which turns off that seeking. Nevertheless, it can be reawakened.

BATESON: Yeah, yes I agree on the whole, obviously.

ROGERS: Not obviously.

BATESON: Eh, what?

ROGERS: Not obviously, that you agree. (*Rogers laughs.*)

BATESON: All right, not obviously, but I do agree. And I agree that from where I sit, dealing with university students and graduate students, about half my problem, perhaps more, is in dealing with that which has been turned off. My sense is of two major frustrations. One, it's been turned off — Carl's phrase — and two, why the hell didn't they tell these people some simple little things? (*Both laugh.*) Things which ought to have been communicated way back, but they were too busy turning things off, I guess.

ROGERS: It seems to me it's possible that we could go to the audience now for some questions.

AUDIENCE MEMBER: I wanted to ask Dr. Rogers: I think both of you clearly take your students seriously, in terms of having faith in their capacities, and I wonder if what I'm really asking is about a shaman tradition, which is the effort to trick people into rediscovering their own power, and whether you can take a person's suffering or desire to learn seriously, but also whether you can provoke a person into rediscovering that power rather than using what Mr. Bateson is calling Dr. Rogers' common language to rediscover that. Could you comment on that?

ROGERS: Yes. Often people are provoked into learning, sometimes by extremely bad teachers. (*Bateson laughs.*) That's a fact. I've known students who have heard an arbitrary, authoritarian lecture and who thought, "I'll prove that bastard wrong if it's the last thing I do." And they begin to really learn and study and go into the field deeply in order to do that. So there are many ways of provoking a self-initiated kind of learning. I was merely trying to state the kind of way I liked.

AUDIENCE MEMBER: I have a little difficulty with the statement that Mr. Bateson made, that it was possible to make either fascists or artists out of students. I really have to disagree with it. Dr. Rogers' statement that he just made now, about a student deciding for himself that his professor is full of bullshit and he's going to do something about it, speaks to the opposite fact, and I'd like to maybe hear a little more about that.

BATESON: Yeah, there's a slippery edge there. I think Carl and I would agree that fascists are made and not born. We might not agree about artists being made and not born, and on that I would hedge. I think I'd move over to his side of the story and say that you could probably use the anatomy of the beetles to stop them from being artists, to frustrate and block them, but whether you can make artists out of them, that's another story. You could, perhaps, love them into being artists with the aid of the beetles.

AUDIENCE MEMBER: I still have this nagging question. I hear you saying that behavior modification can work one hundred percent if you set your mind to it. Now I'm not sure exactly whether you're saying that you can make a fascist. Maybe you're not saying that you can make *anybody* a fascist.

BATESON: I would hedge on the *anybody*, but I would say that you could have an educational system in the country which would make a great many.

ROGERS: Yes, if you modeled —

BATESON: And I think there is empirical evidence for that . . .

ROGERS: Excuse me. If the teacher really models a dictatorial type of behavior, a great many of the students will pick that up as the way in which they should behave with their students, and so on.

AUDIENCE MEMBER: Okay, thank you very much.

ANOTHER AUDIENCE MEMBER: I came this evening, I guess, with an expectation of trying to experience some of the richness of your total life cycle, both at a personal level and at a professional level. And while I realize that's a very heavy expectation, I would like, if it's possible, if you could sort of think of us as a family of grandchildren, and there are just a couple of things that you feel are very, very important for you to share with all of us. Thank you.

ROGERS: Perhaps as the elder I should speak first. (*Bateson laughs.*) I don't know. I suppose that I hope you would find it possible to trust your deepest self. I think that the follies and trag-edies of the world result from people being fearful of themselves, not knowing themselves, and certainly being unwilling to trust the deepest level of selfhood. I think you asked for two things; one is about as far as I can go.

BATESON: And, I suppose, on this side of the house, I would hope that you get an idea that it is possible to think feelingly and with some rigor about a great many of the problems that we have been talking about. They don't have to be dismissed either with clichés or with approximations.

MODERATOR: I would like to take the privilege of the last question myself. It's the other side of the coin of the one the lady previously had asked. It's one that I am very much interested in for both of you. All of us in this room have read your works and have been guided by them. As you think back over the pleasures, and perhaps regrets, of your professional lives, what kinds of things at this stage of your development are you having second thoughts about? Where are you wondering whether or not you said it in the right way the first time you said it? What would you erase if you had a chance to go back and erase the tape? Where did you mislead us, you two, and what, if anything, do you have to say about that?

BATESON: I think the first "double-bind" paper was certainly published two or three years too soon. It reads much too concretistic, and a lot of people have wasted a lot of time trying to count double binds, which is very much like trying to count jokes, you know — you can't do it. But this is part of the process. One's work goes forward, branching, correcting, and so on, and that's how it is. You cannot really regret that the process has that form. You can regret that at that moment you were a bit over to one side, maybe.

ROGERS: I think that I regret that in early writings about therapy we were so fascinated with the enormous learnings from recording interviews that we became too much focused on techniques, and that has misled a great many people in the counseling field. I realize that.

BATESON: Interesting. It's almost the same . . .

ROGERS: I think also that I can look back on specific things that I have said and written and done, research that I've done, too, to impress others, or to prove something when I knew damn well that I already knew the answer. That seems like a waste of time. When it comes to the pleasurable part, I just regard myself as very fortunate that it seems to be a never-ending process of excitement. I don't know whether this book I'm working on will be any damn good, but I know I've had as much urgency and fun and excitement in trying to write it as in anything I've written. And to me that's a very precious part of the process of living.

MODERATOR: I want to thank a very kind and good audience tonight. I want to thank two very generous gentlemen for giving of themselves on behalf of all of us. Thank you both. Goodnight.

FOLLOW-UP CORRESPONDENCE

Editors' Note: After their meeting, Carl Rogers and Gregory Bateson corresponded briefly. While the complete letters were not available for publication, the following two excerpts convey the major part of their exchange and offer another perspective on the dialogue. We do regret that the second letter ends so abruptly.

Dear Gregory:

I am intrigued by the thought you expressed at Tucson [another occasion] that "Gregory" is simply a nexus in a floating web of ideas which exist within your skin and outside of it. I don't entirely share that idea, but I can understand and respect it. What I don't understand is what seems to me to be your failure to realize that you are also a nexus of feelings or personal meanings or whatever you want to call them and that these are just as important as your ideas. If ideas exist and matter then so do feelings in my estimation.

I had a good time imagining how our dialogue might have started out if you had been aware of your feelings at the moment and able and willing to take the risk of expressing them. Dick would have given his flowery introduction. I would have made my statement about education. Then you would have spoken something as follows: "I am bloody hot. I was nauseated by my dinner. I resent the fact that we're supposed to be on display and I feel constrained not to let my opposition show. Yet if you want to know a small part of what I think and feel, it is that when Carl speaks of 'the whole person' he is talking a lot of bunk, because all of his thinking grows out of a basic fallacy. For me that fallacy is (and here I can't fill it out because I don't understand it)."

Now if by some miracle you had started out in that way, with both your ideas and feelings evident, you would have been, in terms of *my* line of thought, much more of a whole person. In that case we might even have met instead of simply talking past each other.

I certainly share part of the responsibility for the fiasco, but I didn't realize the depth of your opposition to my way of thinking because you only gave a hint of it. So I felt that we were just shadow boxing. I somehow couldn't really reach you, whether you exist inside or outside of your skin.

This letter doesn't need a response. I just wanted to write it because your letter, with its free expression of things, makes me feel much closer to you than I did at Tucson or on the platform at Marin. Maybe someday — who knows? — I might even get to understand you. I might even understand you in spite of the fact that "you" do not exist.

> Warmly,
> Carl

Dear Carl,

Let me try to say in my language what I understand by the word "feelings" in yours. (And I think I attempted this from the platform.)

1. There are many sorts of "ideas" (i.e., created patterns of news of complexes of selected differences). The problem is how to establish some sort of classification of these sorts.
2. As I understand it, "feelings" are members of a class within 1 above. Ideas may be "painful," ugly, joyous, comic, sad, etc.
3. You call "feelings" also "personal meanings" and that is a helpful limitation, a step towards definition. (If there could be "non-personal meanings" or "personal non-meanings.")
4. But we get into difficulties with both "meanings" and "personal."
    4a. "Meanings" must surely always have their being *between* at least *two* ideas, so that we can say that "A means B."
    4b. "Personal," we know, means something different for you

from what it means for me. For me, "person" is that "nexus in a floating web of ideas which exist within my skin and outside it." For you, I guess that "person" is all contained *within*.

(In parenthesis, I strongly recommend my version of "person" for use if and when we face the very difficult formal problems of aesthetics. And don't forget that other use of "person" as *mask* — the view of me which I show to others on the outside.)

5. This matter of "location" of ideas, feelings and whatnot is very awkward for both you and me. Where is the "pain" of my big toe? Or where *is* the (very terrible) pain of a phantom limb? I think we can agree to have no localization of anything (ideas, feelings, meanings, etc.) within the person or self (in both your and my usage of "person").

The world of "person" is non-spatial. And Bishop Berkeley was right in asserting that what was not inside "mind" (in my sense) was not.

6. So now we come to the *relationship* implicitly mentioned in your phrase "personal meanings" . . .

III / REVIEWS, SYMPOSIUM, AND CORRESPONDENCE

8
Reinhold Niebuhr

Reinhold Niebuhr was born in 1892 in Wright City, Missouri. He thought his minister father "the most interesting man in town," and followed in his footsteps, attending two years at Elmhurst College, three at Eden Theological Seminary, and receiving his Bachelor of Divinity degree at Yale University in 1914 and his Master of Divinity in 1915. (Niebuhr's brother and sister went on to become respected theologians as well.)

An ordained minister of the Evangelical Synod of North America, which later became part of the United Church of Christ, Niebuhr was pastor of the Bethel Evangelical Church in Detroit from 1915 to 1928. This congregation, composed primarily of automobile workers, grew from forty to more than eight hundred under his leadership. In Detroit, Niebuhr was impressed by the dehumanizing effects of modern industrialism and became a strong and radical advocate of the rights of labor, a "crusading lecturer" and "radical preacher" at forums and college campuses throughout the Midwest. *Time* magazine wrote that the industrialists of Detroit "breathed a sigh of relief" when he left for Union Theological Seminary in 1928. In 1931 he began his lifelong marriage with Ursula Keppel-Campton, a distinguished scholar and theologian. They had two children.

Niebuhr remained at Union as professor of applied Christianity until 1960, as vice-president of the seminary from 1955 to 1960, and as professor emeritus until his death, altogether a tenure of more than forty years at that institution. There he taught Christian ethics, philosophy of religion, many applications of religion to society, politics, and history, and established himself as "the greatest Protestant theologian born in America since Jonathan Edwards."

Once describing himself as "a moralist who has strayed into theology," Niebuhr was a theological conservative. One critic wrote, "He has done more than any theologian to rehabilitate the Christian dogma of original sin in present-day thinking." He criticized those who saw man's redemption in any secular solution — whether Marxism or science — all of which he considered to be rooted in the mistaken belief that the basis for evil lies outside man himself. He argued that total absorption in the "social gospel" was a great mistake, and that liberal Protestantism was "utopian."

Niebuhr wrote more than forty books and one thousand articles on Christianity and society, including *Does Civilization Need Religion?* (1927), *Moral Man and Immoral Society: A Study in Ethics and Politics* (1932), *The Interpretation of Christian Ethics* (1935), his two-volume major work, *Nature and the Destiny of Man* (1941, 1943), *Faith and History* (1949), *Christianity, Power and Politics* (1950), *Christian Realism and Political Problems* (1953), and *Man's Nature and His Communities* (1965). He received numerous honorary degrees from universities at home and abroad.

Ironically, while standing for conservative Christianity theologically, Niebuhr became one of the most influential political liberals of his time. Moving from the socialism and pacifism of his earlier years (he ran for Congress on New York's Socialist party ticket in 1930), he was continually active in anti-Communist, liberal causes, as evidenced by the following roles: chairman of American Friends of German Freedom, which espoused combatting Hitler's rising power and urging U.S. involvement in the war to resist Nazism; vice-chairman of the Liberal Party of New York; a founder of Americans for Democratic Action. He was active in the resettlement of war refugees and influential in the World Council of Churches, in which forum he pressed for a more vigorous expression of Christian involvement in various movements for social justice. He wrote regularly for Christian and secular journals such as *Christian Century, Commonweal, The New Republic*, and *The Nation*, often serving for many years as contributing editor.

His conservative theology explained rather than contradicted his liberal politics. He wrote, "Man's capacity for justice makes democracy possible, but man's inclination to injustice makes democracy necessary." His lifelong attempt to integrate Christian ethics with a practical political philosophy — "Christian realism," as he called it — was aided by "a keen intellect, an understanding of opposing viewpoints, and an encyclopedic knowledge." In describing his style, a reviewer wrote, "It has an amazing wealth of scholarly lore, a richness of insight and perspectiveness [*sic*], an architectural quality of rearing before one's eyes a structure of impressive logical design." In person, he was a striking speaker — over six feet, with blue eyes and blond hair. "Hawknosed and saturnine, he is, nevertheless, a cheerful and gracious (though conversationally explosive) man."

Niebuhr's views on democracy, history, politics, and the problems of the day, founded as they were on a theological base, captured the attention of leading thinkers, politicians, and opinionmakers. One said, "No Protestant theologian has spoken so relevantly to our concerns in the Western world as Reinhold Niebuhr." Another wrote, "No theologian in the United States has been listened to with greater respect by the general academic community and by people concerned with political affairs. . . . He did as much as any other thinker to prepare America for facing responsibly the realities of world power." When he semiretired from Union in 1960, a professorship in his name was established and funded by a cross-denominational group including Jacques Maritain, T. S. Eliot, Arnold Toynbee, and Eleanor Roosevelt. He was awarded the Presidential Medal of Freedom in 1964.

Although serious illness curtailed his activities in his later years, his writing maintained its vigor and relevance. When Niebuhr died in Stockbridge, Massachusetts, on June 1, 1971, *The Times* of London called him "probably the best known and most influential American theologian of our time."

Carl Rogers's review of Niebuhr's *The Self and the Dramas of History* was published in *Pastoral Psychology* in 1956, together with responses by Bernard Loomer, Walter Horton, and Hans Hofmann, and Rogers's final response to these three respected academicians.

208   *Reviews, Symposium, and Correspondence*

Reinhold Niebuhr's
The Self and the Dramas of History

REVIEW BY CARL ROGERS

I was persuaded to read and comment upon this book because in my work as a psychotherapist I have become deeply concerned with the self and its place in our psychological existence. My reactions are not intended as a formal review.

As I lay the book down, I find that I am impressed most of all by the awesome certainty with which Dr. Niebuhr *knows*. He knows, with incredible assurance, what is wrong with the thinking of St. Thomas Aquinas, Augustine, Hegel, Freud, Marx, Dewey, and many, many others. He also knows what are the errors of communism, existentialism, psychology, and all the social sciences. His favorite term for the formulations of others is "absurd," but such other terms as "erroneous," "blind," "naive," "inane," and "inadequate" also are useful. It seems to me that the only individuals who come off well in the book are the Hebrew prophets, Jesus (as seen by Niebuhr), Winston Churchill, and Dr. Niebuhr himself.

So strong is this impression that I cannot help but speculate as to whether in some sense Dr. Niebuhr may be speaking to himself when he says that "religion lends itself particularly to the pretensions of possessing absolute truth and virtue by finite and sinful men"; or when he states that the sin of the self consists of "claiming too much for its finiteness, and for the virtue and wisdom which it achieves in its finiteness." I find myself offended by Dr. Niebuhr's dogmatic statements and feel ready to turn back with fresh respect to the writings of science, in which at least the *endeavor* is made to keep an open mind.

*The Chicago Theological Seminary "Register," January 1956, No. 1.

But I do not wish my distaste for the *form* of the presentation to cause me, or the reader of these comments, to overlook the major issue toward which the book is directed. Stated in oversimplified fashion, Dr. Niebuhr is wrestling with the fact that the trend of social and psychological science is to make man a creature determined by natural causes, and history an essentially predictable sequence. He dislikes this trend and stresses that man is a free self, transcending natural causes, and that history is an unpredictable affair, growing out of dramatic choice.

I feel deeply sympathetic to Dr. Niebuhr's attempt to deal with this problem, because it is one which concerns me sufficiently that I have tried to pose somewhat the same issue for psychologists to consider.* I looked eagerly to find what resolution he might have found for this complex and disturbing problem. I did not find it easy to discover this resolution, because the author is much more clear about what he is against than what he affirms. As I understand him, he points in several directions which seem to him desirable. He wishes to remove both the self and history from the realm of the "structures of nature," a realm which can be understood by empirical science. He justifies this by the fact that both the self and history are compounded of freedom and necessity (determinism), and thus they fall outside of science, which is "absurd" when it endeavors to discover empirical laws regarding the self or historical events. To me, this seems to be roughly equivalent to telling scientists to stop seeking for orderliness in man's inner nature or in his outer behavior, and I am skeptical that they will pay much attention.

Another thread which runs through Dr. Niebuhr's thinking is his tendency to see the universe in terms of contrasting systems in a state of tension. Thus, in the individual there is a tension between creativity and destructiveness, between rationality and faith, between the self as creator and the self as creature, and hence between freedom and necessity. Dr. Niebuhr does not

---

*"Persons or Science? A Philosophical Question," *American Psychologist*, 10, No. 7 (July 1955), 267–278.

seem to recognize that this duality of systems permits him to explain too much. Thus, on the one hand, he states that "no scientific investigations of past behavior can become the basis of predictions of future behavior." On the other hand, in his brief (and to me arbitrary) analysis of history he makes such statements as this: "The tragedy of Germany must be analyzed in terms of a dozen complex historical factors," and he gives various geographical, social, and cultural factors. In this section he proceeds as though he, like the social scientist, sees historical effect proceeding from historical cause. Yet one cannot tax him with inconsistency, since he believes in both freedom and determinism and that the self is both creator and creature. Because he is not specific as to the degree of freedom he believes the self to possess, it is obvious that he need never be at a loss to explain any event, since, if it is not determined, it is the result of man's transcending freedom, and vice versa. This is a comfortable view but to me not a satisfying one.

Another direction which he takes is the advocacy of a biblical faith. Because it combines a specific historical drama which cannot be understood rationally, with the hope of fulfillment of individual selfhood, this supplies for Dr. Niebuhr the most compelling answer. I must confess that it did not seem equally compelling to me.

As a psychologist, I was particularly interested in Dr. Niebuhr's view of the self. In his discussion of the dialogue of the self with itself, I found much with which I could agree. In his concept of the self in dialogue with others, he describes both the potentialities and the limiting mysteries of interpersonal relationships, where the "otherness" of the other poses a barrier which must be accepted in some ultimate way. I found that his insights in this respect were in many ways in agreement with my experience. The search of the self for ultimate meaning is also a concept which has much reality for me.

It is in his conception of the basic deficiency of the individual self that I find my experience utterly at variance. He is quite clear that the "original sin" is self-love, pretension, claiming too much, grasping after self-realization. I read such words and try to imagine the experience out of which they have grown. I have dealt with maladjusted and troubled individuals, in the intimate personal relationship of psychotherapy, for more than a quarter of a century. This has not been perhaps a group fully representative of the whole community, but neither has it been unrepresentative. And, if I were to search for the central core of difficulty in people as I have come to know them, it is that in the great majority of cases they despise themselves, regard themselves as worthless and unlovable. To be sure, in some instances this is covered by pretension, and in nearly all of us these feelings are covered by some kind of a façade. But I could not differ more deeply from the notion that self-love is the fundamental and pervasive "sin." Actually it is only in the experience of a relationship in which he is loved (something very close, I believe, to the theologians' *agape*) that the individual can begin to feel a dawning respect for, acceptance of, and, finally, even a fondness for himself. It is as he can thus begin to sense himself as lovable and worthwhile, in spite of his mistakes, that he can begin to feel love and tenderness for others. It is thus that he can begin to realize himself and to reorganize himself and his behavior to move in the direction of becoming the more socialized self he would like to be. I believe that only if one views individuals on the most superficial or external basis are they seen as being primarily the victims of self-love. When seen from the inside, that is far from being their disease. At least so it seems to me.

So I leave Dr. Niebuhr's book feeling that I too would like to preserve the self as creator, the self as a free and self-determining being. I wish that I knew how to reconcile this desire with the desire, which I share with other scientists, to find the orderliness which I believe exists in the human psyche. But I have not found the answers in Dr. Niebuhr's book. I shall hope for some other book, more open to all the complex facts, with perhaps less certainty in it, to inform me more deeply in this perplexing area.

Reinhold Niebuhr and Carl R. Rogers: A Discussion by Bernard M. Loomer, Walter M. Horton, and Hans Hofmann

Discussion by: Bernard M. Loomer, Professor of the Psychology of Religion, Chicago Theological Seminary

In Rogers' comments on Niebuhr's *The Self and the Dramas of History* he makes two criticisms of Niebuhr's thought (which I shall list in the reverse order in which they were given). First, Niebuhr believes that man's sin is basically that of self-love or pretension, while Rogers has found in his twenty-five years of psychotherapy that the great majority of his clients "despise themselves, regard themselves as worthless and unlovable." Second, Niebuhr does not really reconcile the dual emphases that man is both free and determined. Rogers wants to harmonize his idea that man is free and self-determined with his desire and concern as a scientist to find the orderliness which he believes exists in the human psyche. Rogers feels that Niebuhr's handling of this tension is unconvincing. I shall deal with each criticism in turn, although quite briefly with the second.*

1. On the issue as to what is basically the trouble with man Niebuhr and Rogers apparently disagree quite flatly. This disagreement is not an easy matter to discuss or adjudicate because it involves great divergencies in total outlooks as well as intellectual concerns. The statement of the issue itself requires some brief mention of the context out of which each man speaks.

To the best of my knowledge, Rogers has no parallel to Niebuhr's doctrine of sin. But from his therapeutic experiences he has derived a conception of man's essential goodness: The more fully a client is able to accept himself because of the therapeutic relationship (which Rogers conceives to be an I-Thou relation and which Buber, incidentally, denies), the more trustworthy he

Pastoral Psychology, 1958, Vol. 9, No. 85, 15–17.

feels his own perceptions and judgments about himself and others to be. He becomes more able to evaluate himself objectively. The greater the degree of the client's self-acceptance, the greater his freedom and self-determination. He becomes more self-initiating and self-sufficient. The more he is open to acknowledge emotionally his strengths and weaknesses, the more freely and willingly he accepts others for what they are. The greater the client's self-acceptance, the more fully is he guided by his finer motives and values.

Niebuhr's doctrine of sin (expounded most fully in his *Nature and Destiny of Man*) emphasizes man's self-love, his tendency to deny God and to make himself the center of his own existence. For Niebuhr, man in his finitude is possessed by anxiety which is the precondition of both his creativity and his refusal to acquiesce to his finiteness. This anxiety is bearable if man trusts God, but man chooses to disobey God and to rebel. This lack of trust and rebellion leads to pride in one or more of its several forms. Pride is self-love. It is man's attempt to transform his contingent form of existence into unconditional significance.

To be sure, Niebuhr takes cognizance of sin as sensuality. But it is important to notice that sensuality is a further consequence of man's refusal to trust God. It is a more obviously degraded stage of his pride. Sensuality is "first another and final form of self-love, secondly an effort to escape self-love by the deification of another and finally as an escape from the futilities of both forms of idolatry by a plunge into unconsciousness" (or nothingness).

To put these points in terms that are perhaps more immediately relevant to the issue at hand, we can say that for Niebuhr (and for much if not most of the history of Christian theology) man sins or contributes to his own downfall because he is strong and not because he is weak. His trouble stems from excess and not deficiency. Basically, man tends to think more rather than less highly of himself than he ought to think. This position is taken partly because man's capacity for greatness is directly related to his propensity to sin.

In the present discussion Rogers seems to be saying that man's tendency is to think less highly of himself than he ought to think, that man's trouble arises from weakness rather than strength or from deficiency rather than excess. Only if he is loved sufficiently and with adequate understanding will a man attribute to himself proper worth and status. Since Rogers has no doctrine of sin or its equivalent, I am not clear as to what his answer would be to the question: Why do his clients underevaluate themselves? Because they have not been loved sufficiently? Or have they refused to accept the love that may have been offered to them? If the former, why would no one offer them adequate love? If the latter, why have they rejected love?

Niebuhr's rejoinder would be, in my judgment, that the clients' condition of weakness or deficiency or underevaluation could be characterized in one (or both) of two ways. Either it is temporary, apparent only and ambiguous, in which case it would be an inverted form of pride masquerading as excessive worthlessness, or it is sincere, in which case it is an instance of the strength of pride or self-love which has turned into weakness.

Therefore the question is: Is self-love the basic evil in man under which we can subsume all other forms? If so, it would appear that Niebuhr (when he stresses pride rather than sensuality, or when he stresses the strength of excess rather than the deficiency of weakness) and Rogers are mainly concerned with two different dimensions or stages of the same fundamental fact or process of man's self-destruction. This difference could be accounted for, in part, by the diversity of their vocations and intellectual preoccupations. Or are self-love and underevaluation totally unrelated phenomena? Perhaps we do not have sufficient evidence to make a responsible judgment, although at the moment I favor the first alternative.

This discussion could be carried to a further stage if we ask the question: When Rogers' clients reach the point in their therapeutic relationship where they do have a sufficiently high evaluation of themselves, do they altogether exemplify Rogers' description of the natural and essential goodness of man or do they exhibit some of the qualities that Niebuhr stresses, remembering that for Niebuhr there is a deep ambiguity in man because of the common rootage and interweaving of good and evil? I am not aware that there are any reliable data on this point and so the question is somewhat hypothetical. Yet a resolution of the two points of view will involve a consideration of this dimension of a client's life. Also some account must be taken of the more largely social character

of human existence before a satisfactory evaluation of these contrasting perspectives can be achieved. Rogers and Niebuhr may
each find the other unconvincing because their respective data
and outlooks are at the moment not altogether commensurate,
although I think it must be granted that Niebuhr's are certainly
more inclusive.

2. On the issue of freedom and external determination the issue is much less clear. In the first place I am not sure that Rogers
means the same thing by "freedom" or "self-determination" that
Niebuhr does. I am inclined to think that the latter's notion of
self-transcendence in terms of spirit is not really part of the former's intellectual outlook. Interestingly enough, this idea, which
is the primary basis from which Niebuhr criticizes most if not all
contemporary schools of psychology, is not dealt with at all by
Rogers. This omission on Rogers' part needs to be explained since
the idea is decisive for Niebuhr. This notion is part of the key to
understanding Niebuhr's criticisms of various forms of rational-
ism, including rationally intelligible structures of coherence and
meaning. It would also apply to Rogers' own conceptions of the
good life and the nature of man.

This possible difference in their definitions of freedom ac-
counts in part for their divergence in handling the freedom-
determination question. I am not really clear as to what sort
of a resolution of this tension Rogers is looking for. Apparently he is searching for a concept of the psyche's orderliness under which the freedom of the self can be subsumed.
Possibly the concept of the self's creativity would also be included within the meaning of the self's "orderliness." Does
Rogers want to eliminate the tension between order and freedom by systematizing freedom in terms of self-determination?
At one point he seems to criticize Niebuhr for not being able
to specify "the degree of freedom he believes the self to possess" (although the context of this quotation might lead the
reader to think correctly that Rogers meant this remark fa-
cetiously).

Niebuhr's view of the relation between historical determination and self-transcendence is such that no resolution of this
tension is possible. Both elements are present but interrelated.
(In this connection it seems to me that Rogers is incorrect when

he states that Niebuhr "wishes to remove both the self and history from the realm of the 'structures of nature.' ") Furthermore the tension is desirable. But this does not mean that Niebuhr is opposed to scientific inquiries. But it does mean that in the last analysis he thinks that a strict science of the self, including its self-transcendence, is not possible. For him, the freedom of the self is indeterminate and therefore cannot be systematized into any rationally structural order. This view has theological presuppositions and implications which are probably not shared by Rogers. The differences between the two men are in large part theological.

*Discussion by Walter M. Horton, Professor of Theology, Graduate
    School of Theology, Oberlin College*
    The editor has asked me to comment on Carl Rogers' review of Reinhold Niebuhr's *The Self and Dramas of History* in the January 1956 issue of the Chicago Theological Seminary "Register." Reading Rogers' judgment, springing as it does from a wealth of clinical experience, gives me a strong impulse to spring into the breach (for breach it is) between these two wise and gifted men, and offer a few words of interpretation.

First as to the impression of dogmatism and narrow-minded certitude which Rogers got from reading Niebuhr. I have known Reinhold Niebuhr for a good many years as a fellow member of a small, intimate theological discussion group, and think I can understand the basis of this false impression. "Reinie" does indeed make free use of such terms as "absurd," "erroneous," "inane," in describing false views. His first act in confronting any theological problem is to find two opposing views on the subject and sharpen them both to the point of absurdity, so that the truth plainly must lie somewhere between them. He does not very precisely identify these views with the actual views of their representatives and, in fact, sometimes gives a biased picture of these, so anxious is he to get a real pair of nutcracking opposites. But listen to him from this point on when he tries to suggest the true alternative to these absurdities, and he becomes very cautious and tentative.

On all ultimate questions, the best the religious thinker can do is to point to a mythical or symbolic solution, of which it can always be said, "We are deceivers and yet true" (*Beyond Tragedy*, Chap. I). So great is the peril here of real deception, that Niebuhr frequently whirls on himself in the midst of discussion, and catches himself in the wrong with as much pleasure as if it were someone else. Indeed he *is* "speaking to himself" when he warns against the "pretensions of possessing absolute truth." He is speaking to all and sundry, not just to Roman Catholics, when he develops the paradox of "having and not having the truth" in the second half of his *Nature and Destiny of Man*. Dogmatism is as hateful to him as to Carl Rogers; the appearance of dogmatism is due to the negative side of his didactical method. On the positive side, even his friends have accused him of being too tentative. No scientist could be more so.

That brings us to Rogers' second point, that Niebuhr gives an antiscientific and therefore profoundly unsatisfactory answer to the problem of freedom and determinism, with which every serious student of human nature has to wrestle. By pointing to the "unpredictable" character of history, rooted in "dramatic choice," Niebuhr seems to imply that empirical science cannot formulate laws about man without falling into the "absurd," and seems to be "telling scientists to stop seeking for orderliness in man's inner nature or in his outer behavior." On this understanding, Rogers finds Niebuhr inconsistent when he enumerates causal factors that help one to comprehend the tragedy of modern German history — *either* inconsistent, or else holding the comfortably loose theory that since freedom and determinism are both there, whatever is "not determined" is "the result of man's transcending freedom." But this is not all that Niebuhr means by the combination of freedom and determinism in human events — not "either one or the other," as if they were wholly disparate factors, but "both together simultaneously." His preference for biblical faith and dialectical thinking in ultimate human problems is not at all inconsistent with an empirical analysis of the same events, pushed as far as it can fruitfully go.

Rogers' principal objection, however, is his third and last, that Niebuhr's doctrine of self-love and pretension as the original sin is contradicted by the findings of psychological counseling experience, which indicate unambiguously that man's basic need is to "begin to feel a dawning respect for, acceptance of, and, finally, even a fondness for himself." It is a "superficial" view of man, says Rogers, that supposes his real disease is self-love instead of *lack* of self-love. This is certainly a terrific conflict of findings, in which two very acute observers — one in the realm of public affairs and the other in the realm of the inner life of persons — appear to belie one another completely. Out of such conflicts, real advances in understanding have sometimes come. Let us see if it may be so in this case.

It will not do to press the title of Niebuhr's *Moral Man and Immoral Society*, and reconcile Rogers' view with Niebuhr's by referring one to the personal life of man, and the other to his social life. The distinction between the personal and social spheres is only a relative one in Niebuhr's thinking; self-love and proud pretension are only more massive and obvious in group life than in personal life. There are plenty of texts concerning self-love and pride in *The Self and the Dramas of History*, the most psychological of all Niebuhr's books, to justify Rogers' interpretation of it.

Nevertheless, there is a further twist in Niebuhr's doctrine of man and sin, not nearly so manifest in this recent abbreviated version as it is in the full-length analysis given in *The Nature and Destiny of Man*. This analysis (surely the definitive statement of Niebuhr's position) starts interestingly enough with a psychological insight borrowed from Kierkegaard — to whom Carl Rogers, from a different angle, has also acknowledged a great debt. (See his Nellie Heldt Lectures, "Becoming a Person" [Oberlin, 1954], on Kierkegaard's doctrine of *choosing to be one's self* as the great antidote to despair.) The insight is that *anxiety* is "the internal precondition of sin . . . the inevitable spiritual state of man." Because of his borderline position, both part of nature as determined and above nature as free, man cannot help but be anxious. This is not sin, but it is a mighty *temptation* to sin. Self-love and pride are not the only forms of sin; they are attempts to overcome anxiety through trying to make one's self more secure than any finite creature can be. An opposite form of sin, also listed by Niebuhr, is *sensuality*, which tries to escape from the anxiety of selfhood by trying, like Walt Whitman, to go and be like the animals who are "not forever moaning about their sins." Beneath both these escape-reactions is a fundamental attitude of *unbelief* — unwillingness to trust God and accept his forgiving, empowering grace, which can overcome the threat of anxiety. Thus it is not strictly true to say that self-love and pretension are the very root of sin, for Niebuhr. Beneath these and other prevalent forms of sin are anxiety and lack of faith in God — which, most observers agree, is intimately related to lack of faith in the human Other and in the Self. Is this doctrine so remote as it first seemed from Carl Rogers' emphasis upon the basic need of normal self-love and an "acceptance" rooted in *agape?*

Let us not be too hasty in our eagerness to reconcile these two antagonists. Their approach to the study of human nature and their major emphasis in describing it remain opposed. Carl Rogers takes such an "accepting" and "permissive" attitude toward his counselees that it appears to him as though their nature were fundamentally wholesome, needing only to be released from shackling external bonds in order to heal and save itself by its own internal powers. This at least leans in the direction of Pelagian self-salvation. Reinhold Niebuhr lays such stress upon the essential helplessness of man, and his utter dependence upon divine grace, fears complacency so like the very devil, that he can cry, "Cursed be the man that putteth his trust in man!" Could any view be more opposed to Pelagian optimism than this new Augustinian pessimism? Yet because Niebuhr actually defines God's grace in terms that overlap with Rogerian "acceptance," and because both have deep compassion upon man's anxiety as the deepest source of his distress, there is room for increased agreement if they should continue to converse. Why be discouraged by the first frustrated encounter?

Discussion by Hans Hofmann, Director of the University Project on Religion and Mental Health, Harvard University

I have been asked to comment upon Reinhold Niebuhr's *The Self and the Dramas of History* in the light of the remarks which Professor Carl R. Rogers has made in the January 1956 issue of the Chicago Theological Seminary "Register" on the same book.

Not being totally familiar with either the background or present-day development in theological and religious thinking,

it is sometimes hard for an outsider like Dr. Rogers to appreciate Reinhold Niebuhr's stand and contribution. The undebatable
and surely still most actual merit of Dr. Niebuhr's writing lies in
his constant reminding us that the unwarranted and thus harmful optimism about the nature of man is just as unrealistic and
hence fruitless as it would be to disregard the complexity of the
human predicament and to deflate men to a mere sum total of
deterministic mechanism and the consequent predictability of his
development. Niebuhr is rightly sensitive to the danger that such
a theological or so-called scientific understanding of man will lull
us into being irresponsibly unaware of the creative and unguard-
ed against the destructive abilities of the human nature, which
never conform totally with our philosophical presuppositions or
experimentally gained premature conclusions.

He is, therefore, very keen to discern sharply the diverse factors which constitute the human self-appreciation and its paradoxical impact on the human participation in history. He sees a
permanent and inevitable tension between human creativity and
human enslavement to environmental conditions. These polar
elements in the nature of the human self-awareness Niebuhr is
unable to reconcile but believes them to be immensely essential,
so much that he harps on this wherever he gets a chance — even
with the danger of falsifying the true picture or making mistak-
en accusations. This may account for the embarrassing fact that
as much as he lauds the Christian faith for fitting his own premises, he does not always tell us exactly what he means by Christian
faith, nor does he give us sufficient impression that he is really intimately familiar with the secular aspects of the understanding of
man to be in a position to pass his usually harsh judgments upon
them. This creates certain problems of which we may briefly mention some.

We should never forget that in spite of Reinhold Niebuhr's
ever-growing sensitivity to God's reality and activity through man
in this world which has provoked his interest in a more sweeping
than precise understanding of history, he never really changed
his primary if not exclusive interest in the nature and destiny of
man. The book under discussion sharpens the foregoing thesis
as none of his previous works had ever done.

It is not without significance that Niebuhr credits Martin Buber at the outset of his own book. Very much like Buber, Niebuhr would like to posit the human self as a unique agency in order to have it act and react in its environmental setting. But this is neither theologically nor scientifically proper or useful.

Theologically, the human self is constituted and kept alive by its experiencing itself as a unique and concrete life-expression of God's self-realization in this world. Not that God and man are thereby identified or indiscernibly merged. Nevertheless, whenever the human self is theoretically conceived as either apart from this God-man relationship or prior to it, then the Christian faith claims that we really speak of either an illusory or distorted self-awareness which, by postulating its independence, actually destroys it and, in turn, has the Promethean destructive influence to which Niebuhr is so eager to refer. The true selfhood of man lies in our grateful and joyful acknowledgment that through God's sovereign dwelling in us we are set free to build our own images — be they of ourself, the world, or God.

Original sin is a theological term for that peculiar but constant temptation of man to establish his selfhood in competition with his true nature as it is given by God and that is able to be fulfilled within its own appropriate limitations. Knowing of this, Niebuhr nevertheless is at least guilty of not making it expressly clear, which is evident in his utterly deficient understanding of the Holy Spirit.

From the same mistaken concept of the self stems his inability to differentiate clearly between sin as being exclusively the separation between God and man and its secondary symptoms in man's behavior. Only the latter can be phenomenologically investigated and subjected to any moral or ethical evaluation.

"Self-love," if one should even continue to use this highly ambiguous and misleading term, is not sin — original or otherwise. Nor is it a mere bad habit of man. Niebuhr and other theologians could greatly profit from listening patiently to psychopathologists who make clear to us that undue self-concern is the symptom for a far more profound lack of self-realization and self-confidence. After we have studied how this originates from not being appropriately or sufficiently loved, then we may be ready to reflect upon the theological rootage of such a phenomenon.

When we formulate our theological or philosophical insights and conclusions in scientific terms, then we run the risk of clashing with the experimental scientists who may tell us that their findings contradict our conclusions. In turn, they should not be tempted to exceed phenomenological results and trespass with their own inadequate conclusions into spheres where the explanation of either ultimate cause or future result is beyond the reach of their experimental means.

Basically, the controversy between the theologian, Niebuhr, and the scientist, Rogers, arises where on the part of the scientist the most fitting endeavor, to seek "for orderliness in man's inner nature or in his outer behavior," turns into wishful thinking that knowledge and the proper use of it will in itself eliminate man's need for a source and explanation of his life which is beyond himself. On the other hand, where the theologian is all too hasty to prove the identity between theological concepts and truth, he is tempted to blindly override better evidence instead of taking the burden of rethinking his own premises.

Without question, there is an orderliness in the human psyche, as much as it is constantly endangered by chaotic interference if not destruction. It would be utterly obsolete to even discuss this were it not for the fact that unlike stones and animals, human beings are able to interfere with their own or others' psychic structure. The fundamental reason for so doing may lie in a depth of which the theologian is meant to speak. Its expression with its psychological and environmental results is to be examined entirely objectively by the scientist whose own philosophical presuppositions should be recognized in order not to color unduly the evaluation of his own findings.

One might simply state the paradox of man's being at once creature and creator as most indicative that where man's being creature relates to his real Creator, then the avenue is open for his creative enjoyment and the application of his gifts without abusing or distorting them to achieve the impossible, namely, to posit himself as autonomous, unrelated creator. The latter robs him of the freedom to discover and accept orderliness where it can be found since it may point to the humbling experience that any such orderliness is not authored by us nor is to be exploited by us irresponsibly for our own desires. True human freedom is inseparably linked to genuine and thus self-confident humility, which usually is least available where one is under the compulsion to prove himself and his own ideas. Pastoral psychology can learn from Reinhold Niebuhr to be sensitive for the complexity of human nature and man's place in history, precisely since it is the place where God's wisdom is always above our thoughts but wants to reveal itself wherever we are open for the possibility of being enlightened and delighted by it. I cannot see at all why such a freedom should not allow us to be very unbiased students of secular understandings of man without falling prey to either their unconfessed philosophical premises or to sharing an equally unwarranted optimism or pessimism about man. The experience of those who do not derive their practical observations from preconceived theoretical notions, but conversely, realize the value of intellectual reflections and hypotheses on the basis of their concrete findings, has led them to seek a structured understanding of their insights. Nonetheless, they are open to the challenge to abandon outworn premises and to restructure their understanding in the light of better evidence. Like the incarnate God, proved to be the true God, since man came truly alive through him; so the quiet and unobtrusive truth surprises us always where we expect and like it least, we who are too much enamored of our own insights.

Concluding Comment

BY CARL ROGERS

I find myself much informed by the wise and thoughtful comments of Dr. Horton and Dr. Loomer. I am sure they are correct when they suggest that if I had a closer acquaintance with Dr. Niebuhr and with his other works, I would understand this book in a different way. They have helped me toward this understanding. I even found it interesting to learn that I am seen as a Pelagian. It is useful to know the labels for one's heresies.

I found myself less responsive to, and more puzzled by, Professor Hofmann's comments. I felt that in his world the scientist searches for the truth in the scientific area, and the theologian *has* the truth in the theological area. This must indeed be a comfortable world in which to live, but unfortunately for me, it is not the world I live in. Mine does not contain this built-in division, and I can see why he views me as an "outsider."

As to the major points at issue, I find three on which it might be helpful to present my own views. Horton, Loomer, and Hofmann agree that in his other and major writings Dr. Niebuhr sees an inevitable, permanent, irresolvable tension between the freedom and creativity of the individual on the one hand, and necessity, determinism, enslavement to environmental conditions on the other. I trust they are correct in this understanding of Niebuhr's thinking. The book under review seemed to me to try to resolve this tension in ways which, as I pointed out, were unsatisfying to me.

If this *is* Niebuhr's view, then we are closer than I thought in our conception of this issue. I would only change the adjectives. I would say that the freedom of man, experienced so vividly in psychotherapy, and the determined nature of man's behavior, evident so clearly in psychological research, exist today in a currently almost unnoticed, but certainly unresolved tension. I do not know if the contradiction is inevitable, or whether it is permanent. I tried to hold a place for both these elements of truth in my symposium (or was it a debate?) with B. F. Skinner, when I spoke of

the great paradox of behavioral science. Behavior, when it is examined scientifically, is surely best understood as determined by prior causation. This is one great fact of science. But responsible personal choice, which is the most essential element of being a person, which is the core experience in psychotherapy, which exists prior to any scientific endeavor, is an equally prominent fact in our lives. To deny the experience of responsible choice is, to me, as restricted a view as to deny the possibility of a behavioral science. That these two important elements of our experience appear to be in contradiction has perhaps the same significance as the contradiction between the wave theory and the corpuscular theory of light, both of which can be shown to be true, even though incompatible.

We cannot profitably deny our subjective life, any more than we can deny the objective description of that life.*

I do not know the resolution of this paradox. Contrary to Dr. Loomer's perception of my position, I hold that it is the subjective choice which is prior, and that

> we can choose to use the behavioral sciences in ways which will free, not control; which will bring about constructive variability, not conformity; which will ·develop creativity, not contentment; which will facilitate each person in his self-directed process of becoming; which will aid individuals, groups, and even the concept of science to become self-transcending in freshly adaptive ways of meeting life and its problems.†

I point out that a deterministic behavioral science can lead in these directions if it clearly recognizes its fundamental basis in personal, existential choice, and if it places its emphasis upon the process of becoming, not upon the achievement of end states.

To take up another point, Dr. Loomer quite soundly raises the question as to why clients undervalue themselves. He will not be fully satisfied with my answer, because it is not an absolute or theological answer. I can only report my thinking as far as my experience has carried me. The initial estrangement of the individual from himself — the experience which causes him to distrust and devalue himself, appears to follow this pattern. At some point the infant, to retain the love of his parent, takes over (introjects) the value placed on his experience by his parent, and deserts or distrusts his own organismic valuing of experience. This comes about because the love of his parent is conditional — "I will love you only if you place the same value (good or bad) on your experience that I do." As this distrusting of one's own valuing process is repeated countless times, the individual comes to distrust and scorn himself as a guide to life. All his criteria for attaching values to experience come confusedly from

---

*Rogers, Carl R., & Skinner, B. F. "Some issues concerning the control of human behavior." *Science*, 1956, Vol. 124, 1057–1066.
†Ibid.

others. His feelings, which are the best index of his own valuing process, are denied awareness, and he is now a man divided, estranged from self, or, to use the term I would be more likely to use, psychologically maladjusted. As one partial index to the accuracy of this formulation, it appears clear that the more unconditional the love which the person has received as infant and child, the more secure he is in trusting his own experiencing as a guide by which to live, and the more creative is his adjustment. I am not sure that this highly abbreviated statement of my views will do more than create confusion, but readers may pursue the issue further in more extended writings if they wish.*

Let me bring in one further aspect of my thinking. It disturbs me to be thought of as an optimist. My whole professional experience has been with the dark and often sordid side of life, and I know, better than most, the incredibly destructive behavior of which man is capable. Yet that same professional experience has forced upon me the realization that man, when you know him deeply, in his worst and most troubled states, is not evil or demonic. I tried to express this in a recent article.

> The basic nature of the human being, when functioning freely, is constructive and trustworthy. For me this is an inescapable conclusion from a quarter-century of experience in psychotherapy. When we are able to free the individual from defensiveness, so that he is open to the wide range of his own needs, as well as the wide range of environmental and social demands, his reactions may be trusted to be positive, forward-moving, constructive. We do not need to ask who will socialize him, for one of his own deepest needs is for affiliation and communication with others. As he becomes more fully himself, he will become more realistically socialized. We do not need to ask who will control his aggressive impulses; for as he becomes more open to all of his impulses, his need to be liked by others and his tendency to give affection will be as strong as his impulses to strike out or to seize for himself. He will be aggressive in situations in

---

*Rogers, Carl R. *Client-Centered Therapy*. Boston: Houghton Mifflin, 1951, chapter 11.

which aggression is realistically appropriate, but there will be no runaway need for aggression. His total behavior, in these and other areas, as he moves toward being open to all his experience, will be more balanced and realistic, behavior which is appropriate to the survival and enhancement of a highly social animal.

I have little sympathy with the rather prevalent concept that man is basically irrational, and that his impulses, if not controlled, will lead to destruction of others and self. Man's behavior is exquisitely rational, moving with subtle and ordered complexity toward the goals his organism is endeavoring to achieve. The tragedy for most of us is that our defenses keep us from being aware of this rationality, so that consciously we are moving in one direction, while organismically we are moving in another. But in our person who is living the process of the good life, there would be a decreasing number of such barriers, and he would be increasingly a participant in the rationality of his organism. The only control of impulses which would exist, or which would prove necessary, is the natural and internal balancing of one need against another, and the discovery of behaviors which follow the vector most closely approximating the satisfaction of all needs. The experience of extreme satisfaction of one need (for aggression, or sex, etc.) in such a way as to do violence to the satisfaction of other needs (for companionship, tender relationships, etc.) — an experience very common in the defensively organized person — would be greatly decreased. He would participate in the vastly complex self-regulatory activities of his organism — the psychological as well as physiological thermostatic controls — in such a fashion as to live in increasing harmony with himself and with others.*

It will be clear, I hope, that I have not tried to argue with Dr. Niebuhr or with those who have commented on my views of his work. I have simply tried to set forth my own tentative views on three issues which seem crucial to this whole discussion. The first is the issue of freedom and determinism which phrases itself anew in every era, but with an urgency which never dims. The second is the issue as to the origin of man's difficulties —

---

*Rogers, Carl R. "A therapist's view of the good life." *The Humanist*, 1957, No. 17, 299–300.

whether it is an original, inherent "sin," or whether its source lies in man's human environment. The third is the question as to the basic characteristics of man. It is my hope that the reader will, from reading Dr. Niebuhr's book and the various comments which have flowed from it, find himself impelled to formulate his own thoughts on these issues.

9
Rollo May

Rollo Reece May was born in Ada, Ohio, in 1909. His father was a YMCA field secretary, and May grew up in a household infused with Victorian and Methodist traditions. He attended Michigan State for two years, then completed his B.A. in English in 1930. Having minored in Greek history and literature, he spent the next three years teaching English at Anatolia College, in Salonika, Greece. During two of these summers he visited Vienna, where he attended seminars with pioneering psychoanalyst Alfred Adler and took painting lessons with Joseph Binder.

In 1933 he enrolled in Union Theological Seminary in New York City in order, as he later said, "to ask ultimate questions about human beings — not to be a preacher." After a year at Union, he returned to Ohio for two years for family reasons, and supported himself, his younger brother, and his sister by working as a counselor to male students at Michigan State. Returning to Union, he studied under Paul Tillich and earned his divinity degree in 1938. Becoming a preacher after all, he spent two years as minister in a Congregational parish in Verona, New Jersey. His first two books, *The Art of Counseling* (1939) and *Springs of Creative Living: A Study of Human Nature and God* (1940) came out of this period.

May's eclectic background in the classics, religion, and counseling took on new meaning when he contracted tuberculosis in his early thirties and was given a fifty-fifty chance of survival. For the next decade he confronted this disease and the reality of death. He wrote, "I learned to tune in on my being, my existence in the *now.* . . . It was a valuable experience to face death, for in the experience I learned to face life."

Confronting his own existential anxiety and dissatisfied with the limitations of the ministry for helping his troubled parishioners, May enrolled in Columbia University to study clinical psychology and eventually earned his Ph.D., summa cum laude, in 1949. His dissertation on *The Meaning of Anxiety* (1950) argued that anxiety was not always a negative phenomenon, but was a normal response of the individual to personal peril and social upheaval. Confronted honestly, it could lead to richer, more authentic living.

For the rest of his life, May built on these early insights, along with his understanding of Kierkegaard, Nietzsche, Camus, and Tillich, to eventually become "the best-known and most eloquent practitioner of existentialist psychotherapy." Writing of his eighteen-month stay in a tuberculosis sanitarium in Saranac Lake, New York, he said, "The patients who were gay and hopeful and tried to make light of the disease frequently died. Those of us who lived with it, accepted it, struggled against it, recovered. Whether or not I lived or died depended not on the doctors or medicine but on me." For May, it was in the individual's "will," his intentionality, that hope for recovery lay. It was the analyst's role to help the patient confront the ultimate questions of life, death, and meaning and to find the courage to choose health — that is, life.

May's primary professional association was with the William Alanson White Institute of Psychiatry, Psychoanalysis and Psychology in New York, where he joined the faculty in 1948, became the training and supervisory analyst in 1958, and remained until his move to California in 1975. During this period he had a steady private practice of psychoanalysis and also lectured frequently and widely at the New School for Social Research, Yale, Harvard, Cornell, Princeton, and many other universities. On the personal side, he was married from 1938 to 1969 and again from 1971 to 1975, with three children from his first marriage. As one reviewer described him: "Lean, bespectacled, with brown eyes and longish grey hair, he is professional in manner, almost theatrically good-looking."

May presented his existential viewpoint in many popular books published from the 1950s on, including *Man's Search for Himself* (1953), *Existence: A New Dimension in Psychiatry and Psychology* (co-editor, 1958) for a professional audience, *Existential Psychology* (1961), *Psychology and the Human Dilemma* (1966), *Love and Will* (1969), *Power and Innocence* (1972), *Freedom and Destiny* (1981), and *My Quest for Beauty* (1985). Drawing on Greek mythology, world literature, philosophy, art, and religion for examples and metaphors — or as one critic wrote, using his "close reading of those classics which were once part of the common background of the educated Western reader" — May related the clinical experience of psychotherapy to the everyday and perennial concerns of humans and society. So effective was his writing and so pertinent his observations, he became (along with his own psychoanalyst, Erich Fromm) one of the most widely read American psychologists of the last half of the century.

His own description of the William Alanson White Institute, where he worked for almost thirty years, might well summarize May's own career: "I prize the openness of the institute which . . . crosses the boundaries of narrow professionalism, and is broad enough to encompass humanistic and existential psychotherapy along with the stricter forms of psychoanalysis." May, too, was steeped in the traditions of psychoanalysis, yet along with Carl Rogers, Abraham Maslow, and others, was a founder of the Association for Humanistic Psychology in the early 1960s. He is widely regarded as one of America's leading thinkers on individual and social psychology in the broadest sense.

The following written exchange between Rollo May and Carl Rogers begins with a 1959 review Rogers wrote of May et al.'s *Existence: A New Dimension in Psychiatry and Psychology*. Next, and twenty-two years later, is Rogers's brief commentary on Rollo May for *Perspectives*, the journal of the Humanistic Psychology Institute, in a special issue that was devoted to May's work. May responded to this commentary in "An Open Letter to Carl Rogers," published in the *Journal of Humanistic Psychology*, and Rogers, in turn, answered May in the same publication.

The Way to Do Is to Be

REVIEW BY CARL ROGERS

Rollo May, Ernest Angel, and Henri F. Ellenberger (Eds.), Existence: A New Dimension in Psychiatry and Psychology. *New York: Basic Books, 1958.*

If this book is fully and deeply understood, it is likely to disturb American psychologists, both clinicians and experimentalists. For though its overt purpose is simply to present existential psychotherapy as it has emerged spontaneously and independently in a number of European countries, it has two additional purposes which have deeper implications.*

It is trying to show first of all the kind of therapy which (largely developed by analysts) is gradually supplanting psychoanalysis in Europe. Since psychoanalysis has only in recent years been adopted as the basic creed of clinical psychologists in this country, it cannot help but be upsetting to discover that in its place of origin it is already giving way to the next wave of thought and practice.

Even more challenging is the second underlying purpose, which is to raise insistent and critical questions about our allegiance to positivism as the be-all and end-all of psychological science. Existentialism in its psychological ramifications is pictured as "the endeavor to understand man by cutting below the cleavage between subject and object which has bedeviled Western thought and science since shortly after the Renaissance." Instead of this cleavage existentialism attempts to place science in a broader context of humanistic philosophy in which man as an emerging person is always in central focus. Thus in one stroke May (and to a lesser extent his co-editors) is challenging the favorite theory of therapy of the clinicians, as well as the settled dogma of logical positivism so close to the hearts of our scientists.

Since these deeper questions are not the outward concern of the book, but simply represent its underlying intellectual and emotional current, let me turn first to the manner in which the volume meets its more obvious purpose, that of acquainting us with the new philosophical, theoretical, and practical trends which are now evident in European psychotherapy. Rollo May leads off with two long but excellent chapters on existentialism and its significance in and contributions to psychological and psychotherapeutic thinking. These are followed by a somewhat more technical and definitely more academic picture, by Ellenberger, of the historical development of the phenomenological point of view in psychiatric and psychological work, and its absorption into an existentialist orientation in psychotherapy. The remaining two-thirds of the book is taken up with translations of articles and case reports by several representatives of existential psychotherapy, with Ludwig Binswanger of Switzerland accounting for the lion's share of this section.

The two chapters by May, in my opinion, are exceptional. They give evidence of profound scholarship and wisdom. They are clear and penetrating. They show why a new point of view developed in psychotherapy — in the minds of different men, in different places, at about the same time — in answer to the most deeply felt deficiency in Freudian psychoanalysis, namely its theory of man, its view of him. In the terminology of the book, psychoanalysis was most helpful and most effective in its understanding of the *Umwelt* — man in his biological relationship to his environment, his "world around." It has been less helpful in providing us with an understanding of his *Mitwelt*, the "with-world" of his relationship to his fellow men. (Here Sullivan and Horney have in their own ways endeavored to remedy this deficiency.) But the greatest lack has been in the comprehension of the *Eigenwelt* — the "own world" of relationship to one's self. It is here that existentialism and the psychotherapy which has utilized this philosophy pinpoint their contribution.

Before endeavoring to describe this contribution, May gives a brilliant but brief interpretation of existentialism, studded with quotable statements. He shows it as having distant historical roots, extending back at least to Laotzu (d. 531 B.C.). ("The way to do is to *be*." "Rather abide at the center of your being; for

the more you leave it, the less you learn.") He traces it through
Kierkegaard and his concern with the estrangement of the individual from himself, his passionate pursuit of the problem of
how to become an individual, and his belief that a science which
is independent of man — completely objective — is an illusion.
He analyzes Nietzsche's contribution, that every truth should be
faced with the question, "Can one live it?" He adds his own view.
("Existentialism is an attitude which accepts man as always becoming, which means potentially in crisis.") He even, surprisingly
enough, adds Norbert Wiener of cybernetics fame to the list. ("It
is the greatest possible victory to be, and to have been. No defeat
can deprive us of the success of having existed for some moment
of time in a universe that seems indifferent to us.")

Building on such philosophical views, existential psychotherapy is concerned with what makes man an emerging *human* being. It sees neurosis and maladjustment as behaviors which destroy man's capacity to fulfill his own being. Anxiety occurs when
some emerging potentiality faces the individual and threatens his
security. Transference is seen in a new context as an event occurring in a *real* relationship between two people. The remembrance
of the individual's past is determined by what he has chosen to
become. Truth (and hence insight) exists only as the individual
produces it in action, lives it. The aim of therapy is more fundamental than cure. It is to help the individual experience himself
and his existence as real. These are a few of the characteristics of
an existential form of psychotherapy as it is presented in this volume.

To carry on therapy in these terms involves an understanding
of the person in his world. "Existential analysis treats the patient's utterances quite seriously. . . . [It] refuses absolutely to
examine pathological expressions with a view to seeing whether
they are bizarre, absurd, illogical, or otherwise defective; rather
it attempts to understand the particular world of experience to
which these experiences point and how this world is formed and
how it falls apart." Much of the material in the translated articles
is given over to the attempts to reconstruct and to understand
from within the structure of the world in which the individual
lives, the structure of his existence.

Another emphasis is that which May puts upon full human

presence. One has the impression that Martin Buber's description of an "I-Thou" relationship is close to what is meant by the term *presence.* Frieda Fromm-Reichmann he quotes with approval — her statement that "the patient needs an *experience,* not an explanation." It is expected that the relationship with the therapist is the meeting of two live, real, human beings, with the therapist fully present to his client. This situation is at the farthest pole from the therapist as an expert, analyzing the patient as an object. It is a living together in communication that breaks the isolation of the patient.

Perhaps the foregoing paragraphs give a hint or a suggestion of the form of therapy toward which May sees the professional world tending. As we pass beyond psychoanalysis, we may be moving into this more person-centered type of therapy in which both the therapist and the patient with whom he works appear as individuals who are becoming, who are trying to realize their potentialities.

If we are to ask how May sees the "wave of the future" insofar as logical positivism is concerned, then the answer is less clear. The existential psychotherapists certainly do not give up the positivist point of view in science. In the *Umwelt,* in the relationship of man to his environment, they are, he says, complete determinists. But they think it a serious error to deal with human beings as though their only mode of existence were the *Umwelt.* They believe that it is possible to have a science of man which neither fragments him nor destroys his humanity as it studies him. They see human choice and decision as real and significant in man's relation to himself, and they are firmly opposed to the view of man as an "empty organism," as a passive recipient of forces acting upon him. They regard themselves as more empirical than the positivists, because they are open to all of the actual phenomena of human existence, whereas positivism is limited to tunnel vision.

If this hint of a new science is illustrated by the translated articles, then the picture is a disappointing one. For the most part the thinking is ponderous, the analyses reminiscent of Freudian thinking in their complete avoidance of statements which can be checked. They are, indeed, less heavily burdened with conceptual baggage, as they try to reconstruct the world of the individual rather than fit him into preconceived theoretical constructs. Nevertheless, if this is an example of what psychological science is to be, the act does not live up to its billing.

Much the same can be said for the translations when they are viewed from the clinical angle. The most ambitious is Binswanger's account of the case of Ellen West. She lived, was treated and mistreated by psychiatrists and analysts, was hospitalized, diagnosed, discharged, until finally she committed suicide, before the days of existential psychotherapy. Now Binswanger resurrects her case and reanalyzes it in terms of his current thinking. His reconstruction of Ellen's psychological world is fantastically detailed, but the reanalysis is almost as discouraging as the original handling by Kraepelin, Bleuler, Binswanger, and unnamed others. The author is to be commended for being so brutally frank in presenting a case which was incredibly mishandled. When, however, his final conclusion is that, with the best of his thinking now and the best of modern methods, "it could have been merely a question of postponing the final catastrophe," I cannot but reject his conclusions with some vehemence.

This is a book which gives a compelling hint of what is coming in psychological therapy and psychological science. When it attempts to present the writings of current European psychotherapists as fulfillment of these prophetic hints, then the account is disappointing. While the volume has performed a worthwhile function in making us aware of an important and growing trend, while it will stimulate discussion and debate, nevertheless its initial promise is scarcely fulfilled. In view of the brilliance and depth of the early chapters, I would like to ask Rollo May the time-worn question, "Why don't you speak for yourself, Rollo?" His answer might be even better than this book.

NOTES ON ROLLO MAY

BY CARL ROGERS

I think of Rollo as the leading scholar of humanistic psychology. He is well read, deeply informed, and has developed a wisdom which is evident in his writings.

He has always been critical of trends in humanistic psychology which lead toward trivial or unexamined goals. He has wanted the field to have depth, and to be respected for a high quality of philosophical and theoretical thought. In pursuit of this purpose he was one of the initiators of the Tucson conference on theory in humanistic psychology in 1975. This proved to be a stimulating conference for those present, and Rollo was one of its leading figures. It is almost impossible to evaluate the long-range impact of such a conference. During the experience I felt there was a moderate amount of "one-upsmanship," and not too much clarity of communication. But the highly diverse points of view from such individuals as Gregory Bateson, Jonas Salk, Huston Smith, have, I know, left their mark on me, and this is doubtless true of the others present. Rollo deserves much credit for this enterprise.

I remember with pleasure the seminar Rollo conducted for the Department of Psychiatry at the University of Wisconsin, about 1960, when I was a member of that department. It was part of a series of sessions, each extending over several days, in which we became acquainted with the person, the theories, and the therapeutic practice of a number of different leaders in the field. Rollo did not disappoint us, and it was a pleasure for me to have him stay in my home.

I suppose my major difference with Rollo is around the question of the nature of the human individual. He sees the demonic as a basic element in the human makeup, and dwells upon this in his writing. For myself, though I am very well aware of the incredible amount of destructive, cruel, malevolent behavior in

Perspectives, Summer 1981, Vol. 2, No. 1, Special Issue; Rollo May: Man and Philosopher.

today's world — from the threats of war to the senseless violence in the streets — I do not find that this evil is inherent in human nature. In a psychological climate which is nurturant of growth and choice, I have never known an individual to choose the cruel or destructive path. Choice always seems to be in the direction of greater socialization, improved relationships with others. So my experience leads me to believe that it is cultural influences which are the major factor in our evil behaviors. The rough manner of childbirth, the infant's mixed experience with the parents, the constricting, destructive influence of our educational system, the injustice of our distribution of wealth, our cultivated prejudices against individuals who are different — all these elements and many others warp the human organism in directions which are antisocial. So I see members of the human species, like members of other species, as *essentially* constructive in their fundamental nature, but damaged by their experience. The life of the individual is also partially shaped by his or her choices, and as we can readily observe, those choices may be in the direction of inflicting hurt on others or on the self. Nevertheless, if we can provide a growth-promoting climate, the choices prove to be, quite freely and spontaneously, in a socially constructive direction. I cannot see how this could be true if human nature contained an inherently evil element. So Rollo and I continue to differ on this point.

One of Rollo's major contributions has been his bringing of existential philosophy and psychotherapy into the realm of American psychology. In doing so he challenged conventional psychoanalysis and its mode of therapy. He also was one of the first to undercut the thinking of the logical positivism which at that time was so important in psychological science. His book *Existence* (1958) was a most significant volume, and the best chapters in it were not those of the European existentialists, but the presentation and interpretation of that point of view by Rollo himself.

I like to think that I had some part in building Rollo's confidence in expressing his own thinking as original, not as something derivative. In my review of *Existence*, written in 1959, a year after the book's publication, I pointed out the superiority of Rollo's chapters to those of any of the other contributors, and I closed my review by asking the time-worn question, "Why don't you speak for yourself, Rollo?" In my estimation he has increasingly done so. This has greatly benefited humanistic psychology and psychotherapy, the human potential movement, and also the organization of those interests in the Association for Humanistic Psychology.

THE PROBLEM OF EVIL: AN OPEN LETTER TO CARL ROGERS

BY ROLLO MAY

Dear Carl:

Your letter published in the special issue of *Perspectives* (Rogers, 1981) discussed my contribution to humanistic psychology, and I very much appreciate what you wrote. You do me honor in many ways.

You also went on to point out your major differences with me concerning the problem of evil.

As you rightly say, "The presence of terrorism, hostility, and aggression are urgent in our day." I would add that the importance of our confronting these issues is crucial. Central among these destructive forces is the possibility — or probability, as many people believe — of nuclear war and the related threat of nuclear radiation. A recent Gallup poll shows that seven out of ten people in this country believe a nuclear war will actually occur, or that there is a good chance that it will occur, within the next ten years (*Newsweek*, October 5, 1981, p. 35). It seems obvious that if we cannot deal constructively with the threat in atomic power and the terrorism that goes with it, our civilization will die like those of the ancient Romans, Assyrians, Egyptians, and Greeks.

You wrote, Rollo "sees the demonic as a basic element in the human makeup and dwells upon this in his writing." You contrasted this with your own view, "that it is cultural influences which are the major factor in our evil behaviors. . . . So I see

Journal of Humanistic Psychology, Vol. 22, No. 3, Summer 1982, 10–21. Copyright © 1982 Association for Humanistic Psychology.

members of the human species . . . as *essentially* constructive in their fundamental nature, but damaged by their experience." (Rogers, 1981, p. 16).

It is difficult to write this letter because of my affection for you and our long friendship. But the problem of evil is so crucial that it is imperative that we see it clearly. I shall therefore try to clarify my own position not only for our personal purposes but to help readers confront these problems themselves, for the sake not only of ourselves but our children and our future world. I agree with the statement of Edmund Burke: "The only thing necessary for the triumph of evil is for good men to do nothing."

1. In the first place, I never use the word *demonic*, except to say that this is *not* what I mean. My term is *daimonic*, which is critically different. I quote from *Love and Will*, the book in which I write most on this topic: "The daimonic is the urge in every being to affirm itself, assert itself, perpetuate and increase itself . . . [the reverse side] of the same affirmation is what empowers our creativity" (May, 1969, p. 123).

Thus I am stating that I see the human being as an organized bundle of potentialities. These potentialities, driven by the daimonic urge, are the source *both* of our constructive and our destructive impulses. If the daimonic urge is integrated into the personality (which is, to my mind, the purpose of psychotherapy) it results in creativity, that is, it is constructive. If the daimonic is not integrated, it can take over the total personality, as it does in violent rage or collective paranoia in time of war or compulsive sex or oppressive behavior. Destructive activity is then the result.

You and I have seen many cases in therapy with adolescents who are accused by their parents of being destructive when they are really only trying to establish their own independence, their own self-assertion, and indeed their own right. If we undercut the daimonic, as many therapists do, we do a disservice to our clients. I believe Rilke was right when he wrote, "If my devils are to leave me, I am afraid my angels will take flight as well."

It is true that the concept of the daimonic gives a rationale for demonic activity just as it gives a rationale for creativity. This may be why you describe me (I think wrongly) as writing about the demonic.

2. In your letter you acknowledge the evil surrounding us. You say, "I am very well aware of the incredible amount of destructive, cruel, malevolent behavior in today's world — from the threats of war to the senseless violence in the streets." But you say that you "believe that it is cultural influences which are the major factor in our evil behaviors."

This makes culture the enemy. But who makes up the culture except persons like you and me? You write about "the destructive influence of our educational system, the injustice of our distribution of wealth." But who is responsible for this destructive influence and injustice, except you and me and people like us? The culture is not something made by fate and foisted upon us.

Obviously the culture is a great boon as well as a source of evil. We could say, as well, that the fact that we have an educational system at all and the fact that we have an economic system at all are themselves results of our culture. It takes culture to create self and self to create culture; they are the yin and yang of being human. There is no self except in interaction with a culture, and no culture that is not made up of selves.

True, any group does exert a conformist tendency toward those within it by virtue of the mutual expectations it establishes that make it a group. But this is only one element and it cannot account for the fact that human beings individually and en masse are able to turn into warmongers and individual or collective assassins. I propose that the evil in our culture is also the reflection of evil in ourselves, and vice versa.

You also write, in another context but on the same theme: "The persons of tomorrow . . . will be the ones capable of living in this new world, the outlines of which are still only dimly visible. But unless we blow ourselves up, that new world is inevitably coming, transforming our culture" (Rogers, 1980). But this very culture which you see as being "transformed" is what you also say may blow us up. The seven out of ten people who believe in the likelihood of a nuclear war are also the "persons of tomorrow," but they have a quite different point of view. They obviously do not believe in a new world "inevitably" coming, "transforming our culture." They see other facts: Some of them are aware that a single nuclear bomb dropped on Chicago would result in the deaths of 200,000 people. The United States at the end of this year will have approximately 2,400 more nuclear explosives than it did at the beginning of the year, at a cost of billions of dollars. Norman Cousins (1981), reviewing these facts, states: "A mammoth and deadly illiteracy has seized us." I would call it a collective psychosis, which has got us all in its lethal grip, and we find it attractive enough to participate in it. There is no preordained reason our society should "inevitably" survive or disintegrate as did Rome and Greece and Egypt. What about the "good" in their members? Whether we survive or not depends upon whether you and I and millions like us can and will act to change our destructive directions.

The culture is evil as well as good because we, the human beings who constitute it, are evil as well as good. Our culture is partially destructive because we, as human beings who live in it, are partially destructive, whether we be Russians or Japanese or Germans or Americans.

You have also written on the new world toward which you believe we are moving:

> This new world will be more human and humane. It will explore and develop the richness and capacities of the human mind and spirit. It will produce individuals who are more integrated and whole. . . . It will be a more natural world, with a renewed love and respect for nature. . . . Its technology will be aimed at the enhancing, rather than the exploitation, of persons and nature. It will release creativity, as individuals sense their power, their capacities, their freedom.
>
> The winds of scientific, social and cultural change are blowing strongly. They will envelop us in this new world. . . . We may choose it, but whether we choose it or not, it appears that to some degree it is inexorably moving to change our culture (Rogers, 1980, p. 356).

You paint a seductive and enticing picture, and anyone would like to believe it. But I recall the words of Warren Bennis in the film of you and him, when he characterized your viewpoint as "devilishly innocent."

How do you square this "human and humane" world you predict with the fact (Yankelovich, 1981, p. 184) that the suicide rate in this country has gone up 171 percent in the last thirty years? Most of this great increase is among young people in their teens and early twenties; how can one tell them that their world explores "the richness and capacities of the human mind and spirit"? What about the fact (Yankelovich, 1981, p. 182) that major opinion polls, which showed in the early 1970s that only one in five Americans believed that "next year will be worse than this year," reveal now that a 55 percent majority has been forced into this pessimistic position? How can one talk to those people about releasing "creativity as individuals sense their power, their capacities, their freedom"?

In the 1950s and up to the late 1960s, most Americans believed that the present was superior to the past and that the future would improve on the present. By 1978 this pattern had wholly reversed itself, a "truly historic shift away from optimism to bleakness" (Yankelovich, 1981, p. 183). These "people of tomorrow" do not find the world "enhancing" their "persons and nature."

I wonder also how you square your statements with the famous Milgram (1969) experiments at Yale? You recall that Milgram took subjects from every walk of life (they answered an ad and were paid $4.00 an hour). The purpose of the experiment, as stated to each subject, was to teach the "learner" behind a glass partition by means of giving him electric shocks when he gave the wrong response. But the experiment was actually designed to see how far human beings would go in increasing the voltage to punish the learner for his mistakes. Subjects were told by Milgram to increase the voltage as they went through the experiment.

The results, which shocked Milgram as well as the rest of us who read about them, were that over 60 percent of the people willingly turned the electric current up to a voltage that they knew would kill the person on the other side of the glass partition. Milgram (1969, p. 178) writes that his studies "are principally concerned with ordinary and routine destruction carried out by everyday people following orders." Milgram points out that his results are similar to the phenomena uncovered in the trial of Lt. Calley for his actions at My Lai in the Vietnam war, when women, children, and old men were slaughtered in cold blood by American soldiers when commanded to do so by Lt. Calley.

How also do you deal with Philip Zimbardo's (1973) "prison" experiment at Stanford? You will remember that Zimbardo and his associates divided his psychology class of students into "guards" and "inmates" and had them go through a prison period, planned to last two weeks, in the basement of a building. He found that the "prisoners" began to taunt the "guards" and that the guards would taunt back, and soon the guards were striking the prisoners with clubs. The real violence became so destructive that Zimbardo, to his surprise and chagrin, had to stop the experiments after one week.

These students had no particular enmity toward each other to begin with. They were middle-class persons like you and me and our colleagues, and they certainly would have fit your category of "people of tomorrow." But they had a capacity for destructiveness that became, without much provocation, an evil acted out in reality. The evil possibilities were just beneath the surface. Philip Zimbardo, like Stanley Milgram, is a psychologist of stature who was simply trying to find out the possibilities in human beings for destructiveness and self-control.

Yes, the culture admittedly has powerful effects upon us. But it could not have these effects were these tendencies not already present in us, for, I repeat, we constitute the culture. When we project our tendencies toward evil on the culture — as we do when we repress the daimonic — the evil becomes the culture's fault, not ours. Then we don't experience the blow to our narcissism that owning our own evil would entail.

If you conclude that the trouble lies in the fact that human beings are so susceptible to influence by their culture, so obedient to orders they are given, so pliable to their environment, then you are making the most devastating of all judgments on evil in human beings. In such a case we are all sheep, dependent upon whoever is the shepherd; and Fred Skinner is right. But I do not think you believe that and neither do I.

True, I could cite as many incidents of heroic and altruistic behavior, as after the recent plane crash in Washington, D.C. I am not arguing that we human beings are only evil. I am arguing that we are bundles of both evil and good potentialities.

3. Let us turn to the question of evil as we experience it in our own field, that of psychotherapy. You will recall your own

important experiment, continuing over three years, on client-centered therapy with schizophrenics at the Veterans Administration Hospital in Madison, Wisconsin, some twenty years ago (Rogers, Gendlin, Kiesler, & Truax, 1967). You will also recall that I was chosen as one of the twelve judges, who were experienced and practicing therapists, to assess that therapy.

After listening to the tapes you sent me, I reported that, while I felt the therapy was good on the whole, there was one glaring omission. This was that the client-centered therapists did not (or could not) deal with the angry, hostile, negative — that is, evil — feelings of the clients. It turned out that the other judges, by and large, pointed out the same thing. I quote from the summary written by you and your colleagues of this whole experiment:

> Particularly striking was the observation by all the theorists that the client-centered process of therapy somehow avoids the expected and usual patient expressions of negative, hostile, or aggressive feelings. The clear implication is that the client-centered therapist for some reason seems less open to receiving negative, hostile, or aggressive feelings. Is it that the therapists have little respect for, or understanding of their own negative, hostile, or aggressive feelings, and are thus unable to receive these feelings from the patient? Do they simply "not believe in" the importance of negative feelings? (Rogers et al., 1967, p. 503)

One of your students, Nathaniel Raskin (1978, p. 367), quotes my report as it was discussed in that book:

> Rollo May, as one of the outside experts in the Wisconsin study, "sometimes got the feeling there were not two people in the room. . . . A consequence of a misuse of the reflecting techniques . . . [is] that we get only an amorphous kind of identity rather than two subjects interacting *in a world in which both participate, and in which love and hate, trust and doubt, conflicts and dependence, come out and can be understood and assimilated.*" May was concerned that the therapist's overidentification with the patient could "take away the patient's opportunity to experience himself as a subject in his own right, to take a stand against the therapist, to experience being in an interpersonal world."

In spite of the fact that "client-centered therapists, both individually and collectively, have advocated openness and freedom in the therapeutic relationship," the outside judges focused "upon what they perceive as the therapist's rigid and controlling nature which closes him off to many of his own as well as to the patient's experiences" (Rogers et al., 1967, p. 503).

This same student, who has since become a therapist in his own right, adds some notes about his own experience. I realize that our students develop in their own way, and you and I cannot be responsible for them. But Raskin's (1978, p. 366) comments on his own experience are so relevant to the issues here that I ask your permission to quote it: "I used the early concept of the client-centered therapist to bolster the inhibition of my anger, my aggression etc. I got some feedback at that time that it was difficult for people, because I was so nice, to tell me things that were *not* nice, and that it was hard for people to get angry at *me*." He then goes on to say that he needed to find some new ways within the client-centered approach to take in other phenomena, which I have called the "negative, hostile and aggressive feelings."

I find it important in therapy that the patient be able to take a stand against me, the therapist. This is in accord with what Raskin said, that he realized he was taking something away from the patient when he was "too nice, too much identifying with the other person." What he was taking away was the patient's possibility of becoming independent. Patients' anger is an essential part of their motivation in their assertion of individual steps toward psychological health. The anger of the therapist can also be a powerful aid in helping patients experience what effect their behavior has on their relationships in general.

This means that aspects of evil — anger, hostility against the therapist, destructiveness — need to be brought out in therapy. Personal autonomy occurs not by avoiding evil, but by directly confronting it. Therapists need to be able to perceive and admit their own evil — hostility, aggression, anger — if they are to be able to see and accept these experiences in clients.

I am quite ready to believe that it would be impossible for anybody to sit down in a therapeutic hour with you and not be affected for good by it. But every patient does have the possibility to destroy himself or herself, and some patients will destroy themselves no matter how much or how well you and I work with them. You illustrate this when you speak of the trouble you had with a schizophrenic woman in Chicago.

4. I want to return to the question of inevitable cultural transformation. You write that this "new world" that you describe is "inevitably coming," and later you remark that the new world is "inexorably moving to change our culture." How can you be so certain? There are countless scenarios that can be written as predictions of our future. The persons who committed suicide, mentioned above, lived and died in entirely different scenarios from yours, and the polls indicate that the majority of citizens in our country would also write very different predictions. The scenarios I take seriously are those that see the evil in humankind's development as well as the good.

You also write that "we may choose [this cultural change], but whether we choose it or not, it will still happen." Do you mean it will take place regardless of whether we do anything about it? This sounds like Fred Skinner again: The environment will force us into this brave new world whether we want it or not!

As with Skinner's viewpoint, your statement that it will come regardless of what we humans do about it cuts the nerve of social action. A danger of which I am very aware is that people, hypnotically seduced by rosy predictions of the future, will conclude that it requires no effort from them and will sit back and do nothing. This, as Edmund Burke said so well, is the quickest way for evil to triumph.

There are innumerable issues that cry out for our awareness and our energies, quite in addition to the imminence of nuclear war. There is, for one, the food crunch and the problem of hunger. The President's Commission on World Hunger, 1980, stated that there are more ill-fed people on our planet than ever before, amounting to 800,000,000 (not counting the Communist countries). The number is growing and, as the available food lessens, will approach panic proportions by the year 2000. This includes hundreds of thousands of children who are starving and millions more who go to bed every night hungry. This includes fathers who walk the streets, their self-esteem eroded because they are unable to find work. It also includes despairing mothers who can do nothing but watch their children starve.

If we do get to a new world, it will only be by solving these problems first. If we don't, we will not have the new world you see coming: The price in human suffering will be too high.

5. In *Love and Will* I also wrote:

> It [the daimonic] constitutes a profound blow to our narcissism. We are the "nice" people and, like the cultivated citizens of Athens in Socrates' time, we don't like to be publicly reminded, whether we secretly admit it to ourselves or not, that we are motivated even in our love by lust for power, anger, and revenge. While the daimonic cannot be said to be evil in itself, it confronts us with the troublesome dilemma of whether it is to be used with awareness, a sense of responsibility and the significance of life, or blindly and rashly. . . . When the daimonic is repressed, it tends to *erupt* in some form — its extreme forms being assassination, the psychopathological tortures of the murders on the moors and other horrors we know only too well in this century.
>
> "Although we may recoil in horror," writes the British psychiatrist Anthony Storr, "when we read in newspapers or history books of the atrocities committed by man upon man, we know in our hearts that each one of us harbors within himself those same savage impulses which lead to murder, to torture and to war." (May, 1969, p. 129)

I am pleading for a realistic approach to human evil. A colleague tells me that when you had the discussion with Martin Buber in Michigan you said, "Man is basically good," and Buber answered, "Man is basically good — and evil." I am arguing that we must include a view of the evil in our world and in ourselves no matter how much that evil offends our narcissism.

When we can deal with this evil, then and only then what we say about goodness will have power and cogency. Then we can speak in ways that will genuinely affect our culture, in contrast to the miniscule number of people we see in our therapeutic offices.

You and I have often affirmed the capacities of human beings to be autonomous to some extent, to make decisions, to assert some freedom of choice in interrelationship with their destiny and their culture. These capacities put an added responsibility upon us to affirm realistically the anxiety involved, the precarious and limited nature of this freedom, and the fact that our belief in the human being can work for good only when the individual can face the world with all its inner and outer cruelty, its failure, and its tragedy.

The issue of evil — or rather, the issue of not confronting evil — has profound, and to my mind adverse, effects on humanistic psychology. I believe it is the most important error in the humanistic movement. Thus Yankelovich (1981) can say, in his book *New Rules* (which is concerned, as you and I are, with the persons of tomorrow), that humanistic psychology is the narcissism of our culture. I believe he is right. The narcissists are persons who are turned inward rather than outward, who are so lost in self-love that they cannot see and relate to the reality outside themselves, including other human beings. Some people who join and lead the humanistic movement do so in order to find a haven, a port in the storm, a community of like-minded persons who also are playing possum to the evils about us. I, for one, choose to be part of the minority that seeks to make the Association for Humanistic Psychology an organization that commits itself actively to confronting the issues of evil and good in our selves, our society, and our world.

In my experience, our human adventures from cradle to grave take on a zest, a challenge, an attractiveness when we see and affirm this human potentiality of both good and evil. The joy we experience will have, as its other pole, the self-assertion, the hostility, the negative possibilities that I have been talking about. In my experience it is this polarity, this dialectical interaction, this oscillation between positive and negative that gives the dynamic and the depth to human life. Life, to me, is not a requirement to live out a preordained pattern of goodness, but a challenge coming down through the centuries out of the fact that each of us can throw the lever toward good or toward evil. This seems to me to require the age-old religious truths of mercy and forgiveness and (here I am sure you would agree with me) it leaves no place for moral superiority or self-righteousness.

I recall that in my younger days in the middle 1930s I had a position as counselor at a midwestern college. The vocal portion of the students at this college were pacifists. We believed in the League of Nations and we felt certain that we needed only to outlaw war for the world to have peace. I remember looking at a professor who said that there would be another war as though he were a pariah. How wrong my colleagues and I were! We could not even believe what we read in the papers about the persecution of the Jews in Germany, just as people nowadays cannot believe what they read in the newspapers about nuclear bombs. The important point of this story is that Hitler capitalized on our noble but unrealistic ideals, and this, I believe, contributed to or at least hastened World War II. This is why I wrote in *Love and Will*: "Not to recognize the daimonic itself turns out to be daimonic; it makes us accomplices on the side of the destructive possession" (May, 1969, p. 131).

I am not predicting doom. But I am stating that if we ignore evil, we will move closer to doom, and the growth and triumph of evil may well result.

I am not a pessimist. Yes, I believe in tragedy, as Shakespeare's dramas and Eugene O'Neill and others portray it, because I perceive tragedy as showing the nobility of human existence. Without it life would be pallid, uninteresting, and flat. I smile when I note, in conversations with some of my so-called optimistic friends, that when we get down to fundamental issues such as the possibilities of atomic war or the coming food crunch, or the fact that this planet will in all probability be wiped out in a finite number of years, their optimism turns out to be a reaction formation to their hopelessness; and I turn out to be more hopeful than they. This is because, it seems to me, one needs a philosophy for oneself that can stand regardless of failure in our actions or temporary despair.

All of this goes to demonstrate again that the terms *optimism* and *pessimism* refer to the state of one's digestion, and have nothing whatever to do with truth.

I write this letter, dear Carl, with profound respect for you and your contribution in the past to all of us. If I speak strongly, it is because I believe strongly.

Yours,
Rollo May

REFERENCES

Cousins, N. Thoughts at year's end. *Saturday Review*. December 1981, p. 12.

May, R. *Love and will*. New York: Norton, 1969.

Milgram, S. *Obedience to authority*. New York: Harper & Row, 1969.

Raskin, N. Becoming — a therapist, a person, a partner, a parent. *Psychotherapy: Theory, Research and Practice*, 1978, 15(4).

Rogers, C. *A way of being*. Boston: Houghton Mifflin, 1980.

Rogers, C. Notes on Rollo May. *Perspectives*, 1981, 2(1).

Rogers, C., Gendlin, E., Kiesler, D., and Truax, C. *The therapeutic relationship with schizophrenics*. Madison: University of Wisconsin Press, 1967.

Yankelovich, D. *New rules*. New York: Random House, 1981.

Zimbardo, P.G., Banks, W.C., Haney, C., and Jaffee, D. The mind is a formidable jailor: A Pirandellian prison. *New York Times Magazine*, April 8, 1973, p. 38ff.

REPLY TO ROLLO MAY'S LETTER

BY CARL ROGERS

Dear Rollo:

Tom Greening has sent me your eloquent and scholarly letter dealing with the problem of evil and evil behavior. Your thoughtful analyses and arguments will provoke a lot of good thinking and I appreciate that.

Unfortunately, your material arrives on the eve of my departure for Europe and by the time I return, the editor's deadline will be at hand. Consequently, this must be a hasty reply, which I regret. I cannot possibly touch on all the issues that you raised.

I would like first to deal with a couple of lesser points in your letter, ones on which my feelings are clear.

When you speak of the narcissism that has been fostered by humanistic psychology and how many individuals are "lost in self-love," I feel like speaking up and saying, "That's not true!" Then I realize that what I am saying is that it is not true in my

Journal of Humanistic Psychology, Vol. 22, No. 4, Fall 1982, 85–89. Copyright © 1982 Association for Humanistic Psychology.

experience, but my experience is limited to clients and groups dealt with by my particular brand of humanistic psychology and philosophy. In those groups I simply have not seen the development of a harmful narcissism and certainly not of an excessive self-love. If these characteristics have emerged in other facets of the humanistic movement, I have not been in contact with them. I realize this is quite possible because I am not closely in touch with other aspects of the humanistic movement.

In the groups with which I've had contact, the truth is quite the contrary. Such groups lead to social action of a realistic nature. Individuals who come in as social fanatics become much more socially realistic, but they still want to take action. People who have not been very aware of social issues become more aware and, again, opt for realistic actions on those issues. We have had plenty of evidence of this in our encounter groups and workshops. Irrational anger and violence are sometimes defused, but action of a more realistic sort increases.

One amusing bit of personal evidence on this. When I received the copy of your open letter, I was putting the finishing touches on a very strong statement about nuclear war and what might be done to prevent it. I am taking a stand against the policies of our government, which I feel are making nuclear war more likely. This is but one example of the fact that we agree in so many ways it is difficult to be exactly certain where we differ. I am sure that you and I are both acting to do what we can to prevent this monstrous evil of nuclear war.

You speak at length of the failure of people like myself and client-centered therapy to recognize, accept, and respond to feelings of anger, hostility, and negative feelings in general, perhaps especially those directed toward the therapist. I think that to some extent this was definitely true of me in the distant past, although I have also published examples of the way in which I dealt with bitter hostility toward me in therapy. I have never quite agreed with the opinion of the outside evaluators in our schizophrenic research, that we as a group dodged or evaded the negative or hostile reactions. I have to recognize that possibly the evaluators were correct. Certainly in recent years I feel that I have responded much more adequately to such attitudes. The film *Carl Rogers Counsels an Individual: Anger and Hurt*, of which considerable portions are published in *The Comprehensive Textbook of Psychiatry/III* (1980), show that I was responsive to both anger and to the pain that was discovered to be underlying it. I believe I have learned to be acceptant of anger toward me and toward others. There may be truth in what you say, that client-centered therapists have a tendency not to accept or respond to such feelings. If so, I regret this as much as you.

Now I would like to turn to the more fundamental issue. You have never seemed to care whether the evil impulses in man are genetic and inherent or whether they are acquired after birth. For you they are just there. For me their origin makes a great deal of difference philosophically. I would like to try to clarify my reasons. I feel that the tendency toward actualization is inherent. In this, man is like all other organisms. I can count on it being present. It may take bizarre and futile forms. I have given an example of the potatoes in a basement bin, sending their feeble white sprouts upward in a futile effort to reach the light. I feel similarly about the deprived ghetto youth whose only path to ego enhancement is to be the best mugger or the most daring burglar in his gang. My attitude is similar toward the psychotic in a back ward who is Jesus Christ. But the basic, actualizing tendency operates toward fulfillment.

I find in my experience no such innate tendency toward destructiveness, toward evil. I cannot count on the certainty that this individual is striving consciously or unconsciously to fulfill an evil nature. I do not find this in animals either. There is, however, one rare exception which has stuck in my mind. I saw a television show of African wild dogs. There was one female who was jealous of another. When the second female was absent from her den, the first would go into the den, remove one of the cubs, and kill it. This went on day after day until the litter was totally destroyed. I can still remember my shock at that, because it is so uncharacteristic of animals. They kill, but normally only in the interest of actualizing themselves. I gather that you feel the central tendency in human nature is a dual one, aiming both toward creative growth and destructive evil. With the exception I have just mentioned, I don't find that describes animal behavior, or plant behavior, or human behavior. If the elements making for growth are present, the actualizing tendency develops in positive

ways. In the human these elements for growth are not only proper nutrition, etc., but a climate of psychological attitudes.

So, how do I account for the evil behavior that is so obviously
present in our world? In my experience, every person has the capacity for evil behavior. I, and others, have had murderous and
cruel impulses, desires to hurt, feelings of anger and rage, desires to impose our wills on others. It is well to bear in mind that
I also have a capacity to vomit, for example. Whether I, or anyone, will translate these impulses into behavior depends, it seems
to me, on two elements: social conditioning and voluntary choice.
Perhaps we can use Hitler as an example. His early personal life
and social circumstances certainly made it natural that he would
try to fulfill himself by being a big shot, a leader full of hatred toward those he perceived as responsible for his humiliation. But
beyond that, in acts like the decision to exterminate the Jews, a
personal choice for which he was responsible was also a very real
factor.

I believe that, theoretically at least, every evil behavior is
brought about by varying degrees of these elements.

I will admit that there is much I don't understand about some
evil behaviors. The experiments by Milgram and Zimbardo are a
shocking puzzle to me, as they were to the experimenters. Certainly Milgram's subjects were influenced by our education for
conformity and Zimbardo's subjects by our training in prejudice.
But I would agree with you that those scarcely seem like adequate
explanations.

It is interesting that in our decisions about what to do about
evil behavior and evil situations, we seem remarkably similar.
We take the best action we can see to oppose evil, to destroy the
causes, to try to reach people who are acting in hurtful ways. I
am pleased that I had the opportunity to work with groups composed of hostile and feuding individuals whose evil intentions
toward one another were very evident. In a group we worked
with from Belfast, which included both Catholic and Protestant
extremists as well as moderates, a Protestant young woman said
in one of the early sessions, "If a wounded IRA man were lying
before me on the street, I would *step* on him"! This was typical of some of the bitter feelings expressed. Yet in a climate of
understanding and acceptance those people changed so much in

attitudes in a short sixteen hours of contact that when they went back to Belfast they worked in teams of two to show the film to groups in the interest of reconciliation. So I don't for one minute agree that humanistic psychology, at least my kind of humanistic psychology, "cuts the nerve of social action." It enhances social action.

You talk at some length about the transformation that I believe is coming to our world. Here I am much influenced by the thinking of men like Prigogine. The current perturbations in our society and in our world do seem to me to predict that there is an inevitable social transformation coming. In chemistry, and I believe in our culture, these extremes of perturbation lead to a reorganization, to a higher level of order. As to the person of tomorrow, I think you quite misunderstand my description of that person. I was speaking of the person who would be fit to live in the transformed world, not the average person, and though I believe a transformation is inevitable, it certainly will not be a socially constructive transformation unless we all give it every effort. There I think we can agree.

Curiously enough there is one minor point on which I think you are much too optimistic. You speak twice of our culture deteriorating or disintegrating like the cultures of Greece and Rome. I think that is a possible scenario, but it is not what will happen if we have a nuclear war. In that case, our culture will be utterly obliterated. It will not simply deteriorate or disintegrate.

Rollo, you have raised many profound points and this is, I am well aware, a hasty and inadequate reply. Yet I hope that between the two documents people will be stirred to constructive thought. As I said in my earlier published remarks about you, you have been a great contributor to humanistic psychology and I value you very much for that. I hold you in affectionate regard.

Sincerely,
Carl Rogers